Adorned in Dreams

Fashion and Modernity

Elizabeth Wilson

University of California Press
Berkeley   Los Angeles

University of California Press
Berkeley and Los Angeles, California

© 1985 by Elizabeth Wilson
Published 1985 by Virago Press Limited
Published 1987 by the University of California Press

Library of Congress Cataloging-in-Publication Data

Wilson, Elizabeth, 1936–
  Adorned in dreams.

  Bibliography: p.
  Includes index.
  1. Costume—History.   2. Fashion—History.
I. Title.
GT511.W54   1987   391′.009   87-12143
ISBN 0-520-06122-5 (alk. paper)
ISBN 0-520-06212-4 (pbk.)

Printed in the United States of America

1 2 3 4 5 6 7 8 9

Contents

The feminist condemnation of fashion is rejected, and it is suggested that it is inappropriate to see fashion as a moral problem, or as evidence of inauthenticity, 'false consciousness' or subjection to false values. We should rather see it as an artistic and political means of expression, albeit an ambiguous one.

Acknowledgements

My thanks are due to Richard Dyer, Simon Watney, Angela Weir and especially to Tony Halliday; also to Neil Kearney of the National Union of Tailors and Garment Workers; and last but not least to Ursula Owen for all her editorial help.

You may have three-halfpence in your pocket and not a prospect in the world ... but in your new clothes you can stand on the street corner, indulging in a private daydream of yourself as Clark Gable or Greta Garbo.

George Orwell *The Road To Wigan Pier*

Adornment ... which gathers the personality's ... radiance as if in a focal point, allows the mere *having* of the person to become a visible quality of its *being*. And this is so, not *although* adornment is super-fluous, but *because* it is ... This very accentuation of personality, however, is achieved by means of an impersonal trait ... [for] style is always something general. It brings the contents of personal life and activity into a form shared by many and accessible to many.

Georg Simmel 'Adornment'

Chapter 1

Introduction

'In our country,' said Alice . . . 'you'd generally get to somewhere else – if you ran very fast. . . .'
'A slow sort of country,' said the Red Queen. 'Now, here, you see, it takes all the running you can do, to keep in the same place.'

Lewis Carroll: *Through the Looking Glass: And What Alice Found There*

There is something eerie about a museum of costume. A dusty silence holds still the old gowns in glass cabinets. In the aquatic half light (to preserve the fragile stuffs) the deserted gallery seems haunted. The living observer moves, with a sense of mounting panic, through a world of the dead. May not these relics, like the contents of the Egyptian tombs, bring bad luck to those who have been in contact with them? There are dangers in seeing what should have been sealed up in the past. We experience a sense of the uncanny when we gaze at garments that had an intimate relationship with human beings long since gone to their graves. For clothes are so much part of our living, moving selves that, frozen on display in the mausoleums of culture, they hint at something only half understood, sinister, threatening; the atrophy of the body, and the evanescence of life.

These clothes are congealed memories of the daily life of times past. Once they inhabited the noisy streets, the crowded theatres, the glittering soirées of the social scene. Now, like souls in limbo, they wait poignantly for the music to begin again. Or perhaps theirs is a silence patient with vengefulness towards the living.

Charles Dickens recognized that discarded clothes have their special limbo. He described the second-hand clothing market that then existed in Monmouth Street, London, as the 'burial place of fashions'. Yet clothes, unlike their owners, do not die:

> We love to walk among these extensive groves of the illustrious dead, and to indulge in the speculations to which they give rise; now fitting a deceased coat, then a dead pair of trousers, and anon the mortal remains of a gaudy waistcoat, upon some being of our own conjuring up ... We have gone on speculating in this way, until whole rows of coats have started from their pegs, and buttoned up, of their own accord, round the waists of ordinary wearers; lines of trousers have jumped down to meet them; waistcoats have almost burst with anxiety to put themselves on; and half an acre of shoes have ... gone stumping down the street with a noise which has fairly awakened us from our pleasant reverie.[1]

What is the source of this uneasiness and ambiguity, this sense that clothes have a life of their own? Clothes without a wearer, whether on a secondhand stall, in a glass case, or merely a lover's garments strewn on the floor, can affect us unpleasantly, as if a snake had shed its skin. Similarly, a pregnant woman described how the little frock hanging up in readiness for her as yet unborn child seemed like 'a ghost in reverse'.

A part of this strangeness of dress is that it links the biological body to the social being, and public to private. This makes it uneasy territory, since it forces us to recognize that the human body is more than a biological entity. It is an organism in culture, a cultural artefact even, and its own boundaries are unclear:

> Can we really assume that the limits and boundaries of the human body itself are obvious? Does 'the body' end with the skin or should we include hair, nails? ... What of bodily waste materials? ... Surely the decorative body arts such as tattooing, scarification, cranial modification and body painting should also be considered ... [and] it has been shown that it is insignificant (if not inaccurate) to sharply differentiate between bodily decoration and adornment on the one hand and the clothing of the body on the other hand.[2]

No wonder we feel uneasy as we gaze at the crinolines in the costume court.

Clothing marks an unclear boundary ambiguously, and unclear boundaries disturb us. Symbolic systems and rituals have been

created in many different cultures in order to strengthen and reinforce boundaries, since these safeguard purity. It is at the margins
between one thing and another that pollution may leak out. Many
social rituals are attempts at containment and separation, devised to
prevent the defilement that occurs when matter spills from one
place – or category – into another.[3]

If the body with its open orifices is itself dangerously ambiguous,
then dress, which is an extension of the body yet not quite part of it,
not only links that body to the social world, but also more clearly
separates the two. Dress is the frontier between the self and the not-
self.

In all societies the body is 'dressed', and everywhere dress and
adornment play symbolic, communicative and aesthetic roles. Dress
is always 'unspeakably meaningful'.[4] The earliest forms of 'clothing'
seem to have been adornments such as body painting, ornaments,
scarifications (scarring), tattooing, masks and often constricting
neck and waist bands. Many of these deformed, reformed or otherwise modified the body. The bodies of men and of children not just
those of women, were altered – there seems to be a widespread
human desire to transcend the body's limitations.

Dress in general seems then to fulfil a number of social, aesthetic
and psychological functions; indeed it knots them together, and can
express all simultaneously. This is true of modern as of ancient
dress. What is added to dress as we ourselves know it in the West is
fashion. The growth of the European city in the early stages of what
is known as mercantile capitalism at the end of the Middle Ages saw
the birth of fashionable dress, that is of something qualitatively new
and different.

Fashion is dress in which the key feature is rapid and continual
changing of styles. Fashion, in a sense *is* change, and in modern
western societies no clothes are outside fashion; fashion sets the
terms of *all* sartorial behaviour – even uniforms have been designed
by Paris dressmakers; even nuns have shortened their skirts; even
the poor seldom go in rags – they wear cheap versions of the
fashions that went out a few years ago and are therefore to be found
in second-hand shops and jumble sales. Dress still differs in detail
from one community to another – middle-aged women in the
English 'provinces' or in the American Midwest, or in Southern
Italy or in Finland don't look exactly like one another, and they look
still less like the fashion freaks of Paris or Tokyo. Nevertheless they

are less different than they probably feel, for their way of dressing is inevitably determined by fashion. At 'punk' secondhand fashion stalls in the small market towns of the South of France it is possible to see both trendy young holiday makers and elderly peasants buying print 'granny frocks' from the 1940s; to the young they represent 'retro-chic', to the older women what still seems to them a suitable style. But the granny frocks themselves are dim replicas, or sometimes caricatures, of frocks originally designed by Chanel or Lucien Lelong in the late 1930s. They began life as fashion garments and not as some form of traditional peasant dress.

Even the determinedly *un*fashionable wear clothes that manifestly represent a reaction against what *is* in fashion. To be unfashionable is not to escape the whole discourse, or to get outside the parameters. Indeed the most dowdy clothes may at any moment suddenly get taken up and become, perversely, all the rage. Harold Macmillan, Prime Minister of Britain in the late 1950s and early 1960s, used to wear a shapeless, knitted cardigan – it was part of his country gentleman's persona of 'unflappability'. This (which was also and perhaps even more influentially worn by Rex Harrison as Professor Higgins in the film *My Fair Lady*) became for a season the smart item that every young woman 'had' to have. Since Macmillan himself possibly used the garment semi-deliberately as one of the stage props for his public self, its transformation into a fashion was a kind of double parody.

This is one example of the contradictory nature of fashion, with its ever swinging pendulum of styles. Changes in fashion styles not only represent reaction against what went before; they may be self-contradictory too. A nineteenth century belle might wear military frogging on her jacket as if to undercut the femininity of her gown; in the 1960s young women bared their thighs to the crotch, yet veiled their faces with curtains of hair parted in the middle like a Victorian maiden's. Often the contradictions appear senseless. Constantly changing, fashion produces only conformity, as the outrage of the never-before-seen modulates into the good manners of the

The widespread human desire to change the human body: in this case by body painting or tattooing. John White (active 1585–93) watercolour – a Woman of Florida.
Reproduced by kind permission of the Trustees of the British Museum.

faultlessly and self-effacingly correct. To dress fashionably is both to stand out and to merge with the crowd, to lay claim to the exclusive and to follow the herd. Looked at in historical perspective its styles display a crazy relativism. At one period the breasts are bared, at another even a V-neck is daring. At one time the rich wear cloth of gold embroidered with pearls, at another beige cashmere and grey suiting. In one epoch men parade in ringlets, high heels and rouge, at another to do so is to court outcast status and physical abuse.

Yet despite its apparent irrationality, fashion cements social solidarity and imposes group norms, while deviations in dress are usually experienced as shocking and disturbing. Madame de Sévigné, whose letters describe life at the court of Louis XIV in seventeenth century France, writes of the funny side of a serious fire that broke out in the middle of the night:

> What portraits could not have been painted of the state we were all in? Guitaut was in his nightshirt, with some breeches on. Mme. de Guitaut was bare-legged and had lost one of her bedroom slippers. Mme. de Vauvineux was in her petticoat with no dressing-gown. All the servants and neighbours had nightcaps on. The Ambassador, in dressing-gown and wig, maintained perfectly the dignity of a Serene Highness. But his secretary was wonderful to behold. Talk about the chest of Hercules! This was a very different affair. The whole of it was on view, white, fat and dimpled, particularly as he was without a shirt, for the string that should keep it on had been lost in the scrimmage.[5]

But disarray in dress is forgivable only in such abnormal circumstances, and the moral implications of the clothes we wear are so firmly embedded in our social consciousness that even our language reflects it:

> It is difficult in praising clothes not to use such adjectives as 'right', 'good', 'correct', 'unacceptable' or 'faultless', which belong properly to the discussion of conduct, while in discussing moral shortcomings we tend very naturally to fall into the language of dress and speak of a person's behaviour as being shabby, shoddy, threadbare, down at heel, botched or slipshod.[6]

Fashion as Change: 'Changing with the Times' by Fougasse, 1926.
Reproduced by kind permission of the proprietors of Punch.

CHANGING WITH THE TIMES.

WHAT A WELCOME CHANGE IT WAS WHEN THE UGLY CLOTHING OF THE 70's WAS REPLACED BY THE MORE SENSIBLE FASHIONS OF THE 80's!

AND HOW PLEASANT IT WAS WHEN THE TERRIBLE COSTUMES OF THE 80's WERE SUPERSEDED BY THE ARTISTIC CREATIONS OF THE 90's!

WHAT A RELIEF IT WAS WHEN THE HORRIBLE CLOTHES OF THE 90's SURRENDERED TO THE DELIGHTFUL DRESS OF THE 1900's!

AND HOW DELIGHTFUL IT WAS WHEN THE HIDEOUS RAIMENT OF THE 1900's WENT OUT AND THE CHARMING MODES OF THE 1910's CAME IN!

HOW WE ALL CHEERED WHEN THE UNSIGHTLY GARMENTS OF THE 1910's WERE OUSTED BY THE FASCINATING DESIGNS OF

AND I WONDER WHEN THE GHASTLY GARB OF THE PRESENT DAY WILL GIVE PLACE TO SOMETHING REALLY INSPIRING.

The sense of unease when we are 'improperly' dressed or of disapproval when we feel that others have similarly offended, is no doubt related to the intimate dialogue between our clothes and our body. We use the phrase 'her slip was showing' (although now that slips are ceasing to be worn, by younger women at least, the phrase itself is falling into disuse) to indicate something more than slight sartorial sloppiness, to suggest the exposure of something much more profoundly ambiguous and disturbing; it reminds us that the naked body underneath the clothes and paint is somehow unfinished, vulnerable and leaky at the margins.

Yet at the same time the limits of conventional dress act as a barrier we attempt constantly to breach, a boundary we dare to cross. It is both defence and attack, both shield and sword.

In the twentieth century the morality of dress has become to a large extent disassociated from the rigid behavioural codes that once sustained it. This means that although it remains an emotive subject, it cannot be quite so normative as once it was. Its stylistic changes do retain a compulsive and seemingly irrational quality but at the same time fashion is freed to become both an aesthetic vehicle for experiments in taste and a political means of expression for dissidence, rebellion and social reform. This is possible, also, because in the twentieth century fashion, without losing its obsession with the new and the different, with change and exclusivity, has been mass-produced.

The mass production of fashionable styles – itself highly contradictory – links the politics of fashion to fashion as art. It is connected both to the evolution of styles that circulate in 'high' and avant garde art; and to popular culture and taste.

Those fashion commentators, therefore, who still feel able to discuss fashion in terms largely of social psychology – as primarily a form of *behaviour* – miss its significance for the twentieth century. An investigator of the psychology of clothes might interview individuals to discover their feelings about their clothes and might observe the sartorial behaviour of various social groupings. This could be developed into an anthropological or ethnographic perspective towards western fashion as though this were no more than simply a particular kind of 'sartorial behaviour' similar to the sartorial behaviour of 'traditional' or 'ancient' societies. This is often done, but misses the crucial historical dimension of fashion – as though we were to discuss the films of Antonioni in terms of the conventions of ancient Greek tragedy, as if both expressed some eternal 'human spirit'. To reduce fashion to psychology also excludes, or at best minimises, the vital *aesthetic* element of fashion. Fashion's changing styles owe far less to psychological quirks than to the evolution of aesthetic styles generally.

It is not that the behavioural aspect of dress is without interest, but this book is intended to some extent as a corrective to that approach, which inevitably overplays the unintentional, irrational and seemingly absurd aspects of dress, and particularly of fashionable exaggeration. Of course dress does 'speak' status, it does betray the unconscious of both the individual and the group, it does have a moral dimension. *Adorned in Dreams*, however, explores it as a cultural phenomenon, as an aesthetic medium for the expression of ideas, desires and beliefs circulating in society. Fashion is, after all, 'a form of visual art, a creation of images with the visible self as its medium'.[7] Like any other aesthetic enterprise fashion may then be understood as ideological, its function to resolve formally, at the imaginary level, social contradictions that cannot be resolved.[8] It has in fact been one site for the playing out of a contradiction between the secularity of capitalism and the asceticism of Judaeo-Christian culture, the fashion project at one level an attempt to emphasize the human body and its beauty in a culture that has tended to despise and denigrate the sensual.

Fashion, in fact, originates in the first crucible of this contradiction: in the early capitalist city. Fashion 'links beauty, success and the city'.[9] It was always urban (urbane), became metropolitan and is now cosmopolitan, boiling all national and regional difference down into the distilled moment of glassy sophistication. The urbanity of fashion masks all emotions, save that of triumph; the demeanour of the fashionable person must always be blasé – cool. Yet fashion does not negate emotion, it simply displaces it into the realm of aesthetics. It can be a way of intellectualizing visually about individual desires and social aspirations. It is in some sense inherently given to irony and paradox; a new fashion starts from rejection of the old and often an eager embracing of what was previously considered ugly; it therefore subtly undercuts its own assertion that the latest thing is somehow the final solution to the problem of how to look. But its relativism is not as senseless as at first appears; it is a statement of the unnaturalness of human social arrangements – which becomes very clear in the life of the city; it is a statement of the arbitrary nature of convention and even of morality; and in daring to be ugly it perhaps at the same time attempts to transcend the vulnerability of the body and its shame, a point punk Paris fashion designer Jean Paul Gaultier recognizes when he says, 'People who make mistakes or dress badly are the real stylists. My "You feel as though you've eaten too much" . . . collection is taken from exactly those moments when you are mistaken or embarrassed' (*Harpers and Queen*, September 1984).

In the modern city the new and different sounds the dissonance of reaction to what went before; that moment of dissonance is key to twentieth century style. The colliding dynamism, the thirst for change and the heightened sensation that characterize the city societies particularly of modern industrial capitalism go to make up this 'modernity', and the hysteria and exaggeration of fashion well express it. Whereas, however, in previous periods fashion is the field for the playing out of tensions between secular modernity and hedonism on the one hand, and repression and conformity on the other, in the contemporary 'post modernist' epoch rather than expressing an eroticism excluded from the dominant culture it may in its freakishness question the imperative to glamour, the sexual obviousness of dominant styles.

Fashion parodies itself. In elevating the ephemeral to cult status it ultimately mocks many of the moral pretensions of the dominant culture, which, in turn, has denounced it for its surface frivolity while perhaps secretly stung by the way in which fashion pricks the whole moral balloon. At the same time fashion *is* taken at face value and dismissed as trivial, in an attempt to deflect the sting of its true seriousness, its surreptitious unmasking of hypocrisy.

Writings on fashion, other than the purely descriptive, have found it hard to pin down the elusive double bluffs, the infinite regress in the mirror of the meanings of fashion. Sometimes fashion is explained in terms of an often over-simplified social history; sometimes it is explained in psychological terms; sometimes in terms of the economy. Reliance on one theoretical slant can easily lead to simplistic explanations that leave us still unsatisfied.

How then can we explain so double-edged a phenomenon as fashion? It may well be true that fashion is like all 'cultural phenomena, especially of a symbolic and mythic kind, [which] are curiously resistant to being imprisoned in one . . . "meaning". They constantly escape from the boxes into which rational analysis tries to pack them: they have a Protean quality which seems to evade definitive translation into non-symbolic – that is, cold unresonant, totally explicit, once-for-all-accurate – terms.'[10] This suggests that we need a variety of 'takes' on fashion if the reductive and normative moralism of the single sociological explanation is to be avoided while we yet seek to go beyond the pure description of the art historian. The attempt to view fashion through several different pairs of spectacles simultaneously – of aesthetics, of social theory, of politics – may result in an obliquity of view, even of astigmatism or blurred vision, but it seems that we must attempt it.

It would be possible to leave fashion as something that simply appears in a variety of distinct and separate 'discourses', or to say that it is itself merely one among the constellation of discourses of post-modernist culture. Such a pluralist position would be typical of post-modernist or post-structuralist theoretical discourse (today the dominant trend among the avant garde and formerly 'left' intelligentsia): a position that repudiates all 'over arching theories' and 'depth models' replacing these with a multiplicity of 'practices, discourses and textual play ... or by multiple surfaces'.[11] Such a view is 'populist' and 'democratic' in the sense that no one practice or activity is valued above any other; moral and aesthetic judgments are replaced by hedonistic enjoyment of each molecular and disconnected artefact, performance or experience. Such extreme alienation 'derealizes' modern life, draining from it all notion of meaning. Everything then becomes play; nothing is serious. And fashion does appear to express such a fragmented sensibility particularly well – its obsession with surface, novelty and style for style's sake highly congruent with this sort of post-modernist aesthetic.

Yet fashion clearly does also tap the unconscious source of deep emotion, and at any rate is about more than surface. Fashion, in fact, is not unlike Freud's vision of the unconscious mind. This could contain mutually exclusive ideas with serenity; in it time was abolished, raging emotions were transformed into concrete images, and conflicts magically resolved by being metamorphosed into symbolic form.

From within a psychoanalytic perspective, moreover, we may view the fashionable dress of the western world as one means whereby an always fragmentary self is glued together into the semblance of a unified identity. Identity becomes a special kind of problem in 'modernity'. Fashion speaks a tension between the crowd and the individual at every stage in the development of the nineteenth and twentieth century metropolis. The industrial period is often, inaccurately, called the age of 'mass man'. Modernity creates fragmentation, dislocation. It creates the vision of 'totalitarian' societies peopled by identical zombies in uniform. The fear of depersonalization haunts our culture. 'Chic', from this perspective, is then merely the uniform of the rich, chilling, anti-human and rigid. Yet modernity has also created the individual in a new way – another paradox that fashion well expresses. Modern individualism is an exaggerated yet fragile sense of self – a raw, painful condition.

Our modern sense of our individuality as a kind of wound is also, paradoxically, what makes us all so fearful of not sustaining the autonomy of the self; this fear transforms the idea of 'mass man' into a threat of self-annihilation. The way in which we dress may assuage that fear by stabilizing our individual identity. It may bridge the loneliness of 'mass man' by connecting us with our social group.

Fashion, then, is essential to the world of modernity, the world of spectacle and mass-communication. It is a kind of connective tissue of our cultural organism. And, although many individuals experience fashion as a form of bondage, as a punitive, compulsory way of falsely expressing an individuality that by its very gesture (in copying others) cancels itself out, the final twist to the contradiction that is fashion is that it often does successfully express the individual.

It is modern, mass-produced fashion that has created this possibility. Originally, fashion was largely for the rich, but since the industrial period the mass-production of fashionably styled clothes has made possible the use of fashion as a means of self-enhancement and self-expression for the majority, although, by another and cruel paradox, the price of this has been world-wide exploitation of largely female labour. Fashion itself has become more democratic, at least so far as style is concerned – for differences in the quality of clothes and the materials in which they are made still strongly mark class difference.

Mass fashion, which becomes a form of popular aesthetics, can often be successful in helping individuals to express and define their individuality. The modernist aesthetic of fashion may also be used to express group and, especially in recent years, counter-cultural solidarity. Social and political dissidents have created special forms of dress to express revolt throughout the industrial period. Today, social rebels have made of their use of fashion a kind of avant gardist statement.

Fashionable dressing is commonly assumed to have been restrictive for women and to have confined them to the status of the ornamental or the sexual chattel. Yet it has also been one of the ways in which women have been able to achieve self expression, and feminism has been as simplistic – and as moralistic – as most other theories in its denigration of fashion.

Fashion has been a source of concern to feminists, both today and in an earlier period. Feminist theory is the theorization of gender, and in almost all known societies the gender division assigns to women a subordinate position. Within feminism, fashionable dress and the beautification of the self are conventionally perceived as expressions of subordination; fashion and cosmetics fixing women visibly in their oppression. However, not only is it important to recognize that men have been as much implicated in fashion, as much 'fashion victims' as women; we must also recognize that to discuss fashion as simply a feminist moral problem is to miss the richness of its cultural and political meanings. The political subordination of women is an inappropriate point of departure if, as I believe, the most important thing about fashion is *not* that it oppresses women.

Yet although fashion can be used in liberating ways, it remains ambiguous. For fashion, the child of capitalism, has, like capitalism, a double face.

The growth of fashion, of changing styles of dress, is associated with what has been termed 'the civilizing process' in Europe. The idea of civilization could not exist except by reference to a 'primitive' or 'barbaric' state, and:

> an essential phase of the civilizing process was concluded at exactly the time when the *consciousness* of civilisation, the consciousness of the superiority of their own behaviour and its embodiments in science, technology or art began to spread over whole nations of the west.[12]

Fashion, as one manifestation of this 'civilizing process' could not escape this élitism. In more recent times capitalism has become global, imperialist and racist. At the economic level the fashion industry has been an important instrument of this exploitation, and I devote Chapter Four to a description of the economics of the fashion industry, and to the way in which it today exploits the labour of the developing countries, and that of women in particular.

Imperialism, however, is cultural as well as economic, and fashion, enmeshed as it is in mass-consumption, has been implicated in this as well. Western fashions have overrun large parts of the so-called third world. In some societies that used to have traditional, static styles of dress, the men, at least those in the public eye, wear western men's suits – although their national dress might be better adapted to climate and conditions. Women seem more likely to continue to wear traditional styles. In doing so they symbolize what is authentic, true to their own culture, in opposition to the cultural colonization of imperialism. Yet if men symbolically 'join' modernity by adopting western dress while women continue to follow tradition, there is an ambivalent message here of women's exclusion from a new world, however ugly, and thus of their exclusion from modernity itself.

On the other hand, in the socialist countries of the 'third' world, western fashion may represent both the lure and the threat of neo-colonialism. A young woman doing the tango in high heels and a tight skirt in a Shanghai tearoom symbolizes the decadence, the 'spiritual pollution' of capitalism (although in continued reaction against the Cultural Revolution, Chinese women and men have recently been encouraged to adopt and to manufacture western styles of dress).

Fashion may appear relativistic, a senseless production of style 'meanings'. Nevertheless, fashion *is* coherent in its ambiguity. Fashion *speaks* capitalism.

Capitalism maims, kills, appropriates, lays waste. It also creates great wealth and beauty, together with a yearning for lives and opportunities that remain just beyond our reach. It manufactures dreams and images as well as things, and fashion is as much a part of the dream world of capitalism as of its economy.

We therefore both love and hate fashion, just as we love and hate capitalism itself. Some react with anger or despair, and the unrepentant few with ruthless enjoyment. More typical responses, in the west at least, where most enjoy a few of the benefits of capitalism while having to suffer its frustrations and exploitation as well, are responses if not of downright cynicism, certainly of ambivalence and irony. We live as far as clothes are concerned a triple ambiguity: the ambiguity of capitalism itself with its great wealth and great squalor, its capacity to create and its dreadful wastefulness; the ambiguity of our identity, of the relation of self to body and self to the world; and the ambiguity of art, its purpose and meaning.

Fashion is one of the most accessible and one of the most flexible means by which we express these ambiguities. Fashion is modernist irony.

Chapter 2

The History of Fashion

Fashionable whims affected only a very small number of people. One cannot really talk of fashion becoming all powerful before about 1700. At that time the word gained a new lease of life and spread everywhere with its new meaning: keeping up with the times.

Fernand Braudel: *Civilisation and Capitalism: The Structures of Everyday Life*

Before the beginnings of mercantile capitalism and the growth of cities in medieval Europe, most costume historians have agreed that fashion as we understand it hardly existed, although Stella Mary Newton[1] has suggested that even in the imperial courts of China and Japan there must have been 'fashions' in colours, ornamentation and other details even if the shape of garments remained unchanging. It may also be that a view of the clothing of Greek and Roman antiquity as static is the outgrowth of a now rather outmoded vision of this 'ancient' world and its culture as generally harmonious and stable. This Victorian vision of classical antiquity as some sort of ideal perhaps has lingered on in costume history after its replacement elsewhere by more sophisticated and more relativistic approaches.

There is, however, a clear distinction between all forms of traditional dress and the rapidly changing styles that had appeared in western Europe by the fourteenth century, with the expansion in trade, the growth of city life and the increasing sophistication of the royal and aristocratic courts. This important shift was associated with developments in tailored and fitted clothing.

Eyed needles have been found on Palaeolithic sites (from **40,000** years ago) and it is believed that those remote peoples used a kind of tailoring to sew animal skins into protective suits, much as the Eskimos continued to do until recent times. So tailoring was a very old invention. However, in the classical period, tailors were only mentioned for the first time in an edict of Diocletian (AD **285–303**).

Throughout the classical period fitted clothing was the badge of the barbarian, and both Greeks and Romans wore draped garments. Indeed the most fundamental distinction in dress is not, as we might suppose today, that between male and female, but the distinction between the draped and the sewn.[2]

During the period of the Roman Empire there was an abundance of different fashions in hairstyles, wigs and cosmetics, although garments themselves did not change. Stella Newton again suggests that there were fashions in details such as the positioning of the girdle, but the toga and other draped costumes were less amenable to variation than tailored garments have proved to be.

Fitted hose were unheard of in Rome until they were copied from the tribes of the North, and although despised on account of these origins, they were warm, which made them popular. An early attempt to enforce sumptuary regulations was the decree in AD **397** to prohibit the wearing of hose.[3]

The Emperor Diocletian introduced an almost Oriental hierarchy and magnificence into his court:

> From the time of Augustus to that of Diocletian the Roman princes, conversing in a familiar manner among their fellow citizens, were saluted only with the same respect that was usually paid to senators and magistrates. Their principal distinction was the Imperial or military robe of purple, whilst the senatorial garment was marked by a broad, and the equestrian by a narrow, band or stripe of the same honourable colour. The pride, or rather the policy, of Diocletian engaged that artful prince to introduce the stately magnificence of the court of Persia. . . . The sumptuous robes of Diocletian and his successors were of silk and gold; and it is remarked with indignation that even their shoes were studded with the most precious gems. The access to their sacred person was every day rendered more difficult by the institution of new forms and ceremonies.[4]

After the western Empire, centred on Rome, fell to the 'barbarians' in AD **476**, the eastern Empire, or Byzantium, centred on

Constantinople, came even more under oriental influence. At the
height of its glory, in the sixth century AD, the court of the Emperor
Justinian was extremely hierarchical. The Emperor was a priest
king, his garments were vestments.

This liturgical atmosphere continued for several hundred years,
and life at the Imperial Court was one of 'fixed ceremonies and
slow-moving processions ... ceremonial life of the Court was
passed in a sort of ballet'.[5]

Each dancer in the ritual performances had a distinct costume:

> The tribunes and vicars wear a blue and white garment, with short
> sleeves, and gold bands, and rings on their ankles ... [The second]
> dance is accomplished according to the ritual given above ... except
> that the tribunes and vicars wear a garment of green and red, split, with
> short sleeves and gold bands.[6]

By this time Christianity had become the official religion of the
Roman Empire. The early Christians, on the other hand, had been a
persecuted sect of the poor, influenced by the Stoics, who had had
no interest in art, and by Judaism with its ban on idols and graven
images. At first they had believed that the Second Coming of Christ
was imminent, and worldly matters had been of little interest to
them.

In fact, the Byzantine Court was hardly typical, and across most
of Europe between the fifth and the eleventh centuries AD,
Christian asceticism, or so most costume historians appear to agree,
continued to influence the way men and women dressed. Loose
robes were worn by both sexes, styles were simple and unchanging.
Societies existed for the most part at subsistence level, and were in
many respects free of marked differences in wealth or class. Dress
distinguished rich from poor, rulers from ruled only in that
working people wore more wool and no silk, rougher materials and
with less ornamentation than their masters.

In the twelfth century, however, women's dresses began to be
shaped to the body by being laced in at the sides, and in the
fourteenth century 'something emerges which we can already call
"fashion"'.[7] Both breeches and hose were already being worn, and

Dress in the first half of the fifteenth century: exaggeration and androgyny.
Reproduced by kind permission of the Trustees of the British Museum.

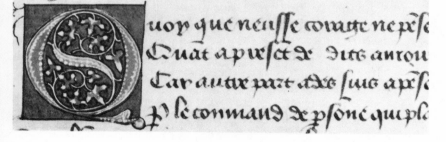

had been for some time. Breeches were trousers, worn tight-fitting by the nobility and looser by the general populace; hose were stockings, sometimes footless, also made of cloth.

The fourteenth century saw the proliferation of much more elaborate styles for both men and women than any seen hitherto. The doublet for men was worn very short and tight, the *cote hardie*, a long tunic buttoned down the front, was also worn tight-fitting by both men and women of the upper classes. At the same time the gown, again worn by men and women, became extravagantly full and long, sleeves became either very tight or very wide, and hems were cut into fantastic shapes, while hats and headdresses burst into the most extravagant and rapidly changing shapes – horns, steeples, turbans and fezes. Shoes became exaggeratedly long and pointed.[8]

In the sixteenth century costume books became popular. These described and depicted fashionable variations in dress in different regions and no doubt contributed towards a speeding up of the fashion process. It was only in the fifteenth and sixteenth centuries that it began to seem shameful to wear outdated clothes, and those who could afford to do so discarded clothing simply because it had gone out of style. This led to the situation which persisted for several hundred years, whereby the humbler classes attempted to dress fashionably but of necessity continued to wear styles that had long ceased to be fashionable among the rich. This class time-lag effect only completely died out after the Second World War.

An intensified aristocratic interest in fashionable clothing seems first to have become noticeable at the Burgundian court in the fourteenth century, at the time when Burgundy was at the centre of the trade corridor that stretched from Flanders towards the Mediterranean. Increased trade was one major reason for the growth of fashion, and fashions developed in a number of geographical centres of trade in Europe. At different times different regions dominated, following movements in the economic balance of power.[9] Cloth, which was enormously expensive, was and symbolized wealth in medieval society. When, at this period, therefore, individuals for the first time (or so it would appear) began to discard their costumes before they were outworn, this represented a new level of consumption.

One reason for what is perceived – whether correctly or not – as the difference between the harmonious stability of classical Graeco-Roman dress and the bizarreries of late medieval fashions is often attributed to Christianity and the changed attitude it brought towards the human body. We feel that the Greeks and Romans accepted and celebrated the body, and that their dress reflected this. In art the unclothed body appeared glorious, and, when clad, it was often merely veiled by liquid draperies that clung to and outlined the limbs.

Cretan culture was an exception. Wall paintings and statuettes show both men and women with constricted and etiolated waists, suggesting that metal belts were worn from childhood to achieve this effect, and it has been suggested that such characteristic forms of adornment may have been influenced by African civilizations, bearing more resemblance to elongated ears or necks than to, say, corsets. But of course, on the other hand, 'Cretan princes only look like Erté fashion plates because the frescoes which portray them were "reconstructed" in the 1930s'.[10] As always, our understanding of past fashions or dress, as of the past generally, is filtered through our own preoccupations and ideologies.

There is no doubt, all the same, that Christianity did induce a new sort of guilt about the body, and that Judaeo-Christian culture suffused sexuality with a sense of sinfulness. Yet early Renaissance society was contradictory, an intensely religious culture that was becoming simultaneously dedicated to secular success, economic expansion and luxurious living, so that from its origins European fashion articulated a tension between worldliness and asceticism, both expressing sexual guilt and subverting it. It spoke all the sins of pride in wealth and rank, and vanity in lust and beauty, and priests, philosophers and satirists hurried to denounce it. Their invective invoked a penitential moralism – although their descriptions of contemporary fashion are often so vivid and accurate that they must at some level one feels, have enjoyed it.

Yet fashionable dress hid sexuality even while displaying it, and drew attention to the body in an ambivalent way. Some parts of the body, particularly the female leg, had at all times to be concealed; others were at one period hidden, at another brazenly revealed, the male fashion for the codpiece being perhaps the most startling exhibitionistic fashion ever, a 'modest' covering for the genitals revealed by the shortened doublet, which managed to draw still greater attention to the sexual organ it was meant to hide. Cosmetics were habitually worn, and styles of beauty remote from the classical ideal of symmetry held sway in the Gothic period. The

Flemish painters celebrated women with bony shoulders, protruding stomachs and long faces, while women shaved or plucked their hairlines to obtain the fashionable egg-domed forehead. (It was not until the eighteenth century, however, that gender difference in dress began to be of overriding importance.)

An effect of the growth of trade and the very beginnings of capitalism in the fourteenth century on dress was to create the notion of fashion as changing styles. Early capitalism was associated with the expansion of trade, with the growth of cities and with the beginnings of the breakdown of the hierarchical society of feudal times and the rise of the bourgeoisie. The development of fashion was affected by each of these, and was in turn integral to them.

The expansion of trade was partly the expansion of the cloth and wool trade, so the production of cloth and clothing played a direct economic role. At the same time the rise of the bourgeoisie was crucial in the development of fashion, although at least until the French Revolution (1789) dress continued to be a courtly affair, and rank continued to dictate styles of dress to a large extent throughout the period from the fourteenth century to the beginning of the Industrial Revolution in the last quarter of the eighteenth century, when the nature of capitalism changed drastically. Dress, however, in the intervening period was the site of frequent struggles for status and freedom.

Members of the poorest classes wore the cheapest cloth: bluett, blue as its name suggests; russet, which was brown or black; or the undyed blanketcloth. Individuals who belonged to various callings and professions at different social levels wore distinctive dress. The master craftsmen of the medieval guilds wore special liveries, or at least hoods. By the late medieval period the merchant class was sumptuously dressed and copied the fashions of the gentry as well as wearing the furs, silk and jewellery supposedly reserved for the landowners and the knights. Later still, the dress of learned callings ossified and diverged from ordinary fashionable dress; in the sixteenth century the clergy, physicians and surgeons continued to wear the long medieval robes discarded by the smartly dressed in favour of short coats, doublets and hose. In humbler sections of society many workmen, street vendors and artisans wore garments associated with their calling. For instance, milk girls in the eighteenth century wore extra ample white aprons and 'bergère' hats; millers, bakers and cooks dressed in white, since they were liable to be covered with flour. It is not always clear whether distinctive dress was worn for practical reasons, or simply to distinguish one kind of street vendor, for example, from another. The female street vendors of the seventeenth and eighteenth centuries, of whom the milk girl is one example, do seem to have worn costumes that differed in certain details, but it appears that working clothes were often not especially functional, or were even dysfunctional, and working people increasingly tried to follow the fashion, sporadically at least. There are, for example, accounts of agricultural workers toiling under the hot sun without removing their wigs.[11]

In the pre-industrial world there were enormous numbers of domestic servants. In the eighteenth century they were still estimated to be the largest socio-economic grouping in England, male servants predominating. At an earlier period, rich landowners might have had upwards of a thousand domestic retainers, and these would often have worn a gorgeous livery in the colours of their master. They might also, like artisans and apprentices, have been given the cast-off fashionable garments of their employer, still in good condition, and thus it was that they were able to parade the city streets in finery that appalled the moralists and conservatives of the day. Upper servants, particularly women, followed the fashions, although perhaps in materials slightly less luxurious than those of their employer. In the sixteenth century, Cardinal Wolsey's head chef, on the other hand, was said to have been as richly dressed as any courtier, while Daniel Defoe complained in 1725 that when a country girl found a place in a fashionable town house:

> Her neat's leather shoes are now transformed into laced shoes with high heels; her yarn stockings are turned into fine worsted ones with silk clocks ... she must have a hoop too ... and her poor, scanty, linsey-woolsey petticoat is changed into a good silk one four or five yards wide.[12]

In many European countries the peasantry continued to dress distinctively. They often aspired to fashion, however, and what is now known as 'national costume' is in many cases a hybrid adaptation of peasant styles to symbolize a newly created national identity when the nineteenth-century nation states were formed. Some of the most seemingly 'authentic' of these costumes may therefore represent the rewriting of history, a kind of sartorial lie.

The period from the fourteenth to the sixteenth century saw the enactment of more sumptuary laws than ever before. These, attempts to restrict by legal means what individuals might wear, constituted a response both to economic and to social change. 'A perfect hurricane' of sumptuary regulations was let loose in all the states and countries of western Europe at this time.[13]

There seem to have been three reasons for this. The regulations represented an attempt to preserve the distinctions in rank, reflected in dress, that were in fact beginning to break down with the rise of the urban bourgeoisie. In the static medieval world 'every costume was to some extent a uniform revealing the rank and condition of the wearer',[14] but now this old order was being replaced by a modern class society in which work with its fluctuating fortunes, rather than rank and hierarchy ordained by lineage, was an important determinant of an individual's status.

Secondly, extravagance was held to be morally harmful. This view was linked to the economic doctrines held by the mercantilists. These believed that wealth and money were identical, and that governments should seek to attract the largest possible share of precious metals. This favourable balance of trade necessitated restrictions on the imports of other goods, particularly luxury goods. It was better, they argued, to encourage home manufacture and to hoard gold. This meant that sumptuary laws were used in an attempt to direct trade and develop particular economic policies believed to be desirable. In England such laws reached a peak in the reign of Elizabeth I (1558–1603), yet James I repealed them all soon after his accession to the English throne in 1603, and in any case in no country and at no time had these laws been enforced, in spite of defining in the most minute detail what the various ranks and sections of society might lawfully wear, and more especially what they might not wear. But by the seventeenth century economists were beginning to understand that high consumption might actually promote economic expansion, and no longer did the hoarding of wealth appear desirable.[15]

Perhaps surprisingly, even the English Puritans of the Commonwealth period (1649–1660) enacted no further sumptuary laws,

Distinctive Dress or accoutrements of street vendors: biscuit seller and seller of knives and writing materials.
Reproduced by courtesy of the Mansell Collection.

although in the previous century the increase of such laws had been associated in mainland Europe with the Reformation as well as with the growth of state power. Yet English puritanism did, after all, in part express a belief in individual freedom, and John Milton, who was a puritan libertarian as well as a poet, wrote that to legislate over clothing was as absurd as to try to regulate music and dancing.

Fashion was also a city phenomenon, and was particularly well developed in the city states of Renaissance Italy. Jacob Burckhardt, nineteenth-century historian of the Italian Renaissance, related the freedom of city life to the development of individualism, and fashion as an expression of the individual:

> In proportion as distinctions of birth ceased to confer any special privileges, was the individual himself compelled to make the most of his personal qualities, and society to find its worth and charm in itself. The demeanour of individuals, and all the higher forms of social intercourse became ends pursued with a deliberate and artistic purpose. ... Even serious men ... looked on a handsome and becoming costume as an element in the perfection of the individual.[16]

With the coming of the industrial revolution and a world dominated for the first time by machines, capitalism was lifted to a new level. Industrial capitalism created vast and turbulent new city centres with new characteristics. Cities had always been places where to some extent the individual's origins could be hidden and in which personal qualities, rather than rank or wealth, were what counted; but the cities of the renaissance were very different from the new, huge industrial infernos where truly the stranger could lose himself or herself, or find a new identity in the anonymity of the surging crowds. The urban landscape created by industrialism might seem hellish as smoke and fumes poured up from the factories, and human beings were crammed together in squalor and misery; it might seem magical as fabulous fantasy buildings – the Crystal Palace, the Eiffel Tower, the Empire State Building – defied gravity and substance, becoming the literal castles in the air of the manufacturing bourgeoisie. What was lost was the still stable rhythm of the pre-industrial order. All that was fixed and unchanging disappeared forever.

To connect these teeming new cities came new forms of rapid communication. Railways, the telephone, the cinema and the mass circulation of newspapers and magazines intensified the rush and pace of modern life. The motor of capitalism whirled everything round in its vortex: 'constant revolutionizing of production, uninterrupted disturbance of all social relations, everlasting uncertainty and agitation, distinguish [this] . . . epoch from all earlier ones'.[17]

The spatial structure of these great new cities intensified the individual's experience of mobility, both geographically and socially; great wealth and dire poverty lived cheek by jowl and the speed with which an individual might run the gamut of experience from one to the other terrified and fascinated a new generation of citizens thus condemned to perpetual over-excitement and over-stimulation. Nietzsche spoke also of the fragmentation of identity caused by the 'tropical tempo' of modernity: 'modern man "can never really look well dressed", because no social role in modern times can ever be a perfect fit'.[18]

This meant that fashion became even more important than it had been in the pre-industrial city. Its circulation of images was itself a form of mass communications. Social roles multiplied. Street life took on a special significance now that it was more sharply divided from the private sphere. For industrial society intensified, or even created, the division between the public and the private zones. This had implications for fashion. The contrast between intimate interiors and busy streets was signalled by clothes that increasingly marked the distinction between being at home and being on display in public.

It was in the eighteenth century that dress began to anticipate its future metamorphosis in the nineteenth century industrial world, and this change came first in England, where the industrial revolution began. The landowning aristocracy and gentry were already effectively rural capitalists, and it was their daily, working dress that became the nineteenth century uniform. Everyday riding clothes – sports clothes – of woollen cloth in quiet colours, evolved into the normal day dress of modern urban man, and quite ousted the brocade, lace and velvet that had once been *de rigueur* for the man of fashion about town. James Laver has suggested that this is only one of the more important examples of the way in which all modern forms of male dress originated as sportswear.[19] What is certainly the case is that the coinciding of the industrial revolution with revolutionary political ideals and with the creed of romanticism resulted in a fundamental change in male apparel. This has been

MORNING WALKING DRESSES

called the 'great masculine renunciation'[20] and many fashion historians have fallen in with the view that from this time men abandoned all pretensions to beauty, women alone continuing to use dress as a form of display. This cliché of fashion history obscures a more complex reality.

The new fashions for men put cut and fit before ornament, colour and display. They abandoned make-up and foppish effeminacy. But the skin-tight breeches of the dandies of the 1800s were highly erotic. So was their new, unpainted masculinity. Throughout the nineteenth and twentieth centuries a variety of male fashions, for example the full beard, Edwardian dandyism, or Clark Gable and Cary Grant's smooth lounge suits in the 1930s, far from being part of a retreat from fashion, represented simply a more oblique, more subtle, more complex approach to glamour than the *ancien régime* courtier's silks and satins.

Fashionable women also modified their dress as cotton, calico and muslin began to be widely used. They adopted styles without exaggerated hoops and panniers, and women, like men, gradually ceased to wear powdered hair and wigs. In Paris these English-women's dresses combined with the influence of classical costumes, which were held to symbolize the revolutionary virtues of simplicity and republicanism. Thus were born the characteristic Empire or Regency styles for women, and, for the first time for several hundred years, corsets were abandoned and legs at times shockingly visible.

Yet at the same period the social and economic roles of men and women began to diverge more sharply; by the early nineteenth century women's role in society was narrowing, dress began to distinguish gender in more exaggerated ways, and fashion was now no longer, as it had been in the aristocratic courts of the seventeenth century, simply a priceless frame for female beauty. Something more subtle occurred; woman and costume together created femininity. By the early Victorian period a ballet-dancer fragility of looks was fashionable for women; they wore their hair parted in the centre and demurely sleeked down and looped to frame a madonna oval face; their gowns had sloping shoulders and pinched in waists; their whole style trembled with meek submissiveness. This divergence between the sexes was about gender as much as eroticism.

It was only in the eighteenth century, after all, that homosexuality had begun to be seen as a permanent psychological condition, as a 'master identity' as well as a sexual practice. In earlier times homosexual acts had been seen as sinful, but as a potential in every individual, given the sinfulness of 'fallen' human nature. Now it was no longer merely a matter of engaging in evil acts; it was rather a case of *being* homosexual, a permanent condition. Much as sodomy had been abhorred, it has been argued that in some ways even greater stigma attached to this new sexual identity than to the old wicked behaviour,[21] so no wonder that it became important to bear witness by your masculine style of dress that you were not effeminate. The increasing sexual stereotyping in dress acted as a defence against new fears.

The ascendancy of the bourgeoisie implied the triumph of ideals of work, thrift and sobriety; and the business or professional man dressed in black represented an ethic quite different from the bedizened courtier or even the gaily dressed merchant of Renaissance Florence. There were, however, two kinds of city dweller, for the urban proletariat also arrived on the scene. The significance to them of modern urban dress was rather that it symbolized their entry to the world of fashion and consumer goods. But although the two are often conflated into the twentieth-century 'democratic citizen', it was not until the 1920s that working men's dress became a fashionable code.

Industrial manufacture transformed the making of clothes as well as city life. In the field of fashion, as in other branches of art and the crafts, the unique and the mass produced developed together.

Although Madame de Sévigné referred in her letters to Monsieur Langlée, a fashionable tailor at the court of Louis XIV at Versailles, one of the new women dressmakers, Rose Bertin, is usually named as the forerunner of the nineteenth-century couturier or dress designer. Even in the late eighteenth century the design of women's

The Early Victorian style of feminine beauty; and children no longer dress exactly like adults.
Reproduced by kind permission of the Trustees of the Victoria and Albert Museum.

LE FOLLET

Boulevart St Martin, 69.

clothes did not greatly alter from year to year; the fashionable difference was made by the choice of ornamentation and detail. Rose Bertin not only designed the dresses Marie Antoinette wore, and advised her on her toilette generally, but she also made fashion dolls, figurines on which her fashions were reproduced in miniature; and these were sent to courts throughout Europe to give news of the latest styles. This device was soon to be surpassed by mass-produced steel engravings which accelerated the circulation of fashion.

The first truly modern dress designer was Charles Frederick Worth, an Englishman who made his name and his fortune in the 1850s at the court of Napoleon III of France by designing the gowns first of the Princess Pauline Metternich and then of her friend, the Empress Eugénie. It was only from this time that fashionable women's wear was seen as the creation of a single designer – just at the time when a clothing industry and mass produced fashion were beginning to appear. Consequently the exclusive dress had to be definitively distinguished from the vulgar copy; the dress designer had to become an Artist.

The Paris of the Second Empire (1850–70) was well suited to become the capital of fashion and to transform the court tailor or the anonymous seamstress into a publicly acknowledged personage; towards the end of his life Worth took to dressing like Rembrandt, with a velvet beret, rich cloak and the flowing tie that was the symbol of the artist amongst the romantics and bohemians. The society of the Second Empire was an expansionist, carpetbagger society in which *nouveaux riches* and old aristocrats, adventuresses and capitalists all sought distinction. In such a society the aristocracy no longer represented an unchallenged dominant class; the Empress Eugénie could not therefore be, as Marie Antoinette had been, an undisputed fashion leader, although her patronage was an essential part of Worth's success. He, not she, however, remained the arbiter. The couturier alone could become the man above court factions and competing classes; he could, because he was an Artist and therefore was 'inspired', create fashions that painters and later photographers then transformed into the symbol or signature of an epoch.

Similarly, the women who wore his clothes, who launched fashions, were actresses or kept women rather than society's social leaders. These *demi-mondaines*, the *grandes cocottes* of mid-nineteenth-century Paris had no name, no family, no class. They came from nowhere, and their success depended entirely on personality and looks. They could therefore afford to wear the most outrageous styles, to create a sensation; indeed it was in their interest so to advertise themselves. Then, once established, the sumptuousness of their dress expressed the wealth of the men who supported them.[22]

In this rapacious world beauty became the passport to social mobility:

> The question of costume ... is one of enormous importance for those who wish to appear to have what they do not have because that is often the best way of getting it later on.[23]

Appearance replaced reality. Whoever wished to crash high society could, provided they looked the part.

The over-ornamented crinolines of the women of fashion contributed to this display. These swaying, trembling bells themselves created the illusion but not the reality of modesty, for they tilted provocatively from side to side when their wearers walked along and when blown up by the wind revealed ankles, legs and drawers. They were decorated with a stylistic rifling from previous periods, a promiscuity that reflected the promiscuity of a society in which bourgeois morality *clothed* the rapacity and animal energy of youthful capitalism. These most artificial works of art, like the painting of the period, tried, paradoxically, to re-invent nature, as the description of her Worth dress by one of his clients, Madame Octave Feuillet, wife of a fashionable novelist, shows:

> He had decided upon a dress of lilac silk covered with clouds of tulle in the same shade in which clusters of lilies of the valley were to be drowned. A veil of white tulle was to be thrown like a mist over the mauve clouds and the flowers, and, finally, a sash with flowing ends should suggest the reins on Venus's chariot.[24]

From the 1830s to about 1900 bourgeois women's dress lagged behind that of men, unadapted to metropolitan life, even as their status declined and they were confined to the vapidity of the bourgeois home. Early street fashions for men adopted the dandy's dark sobriety and clean white linen. They carried this 'uniform' on into the evenings when their womenfolk were brilliantly attired. On the basis of this contrast the myth developed that fashion after the

SKETCH ON THE SEA COAST DURING THE GALE.

Lord D–ndre–ry (*to his Bwother*). " A-a-a, I thay, Tham ! Wather a Dithplay of Figger—Eh ! "

Vicissitudes of the Crinoline – crinolines blowing up in a gale.
Reproduced by kind permission of the proprietors of Punch.

industrial revolution became an entirely feminine affair. It appeared
that women were still stuck in an earlier world. Nevertheless, this
did gradually change.

At first the women of the bourgeoisie had gone out cloaked and
veiled. It was hardly respectable for a woman to be on the streets at
all – and she must of course be chaperoned, or accompanied by a
footman. But there were other, working women in the metropolis.
Already in the 1860s the women of New York City were wearing
'Fifth Avenue Walking Dress' – based on the hunting jacket – and a
few years later the 'mannish' suit, 'with dark jacket, matching
shortened skirt and plain blouse' also appeared.[25] Redferns, an
English tailoring firm who had specialized in riding habits for
women, developed a similar garment for English and French
women of high rank in the next decades, and by 1900 the 'New
Woman' might appear alone on the streets, still outwardly clad in
severe suitings, 'eel' skirts and mannish hats and suits, yet glimpsed
when the skirt was lifted to climb a step or cross the street was a
mass of exquisite flounced and frilled petticoat, which made the

characteristic 'frou frou' sound of the period, an erotic rustling that allegedly sent men's pulses racing.

Fashion speeded up and proliferated to keep pace with modern life. Going off in one direction it matched and expressed the compartmentalized, obsessionally sub-divided life of the bourgeoisie. There were morning gowns, tea gowns, dinner gowns, walking dress, travelling dress, dress for the country, dress (later) for different kinds of sport, deep mourning, second mourning, half mourning; costumes that no longer reflected a clear rank or status, but rather a socially defined time of day, or occasion, or an individual state of feeling. Dress was no longer a gorgeous covering of rich stuff, but was both used as an indicator of social conformity, and, paradoxically, also individualized to the wearer's taste and personality.

In another direction, as many of the old signs of rank disappeared, the uniform was born. Indeed uniforms were the first type of mass produced clothing. The liveries of servants and retainers had been a kind of uniform, but the uniforms of the nineteenth century carried a new meaning. It was all part of the increased classification, docketing and standardization of life in the machine age:

> Since the French Revolution an extensive network of controls had brought bourgeois life ever more tightly into its meshes. The numbering of houses in the big cities may be used to document the progressive standardization. Napoleon's administration had made it obligatory for Paris in 1805. In proletarian sections, to be sure, this simple police measure had encountered resistance ... In the long run, of course, such resistance was of no avail against the endeavour to compensate by means of a multifarious web of registrations for the fact that the disappearance of people in the masses of the big cities leaves no traces.[26]

Uniforms were another manifestation of this bureaucratic attempt to offset the anonymity of the metropolis. They symbolized the advance of the modern state into the life of the individual. They developed earliest in the armies of Europe, one logical extension of the retainer's livery. In the eighteenth century British naval officers adopted a uniform; the lower decks not until the nineteenth century. Uniforms of public 'servants' seem to have started with badges or other insignia of their official, trustworthy status. When such badges developed into fully fledged suits of clothing, however, uniforms became 'sets of clothes stuck in an earlier period'.[27] The first chauffeurs of the early twentieth century, for example, wore leather boots and jodhpur-like trousers as though they were still driving horses, not a machine.

The (private) railway companies were the first to introduce uniforms for their employees; these clothes were intended to give them authority with the public. They were a mark of official status and dignity, yet at the same time signalled that the officials were 'servants of the public' and hence liveried for public service.

The uniform might seem to be the opposite of fashion, meant to submerge the personality rather than to enhance it – with the exception of military uniforms which have traditionally been thought to enhance machismo and glamour. In the eighteenth century the upper maidservants had worn silks and satins. A letter of Byron, dated 1811, however, mentions uniforms:

> I have just issued an edict for the abolition of caps; no hair to be cut on any pretext; stays permitted, but not too low before; full uniform always in the evening.[28]

This seems intended to restrict the fashionable aspirations of his women servants. By the 1890s it had become customary for maidservants to wear black, and, like nurses at the same period, to have women's caps from an earlier period. The dress of women servants was still causing dissension after the Second World War in Britain, as a radio discussion between domestics and employers makes clear:

> Employer: I don't see why we shouldn't say 'would you please wear something dark and plain?' In the average factory you are told what to wear – either dungarees or a white overall. If a girl is going out and she's dressed up to the nines with her hair full of little flowers, she's doing it for a purpose. I want my baby taken to the park, not to the barracks.
> Domestic: It isn't right to keep another woman deliberately in the background by making her dress in dark colours. (*The Listener*, 11 April 1946)

But even uniforms are actually subject to fashion. During the Second World War the uniform coat and skirt designed for the WAVES, the womens's section of the American navy, was fashionably cut in order to attract recruits. In the 1960s and 1970s even

The coat and skirt:modern
street dress for women, 1910.

*Reproduced by kind permission of
the Trustees of the Victoria and
Albert Museum.*

Left: English walking dress.
Reproduced by kind permission of the Trustees of the Victoria and Albert Museum.

Below: Paul Poiret's revolutionary kimono coat; plate from *Les Robes de Paul Poiret racontées par Paul Iribe 1908.*

Below: Regency style dresses of 1908 Paul Iribe.

Twentieth-century dress takes up where the romantic movement left off: similarities in women's dress, 1805 and 1908

nuns updated their habits, while the uniforms of air hostesses, frequently redesigned, always seemed to be just lagging behind what was in vogue. Uniforms, even when intended to suppress sexuality, often have an added sexual charge since they denote the forbidden and the forbidding, and they appear to play a significant role in pornographic fantasy. The uniform is also contradictory in that, intended to quench individuality, it may sometimes enhance it.

If fashion modified uniforms, twentieth-century fashion was itself said to be more and more a uniform. Women's fashions caught up with men's at the end of the nineteenth century. As with men's fashions a century earlier, it was sports styles that were adapted for modern city life. Redferns' coat and skirt and the popular shirt blouse could be copied by the burgeoning fashion industry, for it was between 1890 and 1910 that the mass production of clothes really took off. Paul Poiret, the first major dress designer of the twentieth century, claimed to have abolished the old, tight-laced corset by 1908.

No one individual brought about this change. Yet Gabrielle Chanel, like Worth and Poiret before her, was, as a designer, an important catalyst after 1910. Her biographer, Edmonde Charles-Roux, suggests that Chanel's genius was in doing for women's dress what the English aristocrats and dandies had done one hundred years previously for men's: she adapted sportswear to daily life, and capitalized on 'the feminizing of masculine fashion'.[29]

Chanel took her first steps towards the *beau monde* as the lover of an army and sporting landowner, from whose protection she hoped to launch herself as an actress, singer and music hall star. Riding was her passion, and the influence of riding dress crucial in the formation of the Chanel style. By the time the First World War broke out, she had abandoned her earlier ambitions and was launched as a dressmaker; and at this time she began to design some of the first modern fashions, in beige locknit and grey flannel – cloth that, used for male underwear and blazers, had until then been unheard of for women's fashions. The Chanel style was to become the paradigm of the twentieth-century style.

Chanel created the 'poor look', the sweaters, jersey dresses and little suits that subverted the whole idea of fashion as display; although her trenchcoats and 'little nothing' black dresses might be made of the finest cashmere and her 'costume jewellery' – careless lumps of what looked like glass – were uncut emeralds and diamonds.

Agile and full of movement, this was the spirit of modernity and futurism. As a style, it made a mockery of fashion; Cecil Beaton[30] called it a nihilistic, anti-fashion look, and indeed it was one of the biggest contradictions of all to pay everything for a fashion that was invisible. The aim of this look was to make the rich girl look like the girl in the street, and the black dress and the slight suit were the apotheosis of the shopgirl's uniform, or the stenographer's garb.

The style, developed also by the much less well remembered Jean Patou,[31] clothed every heroine of the 1920s. Evelyn Waugh's first heroine, Margot Beste-Chetwynde, made her first appearance in it:

> An enormous limousine of dove-grey and silver stole soundlessly onto the field ... The door opened, and from the cushions within emerged a tall young man in a clinging dove-grey overcoat. After him, like the first breath of spring in the Champs-Elysées, came Mrs Beste-Chetwynde – two lizard-skin feet, silk legs, chinchilla body, a tight little black hat, pinned with platinum and diamonds, and the high invariable voice that may be heard in any Ritz Hotel from New York to Budapest.[32]

This was the style of an international jet set, yet it was also a classless style. For this reason Chanel designs were soon adapted for the mass market. By 1930 Jane Derby of Seventh Avenue, inspired by Chanel, was already interpreting her for the American mass market.

There was also an American woman designer, Claire McCardell, who disseminated a similar but more democratic image of the modern woman. Active from the 1930s to the 1950s, she never became a household name, but she was one of the most influential twentieth-century designers, and invented tights, flat shoes and soft, easy styles often years ahead of their widespread acceptance. For her the decade of the twenties was the period in which the image of the modern woman gained the ascendancy:

> The big change came in the twenties. Novelists of the time talked about it. Ernest Hemingway describes Lady Brett in *The Sun Also Rises*: 'She wore a slipover jersey sweater and a tweed skirt and her hair brushed back like a boy's. She started all that.' The interesting fashion point is just where Brett wore this 'look' she had started. On a brisk, breezy day

at the Yacht Club? No. On a golf course? No. In a country setting? Anything but. At the exact moment the narrator describes her she is sitting in a bar in Paris.[33]

This is again the migration of sports clothes to the city. Yet the dashing, streamlined 1920s woman was also romantic.

Nancy Cunard was the real-life archetype of all modernist women. Gifted as well as astonishingly beautiful, she was a being so wholly in tune with the epoch that she could only ever *be* it, too closely identified with it to convert it into art, her creativity therefore thwarted. An aura of the tragic surrounded this ultra-modern woman who was recreated as heroine of some of the most famous novels of the period – by Aldous Huxley, by Evelyn Waugh and above all by Michael Arlen in *The Green Hat*. In this best-seller of the period the heroine, Iris Storm, is doomed by having 'a pagan body and a Chislehurst mind'. Her boyish hair, her leather sports jacket, her poster-painted face belie an inner fragility, and although she drives a Hispano Suiza sports car, it becomes the instrument of her suicide. She was what Evelyn Waugh called 'the last of the ... exquisite, the doomed and the damning, with expiring voices ... the ghosts of romance who walked between the two wars'.[34]

In the 1930s fashion was moving back towards romanticism, although Elsa Schiaparelli's use of surrealist motifs (she made hats like shoes, and *trompe l'oeil* sweaters) did prefigure a modernist questioning by fashion of itself. Mainbocher, an American designer who worked in Paris and whose most prestigious client was Mrs Wallis Simpson (he made the dress she wore at her wedding to Edward VIII after his abdication), had actually floated the essentials of the New Look style well before war broke out. The New Look was to be launched in 1947 by another Parisian designer, Christian Dior, when it introduced a full-blown romantic nostalgia into the austerity of the post-war world; but already British *Vogue* was reporting in January 1940: 'In August we were all set to lace in our waists to suit the new waspish lines. ... We were even feeling back to the wide-hipped, close-hemmed pre-[1914] lines.'

The Uniform of Chic: the Twenties.
Reproduced by kind permission of the Trustees of the Victoria and Albert Museum.

During the Second World War *Vogue* was certainly filled with images of sensibly garbed and often uniformed women. Yet there were moments when sexual difference seemed heightened:

> The brave and fair get together. Mars and Venus, he in uniform, she in beauty. . . . Leave days are red letter days, brief snatches of happiness, too short a space for experiments or mistakes. But what to wear, to do, to be? Does Mars want his Venus smart or sweet, grave or gay? Feminine whatever else. . . . Now if ever, beauty is your duty. (*Vogue*, 1941)

There was a whole glamour cult of the male uniform, against which the frivolous, flowery, veiled hats (hats were never rationed)[35] and precious silk stockings of the women appeared in melting contrast.

During the war some Paris dress designers closed down. Chanel spent the war holed up in the Ritz with a German officer. By preventing the wholesale removal of the Paris couture industry to Berlin it has been argued that those couturiers who remained open during the Nazi occupation did France a service. But James Laver in British *Vogue* (September 1944) stated that Paris fashion during the war had been a 'fashion of collaborators and Germans'. It had been tight-waisted, frilly, extravagant and ultra-feminine, and had developed along romantic lines that anticipated the New Look. James Laver hoped and believed that women would move against this reactionary fashion after the war. They did not (although there was opposition to the mode, which I describe in Chapter Ten). But by its development during the Nazi occupation, the post-war romanticism of fashion is revealed as more than merely reactionary, nostalgic and backward looking; it became the persistence in the late 1940s of the romantic styles that had flowered under Nazism, in a world supposedly dedicated to the exorcizing of the fascist creed.

By the late 1940s fashion photography was expressing this romantic, slightly morbid mood with an imagery of women in cloudy tulle dresses floating against castle walls, landscape gardens or a desolating backdrop of bomb damage or slums; or of perfectly

The New Look as interpreted by the British ready to wear firm, Deréta, and drawn by Francis Marshall.
Reproduced by kind permission of Deréta.

elegant women in sheathlike black stepping along like cranes against the façade of a city street. Yet although the New Look was supposed to be so feminine, there was a weird masculinity about it all. The models were tall as guardsmen, and their street clothes resembled those of guardsmen in mufti, or City men leaning against furled umbrellas. They wore the highest high heels, and hobble skirts with sharply jutting hips and flying panels which bore faint memories of Gothic architecture, but the hard hats looked like city bowlers.

Then the angular style of the photographer Horst made way for a newer and more youthful ideal. In 1953 British *Vogue* published a photograph by Antony Armstrong Jones. It showed a model leaning forward across a table to embrace a friend, and inadvertently upsetting a tray of wine glasses. Later, Armstrong Jones drew on candid camera or family snapshot styles as he caught his models supposedly off guard, tripping over in boats or asleep as the tide comes in. Irving Penn, another photographer of the period, was introducing gawky informality into his pictures. The ballerina, gamine Audrey Hepburn look began to represent an alternative to the glacial artifice of Parisian *haute couture*.

During the next thirty years the philosophy of Chanel was to triumph over that of Dior. Her work, as we shall see, laid the basis for a further development of modernist style, which will be discussed in Chapter Seven.

I have sketched the history of fashion in an impressionistic way, and have attempted to draw out trends rather than make an exact chronology. Some concept of the historical is, however, helpful when we turn to examine theoretical explanations of dress, some of which, while trying to explain the *change* that is fashion, actually attempt to find universal explanations based on *unchanging* human characteristics, or else reduce history to a crude economism, or to the simplistically symbolic.

Chapter 3

Explaining It Away

The logic of difference cuts across all formal distinctions. It is equivalent to the primary process and the dream work: it pays no heed to the principle of identity and non-contradiction. This deep-seated logic is akin to that of fashion. Fashion is one of the more inexplicable phenomena, so far as these matters go: its compulsion to innovate signs, its apparently arbitrary and perpetual production of meaning – a kind of meaning drive – and the logical mystery of its cycle are all in fact of the essence.

Jean Baudrillard: *For A Critique of the Political Economy of the Sign*

Because fashion is constantly denigrated, the serious study of fashion has had repeatedly to justify itself. Almost every fashion writer, whether journalist or art historian, insists anew on the importance of fashion both as cultural barometer and as expressive art form. Repeatedly we read that adornment of the body pre-dates all other known forms of decoration; that clothes express the mood of each succeeding age; that what we do with our bodies expresses the *Zeitgeist*. Too often, though, the relationship that of course exists between social change and styles of dress is drawn out in a superficial and cliché-ridden way. The twenties flapper becomes the instant symbol of a revolution in manners and morals after the First World War; the New Look symbolizes women's return to the home (which anyway didn't happen) after the Second World War; the disappearance of the top hat signals the arrival of democracy. Such statements are too obvious to be entirely true, and the history they misrepresent is more complex.

The serious study of fashion has traditionally been a branch of art history, and has followed its methods of attention to detail. As with furniture, painting and ceramics, a major part of its project has been accurate dating of costume, assignment in some cases of 'authorship', and an understanding of the actual process of the making of the garment, all of which are valid activities.[1] But fashion history has also too often been locked into the conservative ideologies of art history as a whole.

The mid twentieth century was a prolific period for the investigation of fashion. Doris Langley Moore, one of the few women then known for her writings on the subject, commented that the subject matter was women, the writers almost exclusively men.[2] Their acceptance of prevailing conservative attitudes towards women led to a tone sometimes coy, sometimes amusedly patronizing, sometimes downright offensive, and itself fundamentally *un*serious, as if the writer's conviction, often stated, of the transcendent importance of his subject matter was subverted from within by his relegation of women to a denigrated sub-caste. Because fashion has been associated with all that is feminine, these writers wrote about it as they would write about women; indeed, Cecil Willett Cunnington, author of many books about dress, even contributed a book to a series called 'Pleasures of Life' – the subject matter *Women*.[3] Other 'pleasures of life' included cricket and gardening!

Art history has also tended to preserve the élitist distinction between high art and popular art. Fashion then becomes essentially *haute couture*, and the disintegration of this tradition, the decline of the Dress Designer as Artist, together with the ascendancy of the mass clothing industry, are alleged to have brought about the end of 'true' fashion. Once we are all in fashion, no one can be, so the hallmark of both bourgeois democracy and socialism is said to be uniformity of dress, that 'grey sameness' by which all fashion writers are haunted. So Cecil Willett Cunnington sighed for the Edwardian glamour of lace and chiffon, and the charm of bustle and crinoline, regretful that

The modern woman no longer finds costume a sufficient medium for the expression of her ideals . . .

As the twentieth century lunges on towards the accomplishment of its destiny it is natural that it should discard those forms of art which have ceased to suffice. This is Progress and part of its price is the Decline and Fall of the Art of Costume.[4]

Quentin Bell, on the other hand, while he comes to the same conclusion, does so for the opposite reason, since he foresees that if abundance became universal

> class distinctions would gradually be swamped from below and the pecuniary canons of taste would slowly lose their meaning; dress could then be designed to meet all the needs of the individual, and uniformity, which is essential to fashions, would disappear.[5]

Those who have investigated fashion, finding themselves confronted with its apparent *irrationality*, have tried to explain this in *functional* terms. The most bizarre styles and fads, they argue, must have some function; there must be a rational explanation for these absurdities, if only we could find it. Yet this gives rise to a dilemma, for how can what is irrational have a function?

This line of argument seems to assume that because fashionable dressing is an activity that relates directly to the human body, as well as being a form of art, it must therefore be directly related to human biological 'needs'. Furthermore, because when human beings dress up they often make themselves uncomfortable and even cause themselves pain, there has been a tendency to explain this 'irrational' behaviour in terms that come from outside the activity itself: in terms of economics, of psychology, of sociology. We expect a garment to *justify* its shape and style in terms of moral and intellectual criteria we do not normally apply to other artistic forms; in architecture, for example, we may all have personal preferences, yet most of us can accept the pluralism of styles, can appreciate both the austerity of the Bauhaus and the rich convolutions of rococo. When it comes to fashion, we become intolerant.

Because the origins and rise of fashion were so closely linked with the development of mercantile capitalism, economic explanations of the fashion phenomenon have always been popular. It was easy to believe that the function of fashion stemmed from capitalism's need for perpetual expansion, which encouraged consumption. At its crudest, this kind of explanation assumes that changes in fashion are foisted upon us, especially on women, in a conspiracy to persuade us to consume far more than we 'need' to. Without this disease of 'consumerism' capitalism would collapse. (Doris Langley Moore argued that this is simply not true of the fashion industry, since the men's tailoring trade, where fashion changed more slowly, has proved far more stable than the fluctuating women's fashion market, where undue risks have to be taken since it is never known in advance which fashions will catch on and which will expire as fads.[6])

Underlying such arguments is a belief that human individuals do have certain unchanging and easily defined needs. The attempt to define and classify such needs has proved virtually impossible, however, and in fact even such biological needs as the need for food and warmth are socially constructed and differentially constructed in different societies. The concept of need cannot elucidate fashion.

Another, related, argument explained fashion in terms of the fight for status in capitalist societies. In such societies costume became one arena for the continuous social struggle of each individual to rise by dint solely of merit and ruthlessness. The old, rigid boundaries of feudal life dissolved, and all were now free to copy their betters. Unfortunately, as soon as any fashion percolated down to the middling ranks of the bourgeoisie, or lower, it became disgusting to the rich. They moved on to something new. This in turn was copied. According to this argument, fashion became an endless speeded-up spiral.

The most sophisticated version of this explanation was Thorstein Veblen's *Theory of the Leisure Class*. Veblen argued that fashion was one aspect of the conspicuous leisure, conspicuous wealth and conspicuous waste he held to be characteristic of an acquisitive society in which the ownership of wealth did more to confer prestige on its owner than either family lineage or individual talent. Veblen, like Engels, also argued that the women of the bourgeoisie were effectively the property of their men:

> It has in the course of economic development become the office of the woman to consume vicariously for the head of the household; and her apparel is contrived with this object in view. It has come about that obviously productive labour is in a peculiar degree derogatory to respectable women, and therefore special pains should be taken in the construction of women's dress, to impress upon the beholder the fact (often indeed a fiction) that the wearer does not and cannot habitually engage in useful work ... [Women's] sphere is within the household,

Veblen's Conspicuous Consumer. French haute couture, 1870.
Reproduced by kind permission of the Trustees of the Victoria and Albert Museum.

which she should 'beautify' and of which she should be the 'chief ornament' ... By virtue of its descent from a patriarchal past, our social system makes it the woman's function in an especial degree to put in evidence her household's ability to pay. ...

The high heel, the skirt, the impracticable bonnet, the corset, and the general disregard of the wearer's comfort which is an obvious feature of all civilized women's apparel, are so many items of evidence to the effect that in the modern civilized scheme of life the woman is still, in theory, the economic dependent of the man – that, perhaps in a highly idealized sense, she still is the man's chattel.[7]

Veblen argued that conspicuous waste accounted for change in fashion, but he also believed in a 'native taste' (that is, some kind of essential good taste) to which conspicuous wastefulness was actually abhorrent. It is abhorrent, he argued, because it is a 'psychological law' that we all 'abhor futility' – and to Veblen the stylistic oddities of fashion were manifestly futile. He explained fashion changes as a kind of restless attempt to get away from the ugliness of the imposed, irrational styles, which everyone instinctively *did* recognize to be ugly. For Veblen, then, the motor force of fashion was a wish, forever frustrated, finally to *escape* the tyranny of irrational change and perpetual ugliness.

Fashion writers have never really challenged Veblen's explanations, and his analysis still dominates to this day. Yet his theory cannot account for the form that fashion changes take. Why did the bustle replace the crinoline, the leg of mutton sleeve the sloping shoulder? Theodor Adorno, a Marxist cultural critic, exposed deeper inadequacies in Veblen's thought, arguing that for Veblen

progress means, concretely, the adaptation of the forms of consciousness and of ... economic consumption to those of industrial technology. The means to this adjustment is science. Veblen conceives of it as the universal application of the principle of causality, in opposition to vestigial [magical thinking]. Causal thinking is for him the triumph of objective, quantitative relations, patterned after industrial production, over personalistic and anthropomorphic conceptions.[2]

In other words, Veblen, according to Adorno, has succumbed to the nineteenth-century obsession with the natural sciences. In Veblen's ideal world there was no place for the irrational or the non-utilitarian; it was a wholly rational realm. Logically, pleasure itself must be futile since it is unrelated to scientific progress. This was the measure of Veblen's utilitarian, clockwork universe, and he therefore hated pursuits such as fashion and organized sport. This ideology led him to reduce *all* culture to kitsch, and to see leisure as absurd in itself. This utilitarian ideology fatally marked the movements for dress reform.[9]

The persistence of Veblen's theories is curious. They have not only continued to dominate discussions of dress by a variety of writers in the fashion history field, but have also influenced recent, supposedly 'radical' critics of 'consumer culture'. In America, Christopher Lasch[10] and Stuart and Elizabeth Ewen[11] have condemned modern culture, including fashion; in France Jean Baudrillard has explicitly made use of Veblen's theory to attack consumerism. Like Veblen, Baudrillard condemns fashion for its ugliness:

> Truly beautiful, definitively beautiful clothing would put an end to fashion ... Fashion continually fabricates the 'beautiful' on the basis of a radical denial of beauty, by reducing beauty to the logical equivalent of ugliness. It can impose the most eccentric, dysfunctional, ridiculous traits as eminently distinctive.[12]

and he regards fashion as a particularly pernicious form of consumerism, since it

> embodies a compromise between the need to innovate and the other need to change nothing in the fundamental order. It is this that characterizes 'modern' societies. Thus it results in a game of change ... – old and new are not relative to contradictory needs: they are the 'cyclical' paradigm of fashion.[13]

Such a view is oversimplified and over-deterministic; that is, it grants no role to contradiction, nor for that matter to pleasure. Baudrillard's vision is ultimately a form of nihilism. The attack on consumerism perceives our world as a seamless web of oppression; we have no autonomy at all, but are the slaves of an iron system from which there is no escape. All our pleasures become, according to this view, the narcotics of an oppressive society; and opera, pop music, thrillers and great literary 'masterpieces' should therefore logically be condemned along with fashion.

What is especially strange about Baudrillard's analysis is that he appears to reject Marxism, while accepting this most conspiratorial

of Marxist critiques of capitalism. He furthermore suggests that
there is some ultimate standard of 'authentic' beauty, while elsewhere he rejects the idea of such rationalistic standards and seems to
suggest that desire, which after all creates 'beauty', in a sense, is
necessarily contradictory and divided, implying that artefacts would
reflect this ambivalence. Where then does the notion of 'true
beauty' come from?

One type of economic explanation of fashion interprets it in
terms of technological advance, and it is of course true that without
the invention of the sewing machine (which Singer patented in
1851), for example, the mass fashion industry could not have come
into being. This, though, does not explain the parade of styles of
the past 135 years.

A more complex economic explanation would include the cultural consequences of expanding trade and expanding economies in
western Europe. Chandra Mukerji argues that Europe was already a
'hedonistic culture of mass consumption' in the early modern
period. According to her, this contradicts the prevailing view,
elaborated by the sociologist Max Weber and popularized in Britain
by R. H. Tawney, that the 'Protestant Ethic' which fuelled capitalist
expansion was one of 'ascetic rationality', that the early capitalists
were thrifty, 'anal' character types who saved rather than spent, and
that only with the arrival of industrial capitalism, and especially in
our own period, did modern consumerism begin. Even the English
Puritans, she suggests, wore costly and elaborate clothes – and in
any case, their clothes were influenced as much by the sober but
fashionable wear of the Dutch as by religious considerations.[14]

Economic simplism was matched by nineteenth-century anthropological simplism. So long as the biblical account of the Creation
was accepted, the wearing of clothes might be not only a sign of
vanity, but paradoxically might also reflect humankind's consciousness of its fallen state. However remote the first figleaf of Adam and
Eve from the peculiarities of Victorian dress, it could be argued that
women and men wore clothes out of modesty, to hide their
nakedness and the sexual parts that reminded them of their animal
nature.

This naive view was shattered as the truth of Genesis began to be
questioned. In addition, the explorations of early European anthro-
pologists, the discovery of lost worlds and 'primitive' societies,
contributed to a gradual, but radical questioning of the nature of

European culture in general and of European costume in particular (although this was usually still in supremacist terms). Anthropology undermined the belief that clothes are 'needed' to shield us from the excessive heat and cold of the climate.

Already in 1831 Thomas Carlyle was writing:

> The first purpose of Clothes ... was not warmth or decency, but Ornament ... for Decoration [the Savage] must have clothes. Nay, among wild people we find tattooing and painting even prior to clothes. The first spiritual want of a barbarous man is Decoration, as indeed we still see among the barbarous classes in civilized Countries.[15]

Later such views were further confirmed by Charles Darwin's description of the people of the Tierra del Fuego. This people, although living in one of the most inclement regions of the world, near the Falklands Islands, wore little clothing:

> The men generally have an otter skin, or some small scrap about as large as a pocket-handkerchief, which is barely sufficient to cover their backs as low as their loins. It is laced across the breast by strings, and according as the wind blows, it is shifted from side to side. But these Fuegians in the canoe were quite naked, and even one full-grown woman ... It was raining heavily, and the fresh water, together with the spray, trickled down her body.

Later, Charles Darwin commented:

> We were well clothed, and though sitting close to the fire were far from too warm; yet these naked savages, though farther off, were observed, to our great surprise, to be streaming with perspiration at undergoing such a roasting.[16]

and when given pieces of cloth large enough to have wrapped themselves in, they tore it into shreds and distributed the pieces, which were worn as ornaments. Darwin, whose writings on this subject were permeated with the racism of his time, poured scorn on the 'savages' and for him this behaviour was merely further evidence of their idiocy. What it actually suggests is that dress has little or nothing to do with the 'need' for protection.

It has as little to do with modesty. As Havelock Ellis, a pioneer sexologist pointed out: 'Many races which go absolutely naked possess a highly developed sense of modesty.'[17]

The growing importance of anthropology in the twentieth

century, and its usually imperialist assumptions, had an impact on western fashion and on the way in which fashion was perceived. On the one hand designers could rifle 'primitive' societies for exotica to give a new flavour to jazz age dress, matching the 'primitivism' of 'Negro music' with African designs and ornaments. (Nancy Cunard always wore an armful of ivory bangles.) On the other hand, the diversity of ways of dressing found in distant lands could make western fashion appear completely relativistic. This implied another kind of conservative explanation. The bizarre varieties of dress could all be seen as reflecting the *sameness* of 'human nature', at all times and in all places. The abstract entity 'human nature', it was argued, always loves novelty, dressing up, self importance and splendour. This cliché reduces all social and cultural difference to a virtually meaningless surface scribble; but actually dress and styles have specific meanings. 1980 mass-produced fashion is not at all the same as Nuba body painting, the sari or Ghanaian robes.

Anthropological discussion of dress tends to blur the distinctions between adornment, clothing and fashion, but is interesting because when we look at fashion through anthropological spectacles we can see that it is closely related to magic and ritual. Dress, like drama, is descended from an ancient religious, mystical and magical past of ritual and worship. Many societies have used forms of adornment and dress to put the individual into a special relationship with the spirits or the seasons in the enactment of fertility or food-gathering rites, for war or celebration. The progression from ritual to religion, then to secular seriousness and finally to pure hedonism seems to have been common to theatre, music and dance – the performing arts – and dress, itself a kind of performance, would seem to have followed this trajectory from sacred to secular. Fashion, too, contains the ghost of a faint, collective memory of the magical properties that adornment once had.

Even today garments may acquire talismanic properties, and both children and adults often become deeply and irrationally attached to a particular item. Billie Jean King, for example, wore a favourite, sixties-style mini-dress for her big tennis matches in the belief that it brought her luck; during the Second World War British Spitfire pilots used to attach their girlfriends' bras to their cockpits for the same reason.

Fashion offers a rich source of irrational and superstitious behaviour, indispensable to novelist and social commentator. And, as

Quentin Bell has pointed out, 'there is ... a whole system of morality attached to clothes and more especially to fashion, a system different from, and ... frequently at variance with that contained in our law and religion'.[18] He suggests that this has to do with a whole covert morality, and is symptomatic not of conformity but of commitment to another, hidden and partly unconscious world, a hidden system of social, collective values.

Alison Lurie sees clothes as expressive of hidden and largely unconscious aspects of individual and group psyche, as forms of usually unintentional non-verbal communication, a sign language.[19] Her vignette interpretations of the sartorial behaviour of both groups and individuals are sharp and amusing, but although dress is, among other things, a language, it is not enough to assume that our choice of dress makes unintended statements about self image and social aspiration. Alison Lurie is always the knowing observer, treating others to put-downs from some height of sartorial self knowledge and perfection; she assumes that even those who most knowingly use clothes to 'make a statement' are letting their psychic slips show in spite of themselves. Her use of the metaphor of language (for it is only a metaphor), far from explaining the 'irrationality' of dress, merely reinforces the view that it is irrational.

Roland Barthes[20] uses linguistics and semiology (the science of signs) in a more sophisticated way, but equally takes it for granted that fashion is irrational. In fact his theory of fashion is based entirely on the idea of irrationality, since for him the sign, like language, is a system of arbitrarily defined differences. He suggests that language works in the following way: the words used to name objects (dog/*chien* and so on) are arbitrary, but the objects named have significance only in terms of their differences from other objects – ultimately our conception of a dog is based on its *difference* from a cat or a cow. Barthes argues that all sign systems work in this way, and like language, fashion is for Barthes an enclosed and arbitrary system, the meanings it generates entirely relative. His exhaustive analysis of the 'rhetoric of fashion' (captions and copy in fashion magazines) places fashion in a vacuum. Fashion has no history and no material function; it is a system of signs devoted to 'naturalizing the arbitrary'.[21] Its purpose is to make the absurd and meaningless changes that constitute fashion *appear* natural.

Barthes, therefore, is not, like Veblen, a functionalist; his theory depends on the belief that fashion has no function. Yet, like Veblen, he does see fashion as morally absurd, as in some way objectionable, and this leads him to argue that at another, ideological, level, fashion does have exactly the conspiratorial function assigned to it by Veblen:

> [The discourse of] fashion describes certain types of work for women ... woman's identity is established in this way, in the service of Man ... of Art, of Thought, but this submission is rendered sublime by being given the appearance of pleasant work, and aestheticized.[22]

He analyses fashion from a hostile point of view that at heart believes fashion to be an unnecessary aberration. Women who like fashion, his analysis implies, suffer from false consciousness. But to banish fashion from the realm of truth in this way is to imply that there exists a wholly other world, a world in which, contrary to his own theory, meaning is *not* created and recreated culturally, but is transparent and immediately obvious. But not only would this be a world without fashion, it would be a world without discourses, a world, that is, without culture or communication. Such a world cannot, of course, exist, or if it did it would be a world without human beings in it.

Even psychoanalysis, which seems to offer a richer understanding of fashion than other psychologies, and which I shall discuss in relation to sexuality, still explains it in terms of its function for unconscious impulses. This is an important dimension. All functionalist arguments nevertheless miss fashion's purposive and creative aspects.

Of all those who have written about fashion, René König[23] has come as close as any to capturing its tantalizing and slippery essence. He sees fashion's perpetual mutability, its 'death wish', as a manic defence against the human reality of the changing body, against ageing and death. Fashion, Barthes' 'healing goddess', substitutes for the real body an abstract, ideal body; this is the body as an idea rather than as an organism. The very way in which fashion constantly changes actually serves to fix the idea of the body as unchanging and eternal. And fashion not only protects us from

Fashion Victims of 1948 by Anton.
Reproduced by kind permission of the proprietors of Punch.

"I must introduce you—you've got so much in common."

reminders of decay; it is also a mirror held up to fix the shaky boundaries of the psychological self. It glazes the shifty identity, freezing it into the certainty of image.

Fashion is a branch of aesthetics, of the art of modern society. It is also a mass pastime, a form of group entertainment, of popular culture. Related as it is to both fine art and popular art, it is a kind of performance art. The concept of 'modernity' is useful in elucidating the rather peculiar role played by fashion in acting as a kind of hinge between the élitist and the popular.

Even the society of the Renaissance was 'modern' in its tendency towards secular worldliness, its preoccupation with the daily, material world, and its dynamism. Characteristic of that world was its love of the changing mode, and a wealthy middle class that already competed in finery with the nobility. From its beginnings fashion was part of this modernity.

The coming of the industrial revolution and a world for the first time dominated by machines transformed everything. 'All that is solid melts into air.'[24] Industrial capitalism tore up the earth, 'dissolved all fixed, fast, frozen relationships' and created a new, turbulent world of motion, speed and change. The perpetual movement of modernity both thrilled and terrified the new citizens of the great industrial centres. It was – and is – experienced both as an explosive kind of liberation and as an annihilating state of disintegration and disorientation.

Machinery not only revolutionized manufacture and material life, but also thought, belief and ideology. The industrial revolution consolidated western faith in the rational and reinforced the scientific attitude. The 'real' was what could be seen, measured, weighed and verified, and the methods of investigation of the natural sciences alone seemed correct. (Veblen's work is stamped with this way of thinking.) Nature no longer seemed so awesome and mysterious, but became an object for human investigation, and a source of raw materials to be exploited. Magic, religion, even artistic endeavour by contrast came to seem irrational. Although art and religion remained important, they now occupied a reduced space. Art was embattled. 'From today painting is dead,' was one response to the daguerreotype, forerunner of the photograph. The appearance of mass-produced artefacts opened a gap between art, including craftsmanship, on one side and machine-made imitations on the other – the unique and the kitsch, high art and the popular.

The Artist found himself both more important and more threatened.

The Romantic movement of the late eighteenth century and early nineteenth century was one early response to the advance of science and the 'dark Satanic mills' of industrialism. It offered a counter-ideology that spoke against the machine age and yet espoused the intense individualism of the new order.

Before the eighteenth century, nature had not been admired; the essence of being civilized was to distance yourself as far as possible from the natural state. Now, nature began to be idealized just at the time when a new and much more wholly urban society was being created by the industrial revolution. The Romantics asserted the superior value of the natural and spontaneous against the mechanical and cerebral, the truth of feeling against reason and the scientific spirit. They cultivated self expression, rebellion against all authority, individual freedom and the refusal of convention. Childhood was idealized as a period of spontaneity and innocence, and children came to be seen as closer to nature and to the quick of experience than adults. Children had traditionally been dressed in adult-style clothes – the paintings of toddling Spanish princesses of the seventeenth century rigged out in ruffs and farthingales, their bodies covered with jewels, is an extreme example – but for some time the artificiality of this had been questioned. Now for the first time specific forms of dress for children appeared.

The liberation of childhood was not matched by an expansion of women's horizons. The Romantics glorified love. Passion defied the patriarchal order and the social bondage of matrimony, and was the most intense form of feeling. Romantic heroines were idealized, but because they were seen as closer to nature, as more emotional and more irrational than men, subtly they were denigrated and reduced to beings less than human. The heroine was simply an excuse for the romantic hero's feelings – for the hero of the Romantic movement was he who gave expression to feeling: the Artist, a man in revolt against the inhumane and unfeeling factory world. Romanticism invented its own fashions – natural, Grecian-inspired styles for women and children, the new sobriety for men.

Throughout the nineteenth century realist artists were enraptured by fashion, that irrational, transient emanation of style so despised in scientific thought. Painters such as Tissot, Constantin Guys and Manet recorded the fashions of their day as central to their paintings. Mallarmé, the French symbolist poet, whose work deconstructed language and questioned the meaning of words, actually edited a fashion journal for a few months in 1874, and appears to have been most upset when he was dethroned by a Baronne de Loumarin, for he wrote to his friend Émile Zola, begging him not to write for the paper under its new editorship and complaining that he had had all his work stolen from him.

He is thought to have written the entire contents of *La Dernière Mode* under pseudonyms such as 'Miss Satin', and the strange contrasts and juxtapositions of ornamentation – juxtapositions as daring as metaphor – seem to have appealed to his poetic sense, so that he speaks of 'une robe ... en dentelle noir semée bizarrement d'acier bleu à reflets d'épée', or 'La neige ... la crème ... ces deux blancheurs toutes contraires mêlent pour moi leur vertu sans leur danger, dans ce produit d'un nom delicieux: Crême-neige.'[25]

Modernism as a movement in art had begun to oust naturalism well before 1900. Modernism was a response to the challenge of nineteenth-century science, which had investigated reality in new ways. Although science regarded the visible world as the real world, by contrast with an unknown, and probably imaginary invisible world, the natural sciences ultimately challenged the 'reality' of what we see and pointed to an underlying structure, showing how the visible world is the result of invisible energy or unseen chemical combinations. The methods of science deconstructed the visible world that art had hitherto been content to reproduce. At first, inventions such as the daguerreotype appeared to threaten the whole artistic project, but later scientific endeavour made possible a new role for art, since art appropriated some of the methods of science. Modernism turned away from the illusion of naturalism and realism, and stated that a painting was just that: a flat representation, not a three-dimensional reflection of the 'real'.

One definition of modernist art has been that it 'lies in the use of the characteristic methods of a discipline to criticize the discipline itself'.[26] Both modernist art and modernist writing placed the artist's own activity centre-stage. The subject of the modernist novel was typically its own creation. Modernist painting was about abstract light, space and colour. In the 1920s fashionable dress simply imitated this angular, two-dimensional style. It was not at that time fully modernist since it had hardly begun to question its own terms, nor to question the whole concept of fashion –

although perhaps Chanel's 'fashion nihilism' and Schiaparelli's surrealism did implicitly do so.

The concept 'modernism', used as an umbrella term to indicate a wide variety of different currents in modern art and aesthetics, has been criticized for its lack of rigour. Yet it does suggest what is *common* to much of modern art: its oppositionalism and iconoclasm, its questioning of reality and perception, its attempt to come to grips with the nature of human experience in a mechanized 'unnatural' world.

The concept 'modernity' is also imprecise. Perry Anderson has argued from a Marxist perspective that 'modernization', 'modernism' and 'modernity' all, as concepts, obscure the actually quite precise kinds of social change to which they refer, veil the rapaciousness of capitalism, and the struggle between classes that it generates.[27]

Yet the word 'modernity' attempts to capture the essence of both the cultural and the subjective experience of capitalist society and all its contradictions. It encapsulates the way in which economic development opens up, yet simultaneously undercuts the possibility both of individual self development and of social cooperation. 'Modernity' does also seem useful as a way of indicating the restless desire for change characteristic of cultural life in industrial capitalism, the desire for the new that fashion expresses so well.

When we look at the relationship of fashion to art, we can see that in the 1920s fashion was directly influenced by modernism. Sonia Delaunay, for example, a Ukrainian who settled in Paris, first of all used Fauve colour schemes, later adapted geometric abstract art to her textile and dress designs. After the Second World War, haute couture, as we shall see later, seemed to aspire to the status of high art, with the couturier in the role of Genius. Some contemporary fashions, those inspired by punk for example, are modernist in questioning the very fashion project itself. Postmodernism, with its eclectic approach to style might seem especially compatible with fashion; for fashion, with its constant change and pursuit of glamour enacts symbolically the most hallucinatory aspects of our culture, the confusions between the real and the not-real, the aesthetic obsessions, the vein of morbidity without tragedy, of irony without merriment, and the nihilistic critical stance towards authority, empty rebellion almost without political content.

Postmodernism appropriates decoratively themes of popular culture. Popular culture, which also has a relationship to fashion, may include both the spontaneous amusements created by the working class for itself, and 'mass entertainment' created for a mass audience by the state or by commercial interests. To some, popular entertainment is democratic, to others it is unworthy. Do the masses actively participate, or are they passive and pulp fed?

Sport, machinery, metropolitan life and the cinema all influenced artists and writers in the early years of the twentieth century, but some of the most influential left-wing critics remained sceptical and ultimately hostile. One group of Marxists, known as the Frankfurt School because their Institute for Social Research was located there, was especially important. Walter Benjamin, also associated with the School, was more sympathetic to popular culture, but Theodor Adorno and Max Horkheimer were the two whose views were best known and most fully spelt out, and they described urban mass society as a cultural nightmare. Influenced first by the rise of Fascism in the Germany from which as Marxists and Jews they were forced to flee, and then by the American culture to which they never assimilated (although the United States gave them refuge until after 1945) they believed popular entertainment to be merely a standardized expression of the ideology of monopoly capitalism. It was art reduced to advertisement, individuality wiped out by mass production, the epitome of false consciousness:

> In the culture industry the individual is an illusion not merely because of the standardization of the means of production. He is tolerated only so long as his complete identification with the generality is unquestioned. Pseudo individuality is rife: from the standardized jazz improvization to the exceptional film star whose hair curls over her eye to demonstrate her originality. What is individual is no more than the generality's power to stamp the accidental detail so firmly that it is accepted as such. The defiant reserve or elegant appearance of the individual on show is mass produced ... the peculiarity of the self is a monopoly commodity determined by society; it is falsely represented as natural. It is no more than the ... French accent, the deep voice of the woman of the world, the Lubitsch touch.[28]

For those writers 'high art' and the mass market were poles apart.

In many western countries the period after the Second World War was one of 'consensus' at home, even if the external situation was threatening. There was agreement, in Britain, for example, across a large part of the political spectrum that certain rights and welfares were established as an essential part of the social structure; popular political programmes of the day concentrated on basic wants clustered around pay, work and social services. A more secure and prosperous base was being created for increased recreation and leisure, or so it was believed. Since it was recognized that 'ordinary people' varied widely in their tastes, abilities and interests, the forms that leisure and recreation would take were left open, and into this vacuum rushed commercial interests. These promoted large-scale, spectacular entertainment. They promoted, too, the desirability of an ever-increasing variety of styles and tastes that impinged on personal and intimate areas of life. This included dress.

British radicals to begin with rebelled against the new commercialization of popular culture. Many Europeans, too, were appalled by the substitution of an Americanized pop culture for traditional working class or national tastes. In the 1960s, in Britain at least, this began to change. The political generation of the sixties grew up to the sound of rock and roll. Pop music had already come to symbolize the rebellion of youth against all that seemed so stuffy and conformist about establishment culture in the 1950s, a culture that, whether managed by conservatives or social democrats seemed stagnant, nostalgic and complacent.

The transformation of one kind of popular entertainment – music – into an expression of the radical spirit meant that it was being taken seriously at an intellectual level. In the years that followed, other aspects of the 'popular' became respectable as objects of study. Unlike Adorno and Horkheimer, the culture critics of the 1960s and 1970s felt it élitist to condemn the masses because they listened to pop, watched football or enjoyed movies or TV soap opera. It was wrong, they argued, to write off popular taste. The crowds at a football match or a pop concert did more than merely passively imbibe predigested entertainment. Their participation was active, and creative.

At first such discussions largely ignored women; men investigated male activities. In the 1970s, however, feminists began to study pulp romances, teenage girls' magazines and TV sit. com. and soap opera – previously rejected as cultural products reeking with anti-liberatory ideologies, inimical to women. But now feminists argued that this feminine culture could not simply be dismissed. Women, it was argued, were far from being the passive dupes of an oppressive, sexist ideology. Rather, the contradictory nature of the romances and magazines themselves, and the way in which their audiences consumed and used them was not mere escapism, but was an attempt to maximize pleasure.

This general accolade still explicitly excluded or at best ignored fashion. Fashion behaviour and popular styles of dress were discussed in relation only to what were predominantly *male* youth subcultures: mods, skinheads, punks. Fashion, as the most widespread medium for women's self-expression, has continued to be largely an absence.

Feminists in the 1970s were reluctant to discuss it. It was simply assumed that – in the jargon of the sixties – everyone now 'dressed to please themselves'; or else that fashion was *obviously* a humiliating form of bondage, confining women to narrow stereotypes of femininity and the 'beautiful', often even restricting their actual movements.

The discussion of feminist attitudes to dress comes under the heading of the politics of fashion. It is mentioned here simply in order to suggest that unlike their male radical counterparts, who had no difficulty in identifying with the macho features of the subcultures they studied, feminists interested in popular culture had to recognize that it was all about the reinforcement of femininity when it catered especially for women. It was particularly hard for them, therefore, to react to fashion, except in rebellion against it. They shared a widespread hostility to fashion. This hostility was massively fuelled by knowledge of the fashion industry, for as soon as we investigate the material base of fashion, we enter a world that is undeniably and inescapably one of cruelty and exploitation.

Chapter 4

The Fashion Industry

It is a curious fact that the production of precisely those articles which serve the personal adornment of the ladies of the bourgeoisie involves the saddest consequences for the health of the workers.

Friedrich Engels: *The Condition of the Working Class in England*

The exploitation of the nineteenth-century garment and textile workers – mostly women – is an all too familiar story, and the hideous contrast between the luxury of fashion and the suffering of those who helped make it possible turned many nineteenth-century reformists entirely against fashion. The fashionable lady, caged in her crinoline or trussed in her bustle, became a symbol of bourgeois hypocrisy both to the workers' representatives and to the feminists. To the old moral disapproval of the vanity of dress was added a consciousness of its injustice.

It was the cotton industry that fuelled the take-off of the industrial revolution in Britain, which was the first country in the world to industrialize. With the coming of industrial machinery the lives of whole communities were shattered and destroyed. E. P. Thompson and John Foster, among others, have described in detail the process whereby the cottage industry of the weavers was transformed to the factories, a process that involved a loss of both independence and living standards, peculiarly harsh conditions, and an exploitation of women and children unheard of before.[1] Within a few years the British cotton industry dominated the world, having destroyed the indigenous cotton industries of the Indian sub-continent and devouring the raw material on which it had been based.

The first cotton cloth, fustian, had been known since the six-teenth century. (The word 'jeans' (as in blue jeans) came from 'Genoa'[2] since one type of fustian was made there.) Manchester developed into a cotton town in the seventeenth century; never a corporate or guild city, it was therefore freer to develop a new form of trade. (Medieval craft guilds had the power to restrict such developments.) At first, cotton was used to make material for linings, pillow covers and other domestic items. But by the early eighteenth century it was being adapted for printed petticoats and waistcoats, and in the second half of the eighteenth century for women's dresses, curtains and chintzes.

Already a fashion had developed in England for the Indian calicoes that the East India Company had been importing through-out the seventeenth century, but which did not become fashionable until towards the end of it. These fine Indian cottons, painted or printed with delicate floral patterns, became fashionable because they resembled the French printed silks that were used to create court fashions, and were fine enough to be pleated and draped in the same way. They were also, of course, easier to keep clean than silk, and therefore more practical. Attempts to restrict the import of French silks also increased their popularity. Yet they were then seen as a threat to the indigenous English wool and silk trades, and they themselves were restricted for a time by a law of 1720. This only led to attempts by native cotton manufacturers to produce a calico substitute themselves; and their success in doing so became one of the pre-conditions for the takeoff of the industrial revolution.[3] After 1750 a whole series of inventions revolutionized the cotton-making processes, weaving and spinning becoming mechanized and eventually steam powered. Methods of printing fabrics were also mechanized. Yet after this spate of inventions, techniques of pro-duction stabilized and even stagnated.

The wool industry, long established in Britain, experienced less upheaval, since it was already highly developed and capitalized. Woollen cloth had been worn by the ordinary people; it was at this same period of the industrial revolution that its use spread to the upper sections of society for formal wear, at least that of men.

An English cotton mill in 1851.
Reproduced by courtesy of the Mary Evans Picture Library.

Before industrialization, the wool industry had been organized on the 'cottage' or 'putting out' system. The weavers, usually although not always male heads of household, obtained the wool from merchants, and the work of spinning and other preparatory processes was carried out by other members of the weaver's household, a patriarchal, family system of work that did not survive the coming of the factories, although the labour force in the factories was, especially at first, predominantly women and children, the overseers usually men.

Although the domestic production of woollen cloth had been widespread in England, the industrial revolution also had the effect of confining it to its centres in the north of England. Although, therefore, the industry was long established, great changes did occur, although some processes, such as knitting, for long continued to be undertaken in the home.

The silk industry was never a major one in England. Dorothy George,[4] however, describes the London silk trade as an important textile industry in the seventeenth and eighteenth centuries. It was a trade in which there were both great fluctuations and major discrepancies, since it included men and women as diverse as the wealthy master weavers and the most exploited women and child workers. Later in the eighteenth century, mills were built in the north of England and in the shires, the result being that by the beginning of the nineteenth century women and children had ceased to be occupied casually as silk winders, but women were now more likely to be weavers, previously an occupation men had striven to reserve for themselves. In the nineteenth century the area around Lyons in France was the western centre of the silk manufacturing industry, and it was greatly assisted by the development of Paris as the world capital of *haute couture*. The production of silk mourning crape was a significant element of this industry. The British firm of Courtaulds, for example, began as producers of this material, for which there was enormous demand.[5]

Unlike cotton or wool, silk is a single continuous filament, not a fibre that requires to be spun into a thread, although the silk is normally 'thrown' by having two or three filaments spun together. Despite the simpler production process, however, silk remained the rarest and most expensive raw material for cloth, because it was the hardest to produce. Only certain climates produce the mulberry trees off which the silkworms feed, and their care is highly labour intensive. Silk was also considered the most luxurious and desirable thread because it could be made into the softest, finest and most lustrous materials, and took colour more beautifully than wool or cotton.

For all these reasons the nineteenth-century search for a synthetic substitute for natural raw materials centred mainly on silk. The first synthetic material was rayon, at first known as 'artificial silk', which was made from wood cellulose treated with chemicals to produce a filament similar to silk. After a treaty of 1860 which reduced import tariffs on French silk and thereby largely undercut the indigenous British silk industry, Courtaulds turned their attention to synthetic fibres. They acquired the patents for the production of viscose in 1904, but the main period of expansion came after the First World War. By 1938, 10 per cent of apparel fibres were synthetic. (In 1966–7 the figure was 38 per cent.)

Companies in Germany, Italy, Japan and the United States have continued to develop new synthetic fibres. After rayon came nylon and polyester, then the acrylic substitutes for wool, and the most recent has been the production of elastic yarn (Lycra) as a substitute for rubber elastic. (It is made by producing a special twist and crimp into filaments of synthetic yarn so that it springs back when stretched out.)

Whereas natural fibres were land or labour intensive, sometimes both, the production of synthetics requires neither a particular type of land or climate, nor abundant supplies of labour. Production is capital rather than labour intensive, and continuous technical advance has tended to encourage ever larger plants. Although, however, the development of these synthetic fibres seemed like a dream come true to the manufacturer during the post-war boom of the 1950s, by the mid-1960s this sector of the textile industry destabilized, and surplus capacity began to become a problem.

In Britain, this was only one aspect of a general decline. Britain's share of the world textile market had begun to shrink by the outbreak of the First World War, and efforts to halt or at least contain this decline have led to fluctuations in policy between free trade and tariffs and protectionism. The decline was especially marked in the cotton industry. The woollen industry was never as dependent on foreign markets, and British woollen goods had an especially high reputation.[6]

The development of the manufacture of clothing was rather

different. The continuing demand for individualized clothes and rapid changes of fashion, particularly for women, have marked the trade, which, like textiles, is an ancient one.

Tailors had been amongst the earliest independent craftsmen, and had set up their own guilds in the medieval towns.[7] These guilds were organizations of employers, who normally worked with their families, one or two trained 'journeymen' and a few apprentices. Then there were tailors who travelled round the countryside, calling at farms and hamlets, staying while they made clothes for whole households, then moving on. In the great houses there would have been those among the armies of servants whose work was to sew and tailor.

Travelling tailors persisted well into the nineteenth century, when they are believed to have become messengers for the embryonic, and barely legal, 'combinations', or trades unions. Indeed, one of the peculiarities of the clothing trade is the extent to which old methods have persisted alongside new. Just as the journeyman tailor survived until well after the introduction of the mass manufacture of clothing in factories, so the sweatshop and the outworker survive to this day.

Until the seventeenth century, customers who wanted their clothes made commercially bought the cloth themselves and took it to a craft tailor. During the course of the seventeenth century, however, the shopkeeping tailor appeared, and this reinforced the division between the skilled craftsman and the mere journeyman. The shopkeeping tailors had capital with which to rent a shop in a smart area, stock it with expensive materials and grant extended credit to the 'quality' who patronized them. Trade was seasonal, and tailoring hands were taken on and laid off as needed. Insecurity and poverty was therefore their lot.

The early eighteenth century saw the beginnings of combinations and associations among the tailoring hands as a response to this insecurity, and the result was a series of demands for shorter working hours and better pay. Meanwhile the craftsman tailors developed into an early form of capitalist élite.

Fine, individualized and hand-done work was carried out in appalling sweated labour conditions in the late eighteenth century and the nineteenth century, both in Britain and elsewhere. Although the original tailors had been men, by the time of the industrial revolution there were many dressmakers making the delicate clothing now in vogue for women, and Engels's description of the working conditions of these young girls in the 1840s would have applied for many years both before and afterwards. The dressmaking establishments as he described them

> employ a mass of young girls – there are said to be 15,000 of them in all – who sleep and eat on the premises, come usually from the country and are therefore absolutely the slaves of their employers. During the fashionable season, which lasts some four months, working hours, even in the best establishments, are fifteen, and, in very pressing cases, eighteen a day; but in most shops work goes on at these times without any set regulation ... The only limit to their work is the absolute physical inability to hold the needle another minute. ... Enervation, exhaustion, debility, loss of appetite, pains in the shoulders, back and hips, but especially headache begin very soon; then follow curvatures of the spine, high, deformed shoulders, leanness, swelled, weeping and smarting eyes, which soon become short-sighted; coughs, narrow chests and shortness of breath and all manner of disorders in the development of the female organism.
>
> In many cases the eyes suffer so severely that incurable blindness follows ... consumption usually soon ends the sad life of these milliners and dressmakers.[8]

For most of these young women the only alternative to this slave labour was the equally hated domestic service; and it was widely believed that necessity drove many of them to casual or full-scale prostitution.

The manufacture of clothing in the industrial societies of the nineteenth century developed in two different ways. There was a demand for the bespoke tailoring and fine needlework that could only be done by hand; at the same time the mass production of clothes was beginning. In France, Britain and the United States factories at first made clothing for the armed forces (and in the US for slaves as well); in the big ports rough clothing for sailors began to be mass produced – a trade accelerated in the United States by the gold rush in the mid century.[9] The process soon began to be extended to ordinary urban daywear for men – the 'snobs' and 'cockneys' of London in the 1830s and 1840s were young clerks and shop assistants whose 'vulgar' pretensions to style were made possible by the ready-to-wear clothing already available.

In 1851 Singer patented the sewing machine, and Symingtons, a

firm of corset makers in Market Harborough in Leicestershire, claim
to have been the first firm to bring sewing machines to England. The
firm of John Barran in Leeds developed the first cutting machine in
1858. This was an adaptation of a band saw used for cutting
furniture veneers. The decline of the linen industry in Leeds at that
time meant that factory space and a pool of female labour were
available in an area in which engineering firms were alert to the
possibilities of adapting machinery.

The coming of the clothing factory deepened the division between
the new bands of casual and semi-skilled machinists and the old craft
workers. In the traditional tailoring trade each garment was made
separately by a single worker. This was known as the complete
garment method. The complete garment method continued on into
the twentieth century, and typically was carried out by a merchant
tailor in a small establishment with the traditional handful of apprentices and journeymen in his employ. He usually designed the clothes
and had a limited supply of materials from which the customer chose.

In Britain and the United States two groups of workers came to
join the ranks of the casual and semi-skilled. These were the women
workers and, towards the end of the nineteenth century, the immigrant workers, especially Jews.

'The tailoring workshop of the eighteenth century had been a
man's world of hard work, hard drinking and tough union politics.'
A few women had been apprenticed, but in the main, 'female labour
was confined to the female wing of the garment industry: the lower-
paid, unorganized trades of dressmaking [and] millinery.'[10] By the
early nineteenth century this relatively stable way of life was under
threat; women began to be apprenticed as tailoresses in larger
numbers, and already by the mid century their increased participation in the trade was being attributed to the loss of control of their
craft by the men, and the appearance of sweated labour.[11] This
development opened an era of struggles among the many tailoring
unions then existing, some specifically for women, in which men
sought to limit the role of women or to eject them altogether,
blaming them for the deterioration in conditions that was actually
the result of industrial upheaval.

Mid nineteenth century London sweatshop.
Reproduced by courtesy of the Mary Evans Picture Library.

The Jewish workers in many cases came already equipped as skilled tailors since, debarred from the professions and from many trades in their countries of origin, they had developed skills in this area left open to them. From among such immigrants to Britain and the United States came many of the innovators and important figures of the twentieth-century clothing industry.

It was during the period from 1890 to 1910 that the mass-produced clothing industry really took off, both in Britain and in America. The expansion of clothing factories, however, did not mean the demise of the sweatshops or the disappearance of out-workers. Rather the factory system perpetuated outwork. Since the clothing trade was seasonal it was cheaper for many of the bigger manufacturers to off-load work at peak periods rather than have spare capacity in their factories for the rest of the year. The un-healthy and often dangerous small workshops were notorious, and one of the worst evils of the system was the middleman who subcontracted work at the lowest possible cost.

At the turn of the century sweating was causing public as well as trade union concern, and a full-scale campaign against it was begun in London. Feminists had been active since the 1890s in campaigns to discover and expose the conditions under which women worked, and in 1909 the campaign against sweating and for a minimum wage in the industry met with success: the Trade Boards Act was passed. This empowered the Board of Trade to set up boards to regulate wages in any branch of a trade where pay was exceptionally low. By 1913 when rates were finally established some of the worst evils of sweating do seem to have diminished; and the First World War strengthened the Trade Boards movement and improved con-ditions of work. Yet Clementina Black's survey of married women's work, published in 1915, demonstrates the still vast differences in pay and conditions,[12] from women cruelly exploited by the middle-men to those few highly skilled workers who earned 'proportionally good wages and live a very comfortable life'.

Other women worked for early forms of the 'madame shop' (what we now call boutiques) and for the big city department stores. Many, having trained in the West End, migrated to the suburbs, where, as Frances Hicks, who became secretary of the London Tailoresses' Union, described, 'they give West End style to neighbouring trades people, upper class servants and a few

wealthier patrons'.[13] Customers provided their own material, a
sewing machine could be hired for about 1s. 6d. (7½p) a week, and
the dressmaker would be assisted by young girls who might pay to
be apprenticed. These young women in turn often aspired to work
in the big, city-centre stores where they might be taken on as
seasonal hands between March and August, and there was a recurring moral panic that they eked out a mean livelihood by
prostitution.

The West End department stores also employed young women
on a permanent but still exploitative basis, characterized by long
hours of work, low pay and no provision for holidays. They did all
kinds of work, from alterations of ready-made clothing bought in
the store to dressmaking from scratch and the copying of expensive
models.

In the United States, and most notoriously on New York's
Lower East Side, conditions were as bad as in the East End of
London. They had already improved slightly before the historic
garment industry strike took place in November 1909. Twenty
thousand workers walked out, and although most of them were
men, the participation of the women who made up the blouse
division made it the largest ever women's strike in America. Suffragists and women in high society took up their cause, and although this particular strike petered out, further action in 1910 led
to an historic agreement being signed with the employers, when at
least some of the workers' demands were met.[14]

Tragically, the following year saw the dreadful Triangle Shirt-
waist fire in which 125 women workers were burnt to death –
another savage testimony to the appalling and dangerous conditions of work. And while these did marginally improve, in an
exploited workforce women were the most exploited, their pay
never more than about half that of their male co-workers.

Yet ironically the development of ready-to-wear and the expansion of the fashion industry reflected an expansion of freedom for
women. By the close of the Victorian age there was a wealthy
middle class, and sections of the lower middle class and the working
class were prosperous as never before. Women's lives were changing, and they were demanding clothes to suit lives in which work
and leisure pursuits were more varied. They were working in offices
and department stores, and engaging more and more in active
recreations and sports.

The ready-made garment trade expanded from producing coats, mantles and outerwear to the 'coat and skirt', the dress, the blouse and the petticoat. 'Separates' were born. The smart city 'coat and skirt' could be mass produced for the new working girl. This style, which became almost a uniform before the First World War, was immortalized by Charles Dana Gibson. His American 'Gibson girl' epitomized the 'New Woman' with free and easy ways, whose almost masculine attire only enhanced her femininity.

The blouses – or shirtwaists, as they were called in the United States – worn with the coat and skirt, formed a staple of the sweated industry. One blouse maker, interviewed by Clementina Black's team, 'was busy upon fine garments of lawn and nainsook, embroidered, and with insertion. One took her three hours to make, and she received 9s. per dozen.' Another 'was making blouses of cheap silk, with two strips of insertion down the backs and one down the fronts and yokes, at 4d. each'.[15]

If Arnold Bennett (writing in the *New Age* under the pen name of Jacob Tonson) is to be believed, the results were often tacky. Reporting on a talk by H. G. Wells at the Times Book Club, he wrote that while the women in the audience certainly 'deemed themselves elegant',

> Being far from the rostrum, I had a good view of the back of their blouses, chemisettes and bodices. What an assortment of pretentious and ill-made toilettes! What disclosures of clumsy hooks-and-eyes and general creased carelessness! It would not do for me to behold the 'library public' in the mass too often![16]

In the United States there was even more scope for mass-produced clothing. The great distances and scattered but rapidly expanding communities in this enormous country meant that clothes could be reproduced in large numbers and dispatched to different centres. Fashion clothing was also a vehicle for the Americanization of immigrants:

> For Italian immigrants in New York City donning ready-to-wear broke ancient taboos. As peasants from [Southern Italy] they had learned that certain lines should not be crossed. . . . To don a hat was the privilege of the signora . . . or the whores. In America a war broke out over such customs. While older women held to the conventions of the past, wearing scarves over their heads and shawls over their shoulders, young Italian women eagerly ate of the forbidden fruit. . . .

For an older generation schooled in the indignities of sumptuary law, fashion was proscribed from desire. For their children it represented a transcendent escape. It was one of the few areas in which the promises of industrial plenty could, at least superficially, be met.[17]

During the First World War women's economic position in Britain improved temporarily. There was also a new social freedom. Respectable women were beginning to appear on city streets openly wearing cosmetics. Cheap fur coats were within the reach of some working women. The design of women's clothes was being simplified, and this went further in the 1920s when chemise dresses and straight coats could easily be factory produced.

In the twenties and thirties there were major changes in the clothing industry. A further swing to factory production further broke down the divisions between the skilled tailor, the semi-skilled workers in tailoring shops, and the factory workers and sweated outworkers. There was a rapid growth of multiple firms, and these specialized in the making of clothing that was at once mass produced *and* made to measure. Men's wear firms with their own factories (for example Montagu Burton and the Fifty Shilling Tailors) were able to translate personal measurements into factory-made clothes. 'Wholesale couture' or 'middle-class fashions' also developed; Deréta, Windsmoor and Harella were examples of firms that developed distinctive 'house styles', and good design was as important as good quality. For the first time the proper sizing of mass-produced clothes was introduced into Britain from America (although American sophistication in this area was not matched until well after the Second World War).

In the factories, methods continued to vary widely. J. Dobbs[18] commented of Britain in 1928 that factories with 5000 employees existed side by side with old-style small workshops, while department stores remained an important source of employment for women dressmakers. Even where new methods were introduced this did not necessarily improve conditions for the workers; the conveyor belt system, for example, was resented because it made the work more tiring than before. In the United States too, where methods of work more advanced than those existing anywhere else had been developed, the old 'complete garment' method persisted. One investigator wrote:

New York City is the exception in a country where section factories are the rule, and like Montreal it still produces women's dresses, coats and suits in small factories by the complete garment method.

Operators are skilled continental immigrant craftsmen whose average age is now between 55–60. In earlier days the craft was handed down through the family but the present generation has no use for such slow methods, preferring the occupations providing high payment more quickly. There is no system of apprenticeship, and manufacturers are therefore faced with a dying craft which permits no interference and opposes mechanisation.[19]

As well as these small workshops, there were sweatshops still turning out cheap clothes. By the 1940s, however, the production of attractive cheap clothing was increasingly associated with the development of modern factory methods. New and often well-designed factories had been built out of town in New Jersey, Connecticut and upstate New York in the 1930s, while in St Louis and Kansas, and in the new fashion centres of California which had developed rapidly during the Second World War, modern inventions such as the Eastman straightknife and circular blade rotary cutter (and American manufacturers were surprised to hear that the band knife was still used in the UK) were in use. Factory owners also pioneered the spreading of the workload throughout the year to stabilize employment.

In Britain the Second World War produced a demand for quality clothes. As in the First World War, men and women were actually financially better off than in peace time. There were military uniforms to be made (and for the first time for women in large numbers). There was also the 'Utility' scheme, which set standards of design for household items such as furniture as well as clothes. To make the best use of materials in short supply British dress designers created smart, attractive models that could be economically mass produced at a price most men and women could afford.

During the war, and for several years afterwards, clothing was rationed, each individual being given a book of coupons, so that there were 'fair shares' for all. After the war the Labour government strove to maintain these standards. Sir Stafford Cripps at the Board of Trade set up a working party into the heavy clothing industry, which reported in 1947. A 'style development council' was proposed, and pay and conditions in the clothing industry were improved.

Utility scheme suit designed for mass production by Digby Morton.
Reproduced by kind permission of the Imperial War Museum.

After the Conservatives returned to power in 1951, however, planning bodies were replaced by voluntary organizations lacking teeth, and the Utility scheme was dropped. Throughout the 1950s the rise in living standards and the development of an 'affluent society' promoted by the encouragement of consumer spending did much to improve design. A further factor in the development of clothing manufacture and dress design was the development of a youth market. By the second half of the 1960s, nearly 50 per cent of all outerwear was being purchased by the age group 15–19.[20] These were teenagers in the full-employment society, who were not yet saving and whose weekly pay packets were immediately disposable; collectively they controlled the spending of millions of pounds.

This 'youth revolution' was centred on Britain, and British dress design for the mass market began to lead the world. (Mary Quant, whose work will be discussed in Chapter Eight, and who was probably the most important of the designers of the 1960s, made good use of American sizing and manufacturing techniques to promote her fashions on an international scale.)

Yet many of the fashion innovators of 'swinging London' relied on the old methods of outwork and sub-contracting. Their rapidly changing styles and short runs couldn't be produced under factory conditions where overheads and labour costs would have been prohibitive, but while outworkers in the late sixties and early seventies were more likely to be employed at agreed rates of pay, it remained true that 'being self employed is economically a good proposition for the contractor, who need not pay insurance or employ her all the time'.[21]

Outwork and homework had been rapidly spreading again since the late 1950s. In 1964 there were 15,000 homeworkers, of whom 85 per cent were women. Ten per cent of these women were under 18 years of age, and 30 per cent under 25.[22]

Meanwhile numbers employed in the industry continued to decline by about 2 per cent per year. Decline at home and competition from the developing countries had contradictory effects. British fashion came to be dominated by a few giant manufacturers, with many of the medium-sized quality firms either bought up or squeezed out of existence. At the same time cheap imports, first from Hong Kong, later from elsewhere in South-east Asia, flooded the market. An attempt by the Labour government of the late seventies to encourage investment in the home industry had some success, and exports increased threefold in 1978–9, but this was cut short by the election of Mrs Thatcher's government. The first Conservative budget, in increasing VAT from 8 to 15 per cent, removing restrictions on investment overseas, and promoting high interest rates during the 'strong pound' period, devastated the industry, and numbers employed fell from 310,000 in 1979 to 200,000 in 1982.

Some firms went out of business, some switched to production overseas, and there was a dramatic shift in the structure of the industry. In the 1970s there were 7000 companies in Britain, with 70 per cent of workers concentrated in 200–300 of these. In 1983 there were only 5000 companies and their average size was much smaller – because of the re-emergence of the sweatshop and small firm. In the large factories, too, conditions worsened rapidly, with summary sackings, the overnight disappearance of factories and sudden shut-downs without warning or redundancy agreements.[23]

It was suggested in 1979[24] that half London's fashion trade output was being produced by homeworkers. Despite economies of size at one end of the market the practice persisted because

> in the clothing industry ... a characteristically low capital investment contributes to the industry's hand to mouth existence, whilst at the same time narrow profit margins, a changing product and highly competitive markets often militate against further investment. It is still true that if wages can be kept at rock bottom levels, small producers can be very competitive and profitable.[25]

Trade unionism in the garment industry has reflected the state of the industry itself and has had a chequered history. The varying kinds and status of workers was reflected in the existence of a mass of small unions throughout the nineteenth century; after a number of mergers a final amalgamation in 1932 brought them all into the National Union of Tailors and Garment Workers (NUTGW). Before the Second World War, *productivity* in the clothing factories of Britain was increasing, despite the Depression when one in five garment workers was unemployed, and despite the fact that actual numbers in the industry began to decline. Women far outnumbered men, and today they form 90 per cent of the workforce, instead of 80 per cent as in the 1950s and 1960s, this again reflecting the increase in outwork.

It was noted in 1941 that 'mechanization is making garment making a mass production industry, [and] it is substituting female machine minders for male craftsmen'.[26] The threat of unskilled and often ununionized female labour to a skilled male labour force is a common one. In the garment industry the deskilling process has intensified the threat, as women are concentrated into assembly processes, while the men who remain in the clothing trade are found in the cutting room, in the stock room and in the mushrooming managerial and supervisory jobs.[27] Women's labour may eventually threaten some of these bastions too. A report in the *Guardian*(8 July 1980) described the introduction at Hepworths of a cutting system which cost £250,000 and 'has meant that a team of girls is now doing jobs which were traditionally a male preserve'. Fifty men's jobs were lost and the young women took only 12 weeks to train, whereas the NUTGW had insisted on a three-year apprenticeship for band saw cutting.

Skilled male labour thus threatened tried to resist the process, but their resistance to change was disliked by employers even in the forties and fifties. Their attempts to preserve skills and maintain wage differentials in practice operated against the interests of the women.

The response of the NUTGW to the massive offloading in Britain of cheap imported goods, and to the modernization that can improve the work but often makes it even more arduous, has been to try to develop policies that protect the home industry. Arguing that free trade as at present practised is harmful to workers in all countries, it therefore favours selective import controls. But import controls, it maintains, must be linked with proper government investment in home industry (as happens in Belgium, France and Italy) and with proper training schemes for all workers (unlike the few that were started in Britain in the 1950s, and which were for boys only, although girls were by far the greater source of recruitment to the industry).

Import controls are sometimes seen as merely the attempt by relatively privileged white male workers to protect themselves and their position at the expense of the 'cheap labour' of the 'third world'.[28] This need not be so, provided that they are introduced as part of a progressive general economic strategy, to include planned trade with the developing countries. The controversy over them, however, does highlight the fearful exploitation of the third world garment factories and sweatshops.

The modernization of all processes continues. There are now cutting machines that are able to deal with 50 or 60 instead of about 20 layers of material at a time, and new 'laying up' machines which automate the preparation of bales of cloth previously prepared and unrolled by hand before cutting. Computerized lay planning (the Gerber system) has developed; laser cutting has even become possible. It is already easier than it was a few years ago for relatively short runs of exclusive clothes to be made profitably in factories where new machinery becomes more and more diversified and sophisticated; the Japanese have developed a machine that can do 'hand' embroidery on very fine material, and factory 'bespoke' tailoring now utilizes machine stitching that imitates the appearance of irregular hand stitching.[29]

This immense technological sophistication coexists with the most dreadful exploitation in the 'third world'. It is nothing less than the re-creation by the multinationals and the so-called 'world market factories' of the worst excesses of the nineteenth-century industrial revolution. The world market factory is typically a wholly or partially owned subsidiary of a Japanese, North American or European multinational.[30] The technological production of the plant, all the advanced processes, in fact, remain within the parent company. The *only* process transferred to the third world country is the part work, and the only reason for this is the 'cheap labour' available. Machinery, fabric, thread, even cut-out garments are sent to the developing country; after the garments have been made up they are returned to the metropolitan parent firm. The technology remains the exclusive knowledge of the original firm – which reaps the profit as well.

This is a mammoth world-scale version of the old putting-out or sub-contracting system – sweating on a global scale. In the early 1970s the 'Polyester Roads' of the South Korean industrial slums were being compared to Manchester in 1840. That situation has spread and worsened in the succeeding decade as it has been extended to Taiwan, Indonesia, Bangladesh and Sri Lanka, while Hong Kong is said to be 'pricing itself out of the world market' because there a generation of workers has developed skills and demands better pay and conditions.[31]

In the new Asian factories it is women – or little girls, as young as 10 or 11 years old – whose labour is exploited. Their situation may, indeed, be even worse than that of their English Victorian forerunners for two reasons. In the 1840s trade unionism was in its infancy, and as it grew it at least made possible some improvements in working conditions. In Asia, on the other hand, there is often a *retreat* from previously progressive trade union legislation, when undemocratic governments, and an indigenous ruling class that stands to profit worsen the lot of the workers. Secondly, whereas in nineteenth-century Britain the introduction of the factory system acted to break up the patriarchal family, in the 'third world' the exploitation of very young women may actually reinforce patriarchal forms.

This occurs because the appearance of the world market factories coincides with the destruction of traditional agriculture (also usually due to 'first world' predators) and of traditional manufacturing systems (such as hand craft weaving in Indonesia). The very young woman therefore goes into the factories to support her whole family. Or, even if she does escape the tutelage of her father, she is liable – as were also the young women of the 1840s – to become the prey of factory owners and supervisors. Once again the spectre of the drift into prostitution becomes a nightmare reality as her eyesight and health are destroyed, and, no longer wanted in the factory, she can become part of a tourist package for the 'tired businessmen' of Japan, the US and West Germany, whose parent companies set up the factories in the first place.

Lest this give the impression that the women who perform their exploited 'cheap labour' in the developing countries do so passively, it is important to remember that this is certainly not the case. Within the past two years, for example, massive strikes in the Philippines and South Korea have erupted, and attempts at international solidarity among women workers have begun.[32]

In the midst of mass production, the exclusive remains an ideal. Polyester Road may seem a million miles away from the Rue de Rivoli, but in both the exploitation of workers goes hand in hand with the creation of a fashionable image.

For a century Paris *haute couture* was the incarnation of the exclusive. Worth inaugurated an age in which fashion was seen as the endeavour of a single creative Artist, a genius. Paul Poiret, whose designs drew on the inspiration of the Diaghilev Ballets Russes and the Cubist and Fauve artists – he often used the bold oranges, purples, blacks and greens of the latter – liked to believe that he alone had revolutionized fashion and was a dictator of styles to women. Indeed, he recounts the story of how on one of his triumphal tours of America he was asked, after a lecture, to advise individually the hundreds of enraptured women from the audience on the colours and styles each of them should wear. As each woman filed past him he looked hypnotically into her eyes and murmured a colour he thought would harmonize – the Svengali of fashion.[33]

He was enraged, during these tours, to discover that his designs were everywhere being pirated and although it was his tragedy never finally to profit from his own brilliance, the couturiers that followed in his footsteps were considerably more canny. Christian Dior in particular, who opened his own salon in Paris after the end of the Second World War, devised a system whereby his designs became almost a species of franchise. Overseas buyers could do one of three things. They could buy a paper pattern of the model; they could buy a canvas copy, which when made up identically or with minor alterations might be labelled 'original Christian Dior copy'; or they could buy the original properly made up and sell copies of it with the label of 'Christian Dior'.[34] And all the Paris *haute couturiers* made strenuous attempts in the post-war period to prevent the pirating of their designs, or even premature publicity by journalists. The creation of each new season's 'collections' was shrouded in exaggerated secrecy, which added to the mystique of inspiration.

Anne Price, for twenty years fashion editor of the British society journal, *Country Life*, explained in a recent interview why this was so:

Those were the days when news editors held the front page for the telephoned word from Paris on the height of the hemline and the status of the waist. Elegantly clad fashion editors, hats askew, handbags flying, would race each other for the phone box with as much ruthless determination as their colleagues from the sports desk displayed at a Cup Final's last whistle.

'Of course,' Anne Price says, 'fashion editors are competitive now, but ... in those days we were reporting one look, *the* look. That was what fashion was about – and it was news. Women all over the world waited to be told whether they should chop two inches off their hemlines and that story on the front page actually sold newspapers. So fashion editors were reporters first; they actually crept around trying to get exclusive previews, bribing employees of couture houses to steal sketches, competing ferociously for a scoop.' (*Guardian*, 23 February 1984)

Dior, like Worth before him, fostered the idea of the couturier as Artist: 'we couturiers are like poets'. He speaks of inspiration giving him an 'electric shock', and likens couture to architecture or painting.[35] Yet his most important contribution was to launch *haute couture* into the realms of big business. Financed by Marcel Boussac, a major French textile manufacturer, his *Maison* was on a far more ambitious scale than the pre-war *couture* firms had been.

Dior dated the emergence of *haute couture* proper not from Worth but from the revolutionary twentieth-century designers, Madeleine Vionnet (who invented the bias cut) and Jeanne Lanvin

> who finally transformed the profession ... by executing the dresses in their collections with their own hands and scissors. The model became a whole and at last skirt and bodice were cut according to the same principle ... Dresses now depended entirely on their cut.[36]

He contrasts this with the situation before their arrival on the scene, when the collections were not the work of a single individual. The 'name' designer accepted one-off designs from a host of freelancers. In any case, originality of design and cut were of less importance than the exquisite trimmings of all kinds which alone differentiated dresses that would otherwise have been almost identical.

Dior dominated French *haute couture* in the 1950s, his main rival being the Spaniard, Balenciaga. A French novelist, Célia Bertin, investigated the world of Paris fashion at this time, and found conditions behind the scenes not so different from those in Whitechapel or the Lower East Side: appalling rates of pay and long hours, the great difference being that they were glamorized by the mystique of Parisian *haute couture*.[37]

She discovered an ununionized hierarchy of workers, from the mannequins (as the fashion models were called) and *vendeuses* (the saleswomen who cared individually for the rich individual clients) at the visible, exciting end of the business, to the *midinettes*, apprentices and senior seamstresses in the obscurity of the workrooms. These skilled craftswomen and the head fitters, the most knowledgeable of all, were 'capable of turning out models which serve as patterns for the whole world' for rates of pay that seldom rose as high as 8*s*. (40p) an hour at 1956 values. Only between 2 and 3 per cent of the work was done by machine.

Despite the exploitation, this esoteric and above all theatrical world fascinated many of the workers, who were proud to dedicate their lives to it. The production of a collection seemed like the world of a film set or theatre. Drama and performance reigned, and the end product, although perishable, was just as much an art as those other perishable art forms, music and the play.

In the 1950s and 1960s, British, American and Italian designers could never quite shake off the dominance of Paris. Then, the ready-to-wear mass market began to change things. Designers recruited directly to this side of the industry wished to do more than simply reinterpret Paris in watered-down versions. The new young market didn't want a dim copy of a Balenciaga original, designed for a rich Frenchwoman of 45 with a lifestyle utterly different from that of the 'working girl'.

It was perhaps Chanel who announced the death knell for old-style couture. She re-opened in 1953, having lived down the disgrace of her wartime collaboration with the Germans, and in an interview she restated her old philosophy from the twenties:

> Elegance in clothes means being able to move freely, to do anything with ease ... Those heavy dresses that won't pack into aeroplane luggage, ridiculous. All those boned and corseted bodices – out with them. What's the good of going back to the rigidity of the corset? Now women go in for simpler lives ...
>
> I am no longer interested in dressing a few hundred women, private clients; I shall dress thousands of women. But ... a widely repeated fashion, seen everywhere, cheaply produced, must start from luxury. (*Vogue*, February 1953)

Soon the Chanel suit was being reproduced everywhere, particularly in the United States, where, Cecil Beaton felt, it had indelibly stamped the American 'working girl' of the fifties; while the bright, sharp Mary Quant style of the 1960s was really a marrying of the style of the Chelsea art student with Chanel.

It is only since the Second World War that mass-produced, ready-to-wear clothing has become the standard wear for everyone. In the 1920s and 1930s, in many regions of Europe and the United States, let alone elsewhere, only the rich wore fashionable dress. In the streets even of large cities you would have seen people dressed

in each of at least three ways. There were the fashionably dressed; then there were the old, and adolescents, who wore clothing distinctive for their age group – the old sometimes continuing to wear the fashions of a past epoch; and there were the poor, who often still dressed in clothes that were both out of date and shabby. Even during the Second World War, for example, some working-class women wore the combination of a tailored suit jacket, a print frock, ankle socks and fashionable wedge shoes, an ensemble devised in the face of both poverty and rationing, but which was regarded as unthinkable by middle-class women – although in the 1970s it was revived as avant-garde, trendy or semi-hippie wear. Again, the long dresses and coats and Edwardian toques that Queen Mary of England continued to wear until her death, only looked truly archaic in the post-1950 period; before that, many rich elderly women had dressed similarly.

Since the 1970s, even Parisian couture has been dominated by the mass-market. The days of a single 'line' dictated from Paris are gone, although there are still style imperatives, and fashion snobbery maintains itself less by exclusiveness of design than by the more hidden perfections of expensive materials and beautiful craftsmanship. One result is that there seems to be disagreement in British colleges of fashion, and possibly in France as well, whether design students should be trained as creative individuals who produce art, or as craftworkers whose main relationship should be to the mass-production industry.[38]

Yet however much the fashion industry and fashion design have changed, its dual nature has remained curiously unchanging: a glamorous façade continues to conceal a life of corrosive toil for the workers hidden from sight. The glamour seems almost inseparable from the exploittion.

The glamour, none the less, continues to entice, and in turning to aspects of fashion specifically associated with the glamorous, we find, perhaps, less the exploitation of the workers than the exploitation of consumers. When we survey the 'glamour' industries of cosmetics and underwear, we discover products that seem often to serve no obvious purpose at all, and which, certainly in the case of cosmetics, are often produced at very low cost, yet sold at a high price as luxuries.

Chapter 5

Fashion and Eroticism

Tattoos, stretched lips, the bound feet of Chinese women, eye-shadow, rouge, hair removal, mascara, or bracelets, collars, objects, jewellery, accessories: anything will serve to rewrite the cultural order on the body; and it is this that takes on the effect of beauty.

Jean Baudrillard: *For a Critique of the Political Economy of the Sign*

It seems so obvious that dress must bear some relationship to sexuality that the assumption goes virtually unquestioned. Even in societies whose members ordinarily wear few clothes, it is said to be customary to dress up for dancing ceremonies and other occasions on which sexual interest is likely to be aroused. It is often said that dress enhances sexual attraction because it both reveals and conceals the body. Articles of dress even become, for some individuals, essential to erotic arousal.

Yet the attempt to explain fashion in purely or even in predominantly sexual terms is doomed to failure. In the first place standards of beauty – what kinds of looks and appearance get defined as sexually alluring – vary so widely from one culture to another that objective judgments of whether dress heightens attraction or not become impossible. Any garment *could* be defined as erotic; the reason for *changing* tastes in beauty must be sought elsewhere.

Dress bears some relation to sexuality, but is expressive of many other impulses as well. In any case, sex cannot be conceptualized as a discrete and tangible thing; it is a current in life, fluid and elusive, relational rather than separate. Many women as well as men, for example, dress as much for reasons of status as for sex appeal; but does not power bear a relationship to sexual allure? Women, and men, may dress to defy parents, spouse, a whole community; equally they may dress in a way that they hope will mean that no one ever notices them. Women certainly do not always dress 'for men'. The belief that they do has confirmed many fashion writers in their view of women as essentially silly, since they have seldom questioned the idea that it is every women's chief preoccupation to arouse male desire. Even, therefore, when women wear status garments, this is interpreted as sexual rivalry – for a woman to dress 'for other women' means simply in order to compete. And it is true that triumph and assassination by dress are by no means infrequent.

James Laver[1] went to great lengths to relate the erotic charge of dress to changes in fashion. He did this by inventing the theory of the 'shifting erogenous zone', arguing that at any period one portion of the female body must be emphasized, but that this emphasis must continuously shift since otherwise men will become satiated. This accounts only for women's fashions; but throughout his work Laver regarded male fashion as essentially defunct. He used his theory to explain particularly 'irrational' fashions such as the bare back dresses of the 1930s; he argued that the back was eroticized because men were no longer turned on by legs, which had been over-exposed in the 1920s, although in fact low backed dresses were also seen then. Yet it seems more likely that one reason for the bare back style was the influence of Hollywood; the imposition of a much stricter censorship on Hollywood films in 1934, the Hays code, meant that dresses cut revealingly low in front were now taboo, but they could still be cut completely away at the back and sides. The bare back dress was less an eroticization of the dorsal area than a surreptitious violation of the censor's ruling. It was also an indication of the influence of sportswear on mainstream fashion, taken over from bathing suits which were cut low at the back simply so that a larger portion of the total body could be tanned.

It is often impossible to interpret clothes in terms of the shifting erogenous zone: trousers might count as revealing the leg *or* the bottom, or equally it would be possible today to

The eroticization of the back? Low back dresses of the 1930s.
Courtesy Condé Nast Publications.

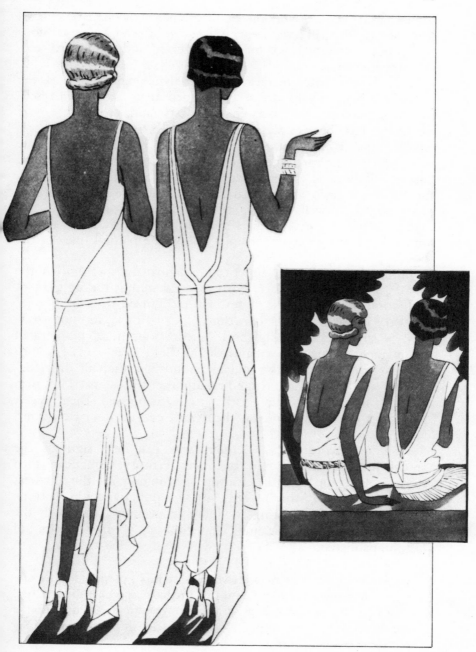

understand them as working clothes. Since women have entered the labour force in ever larger numbers, at least some fashions have been designed to muffle eroticism and rather to emphasize efficiency.

J. C. Flugel[2] attempted a psychoanalytic explanation of the relationship of sex to dress. He argued that fashion is a self-renewing compromise between modesty and eroticism; overt sexuality has been necessarily largely repressed in 'civilized' society, and it must therefore express itself in furtive or oblique ways, always fighting the 'reaction formation'[3] of modesty and shame. Fashion is therefore analogous to a neurotic symptom, or, as Flugel says, 'a perpetual blush on the face of civilization'. This approach well captures the ambivalence of fashion, yet, like Veblen's theory, assumes that fashion is irrational – ugly and absurd whenever it does not follow the natural lines of the body.

Edmund Bergler,[4] an American psychoanalyst writing in the 1950s, went much further, both in condemning the ugliness of fashion and in relating it to sex. He recognized that the fashion industry is the work not of women, but of men. Its monstrosities, he argued, were a 'gigantic unconscious hoax' perpetrated on women by the arch villains of the Cold War – male homosexuals (for he made the vulgar assumption that all dress designers are 'queers'). Having first, in the 1920s, tried to turn women into boys, they had latterly expressed their secret hatred of women by forcing them into exaggerated, ridiculous, hideous clothes.

Fashion, according to Bergler, was just one sign of the sexual malaise of the mid twentieth century. American men were growing up infantile, fearing yet longing for the 'giantess of the nursery' ('Mom'). This grown-up baby could become aroused only by indulging in 'infantile peeping', to which the fetishism and half-revealing, half-concealing artificialities of fashion pandered:

> We know that clothes are a masculine invention, propelled and maintained by man's inner fear ... Clothing reflects a peculiar distortion of sex based on a progressive, psychologically conditioned, diminution of the biological drive proper ... aphrodisiacs for man's vanishing potency.[5]

Underlying *all* these attempts to explain dress in terms of eroticism lurks Veblen's view. It repeats the false assumption so often buried in theories about fashion: that humanity could find its true essence by abandoning the 'civilization' that alone distances us from the animal state.

Yet we cannot return to that state. Among animals mating is regulated by biologically controlled cycles and by instinctive responses to the signals of female receptivity. Among human beings this mating cycle – in the sense of a 'mating season' and specific periods of the year when the female is 'on heat' – has disappeared; we substitute for it subtler signals of socially defined behaviour, in which dress does play some part. The part it plays is muffled and ambivalent, however, since clothing is much more than a sexual signal.

When we examine the two aspects of fashion, underwear and cosmetics, that are particularly associated with sex in the popular mind, we find that fashion is, among other things, a continuous dialogue between the natural and the artificial. Fashion, indeed, brings the two together in an intimate relationship, and the offspring of this relationship is fetishism. This – constriction and other sexual tastes dependent on specific articles of clothing – is a third aspect which reveals less a relationship between nature and artifice than the dependence for sexual arousal of certain individuals on stimuli with no connection whatsoever with biological function. For fetishists sex is in a peculiarly stark way 'in the mind'; but for many more women and men dress must articulate sexual fantasies in a less specific way.

Jean Baudrillard has written that today the term 'fetish'

> refers to a force, a supernatural property of the object and hence to a
> similar magical potential in the subject ... But originally it signified
> exactly the opposite: a *fabrication*, an artifact, a labour of appearances
> and signs.[6]

It originates from the Latin *facere*, which means to do or to make, and, through 'make' (from Anglo-Saxon and German) it is related to 'make-up' (in French, *maquillage*). A fetish is an alienated object that we ourselves make, but into which we then project magical properties. The magic of the fetish wards off or neutralizes fear.

Freud used the idea of the fetish in a particular way, to indicate forms of sexual activity in which, because of the fear of castration, desire is displaced on to a fetishized part of the body or adjunct to it.[7] Because of its proximity and relationship to the body, clothing is especially apt to be fetishized.

It is possible that in all cultures this occurs to a greater or lesser extent. In eleventh-century Japan, for example, the natural appearance was not admired at all. Not only did the court ladies shave their eyebrows and blacken their teeth (gleaming white teeth were considered hideous), but they muffled their bodies in elaborate robes:

> The importance attached to women's dress has already been noticed as an aspect of the rule of taste. A woman's skill in choosing clothes, and particularly in matching colours, was regarded as a far better guide to her character and charm than the physical features with which she happened to have been born. Feminine clothing was immensely elaborate and cumbersome, consisting . . . of a heavy outer costume and a set of unlined silk robes (12 was the standard number), all carefully selected with an eye to the most attractive and original colour combinations. So that their fastidious blending of patterns and colours might be properly admired, women wore the robes in such a way that each sleeve was longer as it came closer to the skin.[8]

In the capitalist West with its different aesthetic, dress always *hints* at the secret, hidden body. Gustave Flaubert's novel, *Madame Bovary*, expresses such fetishism to a high degree. Throughout the book, the desire men feel for Emma Bovary, its heroine, is displaced on to her clothes. When Charles Bovary begins to fall in love with her, Flaubert describes not her body, but her dress:

> He loved the little *sabots* of Mlle. Emma on the washed tiles of the kitchen floor; her high heels made her a little taller, and when she walked in front of him the wooden soles . . . creaked with a dry noise against the leather of the uppers.[9]

while in the most crucial scene in the book, Emma's arrival is described simply as 'a rustling of silk on the paving, the edge of a hat, a black cape . . . it was she!'[10]

In bourgeois life, as Flaubert describes it, the appearance of everything, including the clothed body, is described in minute detail. There is, however, always a suggestion that the body hidden by clothes and coverings is repulsive rather than alluring. In one scene, Emma is described as presenting a sparkling appearance to her husband when he returns from his doctor's round. He, on the other hand, has spent his day plunging his arms into tepid beds and dirty linen while blood and pus spurt in his face. And Emma's death is described in long drawn-out detail as above all the disintegration of a body rather than the extinction of an individual.[11]

Aspects of dress sometimes become the direct object of sexual gratification. Restif de la Bretonne, a self-confessed eighteenth-century fetishist, fell in love with the shoes of his employer's wife, and was, on one occasion, carried away by possession of a discarded pair of rose-coloured slippers with little tongues and green heels: 'my lips pressed one of the jewels, while the other, deceiving the sacred end of nature, from excess of exultation replaced the object of sex'.[12]

Constriction of the body may become a fetish. There are those who derive sexual satisfaction from the experience of having the body encased in a skin-like rubber body suit, but the best known and most long-term of such fetishes is tight-lacing. Laced up corsetry was worn for several centuries and tight lacing was widely practised until the close of the nineteenth century. Then, in the space of a few short years, it was reborn as a sexual perversion. It died as a fashion just at the time when sexologists, such as Havelock Ellis, were classifying, defining and describing, and thereby, some have argued, virtually creating sexual deviations; it has remained the sexual secret of small numbers of 'tight lacers' ever since.

David Kunzle[13] has written an exhaustive history of the practice. He has challenged contemporary feminists who have too readily assumed that the tight corsets of the Victorian era were just one aspect of the general subordination of women. Hélène Roberts, for example, writes:

> The clothing of the Victorian woman clearly perfected the message of a willingness to conform to the submissive masochistic pattern, but dress also helped mould female behaviour to the role of the 'exquisite slave'.[14]

In reality, Victorian women, on either side of the Atlantic, by no means all conformed to the 'submissive masochistic pattern'; tight lacing cannot have been, as Hélène Roberts suggests, a simple reflection of the subordination of women. David Kunzle argues that, on the contrary, it was the reactionary, anti-feminist moralists of the period that inveighed against the 'unnatural' practice, and that it actually expressed a covert form of rebellion. It was also

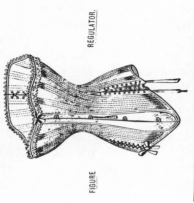

upwardly mobile women who tight laced most enthusiastically, and it therefore indicated, he suggests, social aspiration and aggression rather than conformity.

Kunzle's evident enthusiasm for the aesthetic of tight lacing leads him to downplay the real discomfort and even danger of the practice. Betty Ryan, a Wimbledon tennis star before the First World War, recalled that women's dressing rooms in English tennis clubs up to and during the First World War provided a rail near the fireplace on which the steel-boned corsets in which the women played could be dried: 'It was never a pretty sight, for most of them were bloodstained.'[15] Kunzle tries to invoke nineteenth-century feminist support for the practice of tight lacing, citing Elizabeth Cady Stanton's defence of fashion (not corsetry itself), but it seems unlikely that she, one of the foremost American feminists, would have supported Kunzle in his raptures over the thirteen-inch waists illustrated in his book, since, apart from anything else, she also tried – unsuccessfully – to promote dress reform. (Emily Davies, a British feminist, although a member of the Dress Reform Society, did argue that a corset, moderately tightly laced, offered comfortable support.)

Yet ultimately Kunzle is surely right to challenge the simplistic equation of fetishized fashions with women's subordination, especially since men as well as women wore corsets in the early nineteenth century. The contrary position, taken by Hélène Roberts, too readily positions women as victims, passively submitting to their fate.

At least one contemporary feminist has put an alternative view: that women may seek and actively participate in erotic arousal from forms of dress:

> High heels and corsets provide intense kinaesthetic stimulation for women, appealing to the sense of touch but extending more than skin deep. These frivolous accessories are not just visual stimuli for men; they are also tactile stimuli for women . . .
>
> Those women who were young in the fifties and sixties may remember modest but sustained arousal from comfortably tight girdles and

well-fitted high heels ... Walking in high heels makes the buttocks undulate about twice as much as walking in flat heels with correspondingly greater sensation transmitted to the vulva. Girdles can encourage pelvic tumescence and, if they are long enough, cause labial friction during movement.[16]

This author argues that fashion, including cosmetics, *is* women's pornography, gratifying women's highly developed sense of touch and their pleasure in their own bodies.

But this is surely a minority view among feminists. Simone de Beauvoir explored the idea of 'elegance as bondage' in *The Second Sex*, published in France in 1949, and this negative judgment on elegance has become the 'orthodox' view within feminism. It may be significant that Simone de Beauvoir was writing at a time when fashions, with Dior's New Look, had become unusually nostalgic, backward-looking and shackling.[17] These fashions suited the gloomy, decadent romanticism of the times. This was an era, for example, of the revival and cult of the classical ballet; the 'ballerina look' – an early Victorian pastiche, with flat slippers, sloping shoulders, full skirts and hair drawn back in a chignon – was one popular post-war fashion style. In a world dominated by queues, shortages and the Cold War, crinoline ball gowns, sweeping skirts and an encased elegance gestured towards a more leisurely and more romantic age. The French in particular capitalized on the nineteenth century on a grand scale. Madeleine Renaud and Edwige Feuillère, two of the best known stars of the French stage and screen, launched the period figure and style, clad in the gowns of Marcel Rochas and Pierre Balmain (along with Dior, the couturiers of the moment) both in life and in their films. Stars of course wore New Look styles in modern films, but more significant was the spate of period films. In the United States the modern *film noir* spoke the mournful contradictions of the 1940s, and there were also many period films; in Europe the French, nineteenth-century romantic film best expressed an erotic desire that was fettered and forbidden. Arletty in *Les Enfants du Paradis*, Danielle Darrieux in *Madame de*, Martine Carol in *Nana* and *Caroline Chérie*, Simone Signoret in *Casque D'Or* and a galaxy of stars in *La Ronde* acted out this theme. Edwige Feuillère endured thwarted lesbian love in bustles in *Olivia*, and even Brigitte Bardot went period in *Les Grandes Manoeuvres*.

A connection between the romanticized dress and outright pornography is made in *The Story of O*, a 'classic' pornographic celebration of bondage, flogging and mutilation, which dates from this period, and which is intensely preoccupied with the fetishism of fashionable clothes. In preparation for her first sado-masochistic ordeal, O, the heroine, is dressed in a semi-antique costume:

> Over a whalebone bodice which severely constricted the waist, and over a starched linen petticoat, was worn an ample gown, the open neck of which left the breasts, raised by the bodice, practically visible beneath a light film of gauze. The petticoat and gauze were white, the bodice and gown a seagreen satin.

Later O is permitted, for the time being, to resume her normal life. Significantly, she is herself a fashion photographer,

> which meant that, in the studio where they posed hour after hour, she took the pictures of the strangest – and prettiest looking – girls whom couturiers had selected to model their gowns.

Jacqueline especially takes O's fancy:

> She'd bend her head ever so slightly towards her left shoulder, leaning her cheek against the upturned collar of her fur ... O caught her once that way, smiling and sweet, her hair faintly lifted as though by some gentle breeze, and her soft but hard cheek grazing silver-fox, as grey and delicate as fresh firewood ash. Her lips were parted, her eyes half-closed. Under the cool brilliance of glossy paper one would have thought this the picture of some blessed victim of drowning; pale, so very pale.

What O understands and describes is more than just a pornographic image; the author has seized on the pornographic element in fashion itself, and especially the fashion of that period:

> Jacqueline ... was wearing an immense gown of heavy silk and brocade, red, like what brides wore in the Middle Ages, going to within a few inches of the floor, flaring at the hips, tight at the waist, and whose armature sketched her breasts ... it was what couturiers called a show gown.[18]

– and at once O saw that this exaggerated New Look gown resembled exactly the costume in which she was dressed for the ritual of flagellation. *The Story of O*, then, explores the latently pornographic nature of the *haute couture* outerwear fashions of the late 1940s, with their almost morbid romanticism.

It is more usually underwear that is associated today with the erotic, yet underwear was unknown before the nineteenth century. In 1951 the subject was still so risqué that Cecil Willett Cunnington and Phillis Cunnington prefaced their learned work on the subject with the following disclaimer:

> The historian must regard it as unfortunate that underclothes are so generally associated with eroticism, often to a pathological extent. . . . It is perhaps sufficient for the authors of the present book to claim, as doctors, that they approach the subject in a scientific spirit surveying impartially the various aspects of this subsidiary – though important – element in costume.[19]

Various kinds of linen shift had been worn for centuries; they protected the bodies of the rich from the stiff, scratchy materials of which clothing was often made, and at the same time protected the sumptuous costumes from the dirt of the bodies they adorned. For hundreds of years women swelled out their skirts with farthingales, 'bum rolls', cages, hoops and crinolines, or simply with petticoats. Then, for the first two decades of the nineteenth century, when their dress consisted of a narrow clinging robe, they wore tights and for the first time long underpants, or drawers, often visible beneath the diaphanous skirts. There was a return to heavy petticoats, but in the 1850s these were replaced by the metal crinoline. Then drawers ensured the preservation of modesty should the cage fly up in a wind, but these drawers, indecently to the modern eye, were joined at the waist only and were otherwise open and crotchless. 'Closed' knickers did not appear until the twentieth century, or shortly before. Victorian underwear seems to have been utilitarian and voluminous, but by the turn of the century the word lingerie was coming into use to denote glamorous garments made of delicate materials.

The year 1901 saw the launching in Paris of *Les Dessous Élégants*, the first trade journal to be devoted exclusively to underwear; and the first decade of the twentieth century was one of unprecedented luxury and innovation. Silk was more readily available from the Far East than ever before, yet there were still plenty of penniless needle-women in the cities of the West to transform it into the dainty teagowns, camisoles and lace-trimmed petticoats and nightdresses in the sweet pea colours dear to the boudoirs of the *Belle Epoque*.

The sexually emancipated woman was becoming almost respectable, birth control was accepted by the bourgeoisie, morals had relaxed in an atmosphere of materialism and the 'Indian summer' of imperial expansion. Edwardian lingerie was thought daring because designers such as Lucile (later Lady Duff Gordon, and sister of Elinor Glyn, celebrated author of outré best-sellers) used colours as well as filmy materials, 'a cascade of chiffons',[20] crêpe de chine and satin, lavishly embroidered and decorated with lace and ribbons.

Vice was no longer so rigidly separated from virtue, and although it was certainly possible for a woman to slide down the social scale into disrepute, there was a new 'half world' that began to dissolve moral barriers. Edwardian society, on both sides of the Atlantic, cared even more about money than about breeding; Edith Wharton's heroine Lily, in *The House of Mirth*, met her social downfall not because she was immoral, but because she failed sufficiently to respect money and superficial appearances. As a result, she found herself in a strange sub-world of unanchored luxury:

> The environment in which Lily found herself was as strange to her as its inhabitants. She was unacquainted with the world of the fashionable New York hotel ... Through this atmosphere of torrid splendour moved wan beings as richly upholstered as the furniture, beings without definite pursuits or permanent relations, who drifted on a languid tide. ... High-stepping horses or elaborately equipped motors waited to carry these ladies into vague metropolitan distances, whence they returned, still more wan from the weight of their sables, to be sucked back into the stifling inertia of the hotel routine ...
>
> [Their] habits were marked by an oriental indolence and disorder ... [They] seemed to float together outside the bounds of time and space ...
>
> Through this jumble of futile activities came and went a strange throng of hangers-on – manicurists, beauty-doctors, hair-dressers, teachers of bridge, of French, of 'physical development'.[21]

It was to the women of this world that Elizabeth Arden was soon to ministrate.

After 1918 the increasing use of artificial fibres meant that fancy undergarments could be mass produced, although good quality lingerie continued to be hand made from natural fibres until the Second World War. Films, as James Laver points out, influenced taste:

It was not until the middle 1920s that the film makers realised that the medium had . . . possibilities which can be summed up in one word – sex. Motion pictures began to bear such titles as *Sinners in Silk* . . .

Undressing scenes were frequently shown and had the curious effect of immensely improving women's underwear in real life: the abandonment of linen and the substitution of real or artificial silk.[22]

By 1908 Paul Poiret claimed to have killed off the Edwardian figure by ridding women of tight-laced corsets. Such a claim must over-personalize and over-simplify a gradual change, and in any case corsets did not disappear, but evolved eventually into the modern 'foundation garments' which compressed the female form with elastic rather than with steel and whalebone. Between the wars corsets still appeared rigid rather than supple and often still used laces and boning. After the Second World War Marie Lebigot in Paris revived 'waspies', and her elaborate, pinched-in corsetry complemented the New Look, although many New Look dresses were themselves constructed with boning and interfacing. In the 1950s the girdles and pantie-belts that became fashionable were very modern in their use of elastic rather than whalebone. Yet to the eye of the 1980s, both the girdles and the bras like rocket caps appear bizarre, because the 1960s not only brought Lycra and the body stocking, the eroticization of the total body and the cult of nudity, but made overweight appear immoral as never before.

It was at this period that tights began to replace stockings, and they seemed at the time to symbolize a new freedom by contrast with elaborate suspenders and a multiplicity of undergarments. More recently some feminists have insisted that they perceived tights as offering greater protection in sexual encounters than the underwear of the 1950s. Tights are conventionally judged unaesthetic, since they compress the lower part of the body into a bifurcated sausage; yet they did simplify dress, and may be an example of clothing in which function and usefulness do triumph over aesthetics.

Tights were also simultaneously both outerwear and underwear; as such they anticipated the more recent blurring or even abolition of the distinction between the two. This blurring is one element in the aesthetic of recent fashionable dress.

Glamorous lingerie of the early 1930s.
Courtesy Condé Nast Publications.

There has been a popular, although over-simplified equation between the demise of underwear and the advent of the contraceptive pill in the 1960s. The origins of the 'freedoms' of that period were far more complex than this suggests, and sexuality, especially for women, was never 'liberated' in this simple way. Both sexual behaviour and fashion often expressed confusion and ambivalence. Bralessness, for example, was associated both with a feminist rejection of sexual objectification and with the sexual free-for-all of the 'permissive era', erect nipples visible through blouses and T-shirts a direct sexual come-on. With 'girdles' discarded, for the first time the bottom was visible in two halves instead of a single upholstered cushion. Rubber corsetry, it appears, was rejected both because it was seen as a symbol of enslavement to male standards of beauty *and* as a form of 'cheating', both as an attempt to disguise 'flab' *and* as an unaesthetic garment that turned men off, and akin for some young women to false teeth.[23] Buttocks outlined in tight jeans represented both emancipation and sexuality, both a rejection of male-defined beauty and its acceptance, both honesty and allure.

In the 1970s glamorous underwear made a dramatic reappearance. In Britain its promotion is associated with the name of Janet Reger, a small firm that made a great success out of up-market luxury lingerie before going bankrupt in 1982. But Janet Reger herself is still designing for a larger firm; under-capitalization caused the crash, not the failure of the idea. On the contrary, the designs were so successful that today camisoles, camiknickers, French knickers and even suspender belts and 'waspies' are on sale in every chain store.

But what are these garments really for? In her meditation on the Janet Reger catalogue, Angela Carter points out that 'however informal, these garments are obviously public dress'[24] – and they are sometimes so worn; camisoles are used as party tops, French knickers as even more daring party wear.

Paradoxically, the marketing in the early 1980s by the American designer, Calvin Klein, of a completely different style of 'underwear for women' – in fact modelled on Y-fronts, boxer shorts and boys' vests – illustrates a similar point. It has been explained as the marketing of androgyny interpreted as diluted masculinity[25] – and here again we might make a Freudian point, and speculate whether this androgyny masks the fear of feminine passivity he claimed to have detected beneath the social and psychic structures of gender difference. They also support Angela Carter's point, for they could be and no doubt are used as outerwear. Undergarments may even turn out to have been a brief interlude in the history of fashion, a transition between the distant epochs when cleanliness was a rarity and 'true' underwear an impossible concept, and the late twentieth century when it is assumed, however inaccurately, that everyone can afford to be clean, and when at least cleanliness has become one of the conventions of the 'civilized life' of which fashion is a part.

On the other hand, the distinction between underwear and outerwear reflects the distinction between the public and the private that has become so important a part of modern life, and which was less developed before the eighteenth century. Perhaps its ambiguous status as a useless form of dress (underwear, Angela Carter suggests, is to clothing as ice-cream is to food), and increasingly its deliberate visibility, parallels the late twentieth century ambiguity surrounding privacy, intimacy and sexuality. For the latter, which is supposed to represent the heart of privacy, is simultaneously a publicly elaborated discourse – the counselling session, group therapy, the jacuzzi bath, the confessional 'true life' stories, and, indeed the playground beaches of the western world all make public its private secrets.

Perhaps also the camp crudity and rather parodied style of some 'French lingerie' is another example of the dressing up and 'play' element present in much contemporary fashion. Too often, however, it seems steeped in the prurience so disliked by the Willett Cunningtons, over thirty years ago, but still with us today:

> For though that former reticence, which shrouded the subject in mystery seems at first sight very unlike the modern attitude, there is a psychological affinity.
>
> Feminine underclothing, for instance, now claims to be 'amusing' and it is given playful nicknames – or pet names – with an air of coy audacity which betrays ... an erotic prudery still lurking about them.[26]

Cosmetics, like underwear, are in one sense also 'useless', despite the claims made in some cases for their protective properties. Like underwear, too, they are associated with sexuality and eroticism. They do not arouse the same kind of prurience, yet they are similarly tainted with moral ambiguity. They also trouble us because they are unnatural. Their use, by women or men, has long been associated with moral infirmity – with effeminacy in men and unchastity in women, because in using cosmetics we at one and the same time indicate our readiness for flirtation and dalliance, and attempt to improve on Nature's – or God's – work.

Like underwear, cosmetics have been transformed since 1900, but their origins are far more distant. The kohl of the Ancient Egyptians appears to have been used partly to protect the eyes from suppuration caused by the hot sun, and unguents, pomades and oils were, like perfumes, widely used, but although cosmetics today are held to preserve youth, they were originally associated with death, since they were first used in the ceremony of mummification.[27] In ancient Egypt and the Near East, lipstick was worn as a sign of their calling by prostitutes, but in general women and men painted themselves freely.

The Romans used cosmetics with enthusiasm, and their little palettes for *maquillage* are startlingly similar to the plastic ones produced today. The early Christian church was unable to root out the use of make-up and it persisted through the medieval period. From the sixteenth to the eighteenth century an artificial pink and white face was the fashion. It was produced by the combination of ceruse (the poisonous white lead) and ochre rouge, painted over with egg white or some other lacquer to create what would seem to us a grotesquely artificial appearance.

Despite the dangers of lead, its use persisted until revolutionary romanticism made it unfashionable. It was a part of the ideology of the Romantic period to reject the 'unnatural' and in the early nineteenth century the pale, unadorned face became part of an aesthetic ideal. The Victorian cult of virtue certainly meant that to rouge or powder openly was to advertise moral ambiguity, or worse, but the women of the Victorian leisured classes did not entirely give up the secret, or at least furtive, application of rice powder and possibly rouge.

If older women did still paint, this was assumed to be the continuance of the custom of a bygone age. When Charles Dickens in *Dombey and Son* (1848) described Mrs Skewton, her use of artifice seems to arouse a horror akin to Flaubert's at the disintegration of the body:

Mrs Skewton's maid ... should have been a skeleton, with dart and hour-glass, rather than a woman ... for her touch was as the touch of Death. The painted object shrivelled underneath her hand; the form

collapsed, the hair dropped off, the arched dark eyebrows changed to
scanty tufts of grey; the pale lips shrunk, the skin became cadaverous
and loose; an old, worn, yellow, nodding woman, with red eyes, alone
remained ... huddled up, like a slovenly bundle, in a greasy flannel
gown.[28]

Rouge was unfashionable in the era of pale complexions; but
instead women used lotions and even arsenic to whiten the skin. In
the United States powder and paint were associated with the *ancien
régime* and were therefore seen as unfitting for the daughters of the
American revolution; yet by the mid nineteenth century it appears
the Paris fashions were again being worn with heavy make-up, at
least in New York City.[29] Like so many of our ideas about that
period, the stereotype of the unpainted Victorians must be
modified.

Women continued to rely on homemade creams and lotions to
whiten and soften the skin; these, rather than powder and paint, led
to the beginnings of the huge modern cosmetics industry (the sixth
largest in the United States). The development of modern make-up
was due in large part to a few pioneering women. Both Helena
Rubinstein and Elizabeth Arden began their work in the late nineteenth century, by making face creams rather than cosmetics as
such. Each established her business in the first decade of the
twentieth century – heyday of the beauty parlour. Helena Rubinstein began, while on holiday in Australia from Poland, by marketing a traditional family recipe;[30] Elizabeth Arden was an obscure
beauty therapist who made up a cream to improve the efficacy of
the treatments she offered the leisured women of New York City.

At the same period the fashionable women of Harlem were being
offered skin lightening creams and hair straightening lotions, and
there were black counterparts to Helena Rubinstein and Elizabeth
Arden, in particular Mme. C. J. Walker, whose hair straightening
system became the basis for beauty parlours and for the Walker
College of Hair Culture, and on which she built a fortune. Her
daughter, A'Lelia Walker, became a famous Harlem hostess in the
1920s, and even appeared in a novel by Van Vechten, *Nigger
Heaven*, as Adora Boniface. (Although *Nigger Heaven*, a novel
about the life of the Harlem intelligentsia, was a best seller and
much praised by white writers and critics, its title bitterly offended
blacks, who took issue with its author. 'Nigger Heaven' was a

phrase used by blacks themselves for the gallery of a theatre, where
the black audience was herded in while denied access to the rest of
the theatre. Not only did blacks resent its use by a white writer, but
in any case it was a misrepresentation of Harlem in the 1920s,
which was then the world centre of black culture and the scene of a
'black renaissance' of writing, painting and art of all kinds.) This
author described her as 'even beautiful, in a queenly African
manner'.[31] But at this period to be black was in the last analysis to
be defined as *not* beautiful, and beauty culture for black women was
the attempt to imitate the looks of their white sisters.

   Pioneers of beauty culture such as Helena Rubinstein and
Elizabeth Arden did not, however, see their products as part of
female bondage. On the contrary, at this period cosmetics were
presented as a part of the freedom for which women were striving.
Elizabeth Arden, no suffragist herself, once joined a suffrage march
in the hope of attracting customers – for at this period in New York
fashionable society and feminism mingled. In the 1920s she was
taken up by Elisabeth Marbury, a society woman who was politically progressive and a lesbian. She, along with her friends Elsie de
Wolfe, Anne Morgan and Mrs William Vanderbilt, were leading
figures in the fashionable New York homosexual underground,
although her biographers think it unlikely that Elizabeth Arden
appreciated the nature of their relationships. Her life, like that of
her rival, Helena Rubinstein, seems to have been emotionally
thwarted, despite its great worldly success. It is ironic that both
turned their will to succeed in full force on a product so redolent of
female frailty – but the cosmetics industry, a new field, was one of
the few avenues of business success open to women.

   Elizabeth Arden's biographers comment:

> The fact that these two [sexually] unresponsive women invented the
> cosmetic look makes as strange a comment on twentieth century stand-
> ards of feminine beauty as does the fact that most dress designers are
> homosexual on twentieth century standards of feminine taste. .... They
> created an image of beauty that was framed by the mirror instead of lit
> by the eyes of the beholder.[32]

This rather homophobic comment ignores the function of
maquillage as a signal of women's emancipation in the early decades
of the twentieth century. In her books Helena Rubinstein described
beauty and youthfulness as every woman's right, even that it

was her duty to cultivate them in order further to assist her emancipation:

> Most women are finding that the home and the nursery are not enough. Bringing up children is not a life work ... There are long years ... when useful, profitable and stimulating activities outside the home are to be found.[33]

Beauty became a moral, even a eugenic obligation:

> Above all, stop thinking that there is anything frivolous or vain in wanting to hold onto youth, in striving to be beautiful. To preserve one's beauty is to preserve health and prolong life. Through their determination to achieve these ends women are helping to develop higher health standards ... The beauty loving, beauty seeking woman – especially if she happens to be a mother – is making an important contribution to the building up of a finer race.[34]

Helena Rubinstein emphasized her expertise as a scientist and healer, while discussing her beauty routine in terms more suited to military or boy scout ritual, and she used the arguments of eugenics (discussed in Chapter Ten) to support her case.

Cosmetics were equally discussed in the language of 'democracy' and the 'people's century'. The pseudo-democracy of the era of mass-communications in the period between the two World Wars seemed to offer all women the 'right' to slenderness, youthfulness and beauty. In theory, the fashion magazines, the diets and the cosmetics promised every girl film star looks. The theatre, and, even more importantly, the cinema, made cosmetics not only desirable but also respectable.

Yet when every woman could paint a mask of fashionable beauty on to her face, the democracy of beauty failed to appear. Cheap make-up, at least before the Second World War, did not look the same as the expensive brands, and John Osborne, a British play-wright, describes in words still sharp with disgust, his own mother's efforts:

> My mother's hair was very dark, occasionally hennaed. Her face was a floury, dark mask ... Her lips were a scarlet-black sliver covered in some sticky slime named Tahiti or Tattoo, which she bought with all her other makeup from Woolworth's. She wore it, or something like it, from the beginning of the First World War onwards. She had a cream

base called Crème Simone, always covered up with a face powder called Tokalon, which she dabbed all over so that it almost showered off in little avalanches when she leant forward over her food. This was all topped off by a kind of knicker-bocker glory of rouge, which came in rather pretty little blue and white boxes – again from Woolworth's – and looked like a mixture of blackcurrant juice and brick dust.[35]

The only time cosmetics became truly democratic was during the Second World War, when they were in such short supply that hardly any women had any. In wartime it became even more important to look nice in order to keep up morale. The richer and more fortunate could repair to the basement of the Dorchester hotel in London for a hairdo during air raids, while for young women in the factories:

> Our one aim in life seemed to concern our faces and hair. Pond's cold cream was slapped on by the potful to rid our skins of real and imagined grime. A touch of Vaseline on our eyelids gave our eyes an irresistible look when going to a dance – or so we thought. A beauty spot would be marked on with a black eyebrow pencil, like the one Margaret Lockwood, the film star, had on her chin.[36]

In the 1950s make-up, once the sign of the fast woman, became a badge of conformity. In 1957 Brigitte Bardot starred in *And God Created Woman*. In it she played the part of a 'free' although essentially innocent young woman; and the film contained a nude scene. Her new style of looks, pale, pouting lips, accentuated eyes and long, flowing hair, prefigured the styles of the 1960s[37] and coincided or fitted with the more exaggerated beatnik style. The new pallor, eyes rimmed with black and straight, tousled hair, suggested heavy nights and drug addiction, weekend raveups and purple hearts; by contrast tight perms and primly outlined red lips seemed respectable and even reassuring.

The naturalism of the 1960s was then a different social and aesthetic fashion. The apparent abandonment of make-up seemed related to the abandonment of underwear – and of sexual morality. Yet most women continued to wear make-up. It was simply paler.

A woman's duty to be beautiful . . .
Courtesy Condé Nast Publications.

SCULPTURE

Model your face with make-up to create an illusion of beauty; make an irregular contour appear a lovely oval; play down an imperfect feature, spotlight a good one

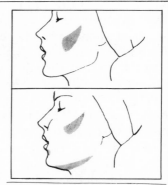

A FLAT FACE can be given better contours by applying dark powder beneath cheekbone. The same two-powder technique will help to diminish a HEAVY JAW or DOUBLE CHIN

CLOSELY-SET EYES. To give eyes a wide-apart look apply eye-shadow to outer corners of eyes. To flatter DEEPLY SET EYES blend eye-shadow from the centre of lid up and out

THIN LIPS. Use lipstick to build up the curves of the lips and carry fullness out to the extreme corners. Give soft and full curves to BROAD LIPS to reduce apparent jaw width

When Mary Quant marketed a foundation cream called 'Starkers' advertisements displayed an apparently naked young woman, crouched clasping her knees so that she was decently cloaked in curtains of Lady Godiva hair – but it was still make-up, not nature.

In the 1970s naturalism was displaced by the 1930s vamp look promoted by Biba (see Chapter Eight), and by camp 1940s styles – dark lipstick and nail varnish, for example, and brighter eye shadow. In the 1980s youth groups took the artificiality of make-up into new realms of exaggeration. Yet the use of cosmetics has become a banal convention. A kind of hyper-naturalism is the norm on the streets of every city, large and small: lots of blusher, lots of foundation colour, lots of lipstick in a 'subtle' shade, the same with eye make-up. Women seem to wear this cosmetic 'uniform' in much the same spirit as most men wear ties – in order to look 'dressed', in order not to stand out from the crowd. The standardized styles of make-up 'art' are there, one feels, to reassure the wearer that she has not strayed too far outside the norms of reasonable good looks, of ordinary prettiness, rather than to 'make a statement' or 'express her personality'. Indeed, although women's magazines have ceased to offer the advice that was so freely given in the 1950s – how to make all shapes of face approximate more closely to the perfect oval by the careful placing of rouge, lightener and shadows – and these days are more likely to suggest that readers make a 'feature' of 'bad' features ('A high forehead? Thick eyebrows? – Flaunt them!'), cosmetics are more something that you can't be seen without (like underwear again) than the daring display of emancipation and sexuality they once seemed. But no doubt it is the fate of all fashions to describe a trajectory from the outrageous to the banal.

The cult of the slender figure has been publicly questioned in recent years in a way that the cult of conventional prettiness has not. It is easy for us to assume that the modern preoccupation with dieting is simply part of a western obsession with thinness, and in particular that 'slimming' is just one aspect of the oppression of women. Diets and dieting have, however, preoccupied western societies at least since the seventeenth century. Diets formed a part of traditional medical regimes as well as of religious asceticism. George Cheyne (1671–1743), an influential Scottish medical practitioner in the period shortly before the industrial revolution, tended fashionable patients in London and Bath. He was concerned with the diet and health of urban, sedentary, upper and upper-middle-class *men*. His regimes were secularized versions of the rules of life enjoined on Protestants for their *spiritual* health.[38] According to one view, the increasing thought given to such dietary disciplines and regimens at the time of the industrial revolution indicates that they formed part of the general culture of regimentation, assisted the work ethic and the obsessional time-keeping of the industrial world, restrained the human passions and thereby maintained law and order. A rational diet would keep men calm and happy; rash eating and drinking inflamed the passions and led to riot and dissolution.

Cheyne's diet was based on milk and vegetables, plus regular sleep and exercise, and temperance. The poet Byron's constant anxiety about his weight cannot have been unique around the period of his youth (1810); his cure was to subsist on potatoes laced with vinegar. He writes to his mother:

> For a long time I have been restricted to an entire vegetable diet, neither fish nor flesh coming within my regimen; so I expect a powerful stock of potatoes, greens and biscuits; I drink no wine.[39]

Later on in the nineteenth century the low carbohydrate diet became the fashionable slimming diet. Devised for a man, Charles Banting, it became so popular that 'banting' was a colloquialism for dieting well into the twentieth century.

So the moral uplift of Helena Rubinstein is part of a long tradition. One of the clichés of fashion history is the 'triumph of the thin woman over the fat woman', and feminists today often assume that the twentieth-century female obsession with slimness and slimming is yet more evidence of the oppression forced on them by society. Clearly it is much more complicated than that, and the emergence of the thin woman as an aesthetic and fashionable ideal reflects wider concerns.

It is, of course, an ideal of *western* cultures. In other societies the plump woman may still be an aesthetic and erotic ideal. My argument, however, is that 'fashion' (changing styles in dress) is peculiar to western capitalist culture, but tends to overrun and eventually dominate other cultures. The ideal of slenderness is therefore of relevance to all cultures. Moreover, the existence of different ideals of beauty in other societies does not explain why thinness has become an ideal in ours.

One explanation[40] is that photography accentuates width. Both film stars and fashion models have, especially since the photograph came to dominate fashion journalism, contributed to the fashion for extreme thinness and length of leg. Paradoxically, the *real* requirements for the creation of the photographic *illusion* have influenced and changed the actual appearance of the 'woman in the street'.

This is an explanation in aesthetic terms. There are also the more familiar sociological explanations for this change of taste in the West. In rural, peasant societies plumpness was valued as an outward and visible sign of prosperity, while thinness was all too reminiscent of famine. And only in the ageing societies of the West was youthfulness more highly prized than any other aspect of beauty. In an era of over-population the plump woman, who represents fecundity, is displaced by the slender, girlish figure suggestive of the pre-pubertal.

Yet it is just as likely – and neither explanation rules out the other – that the slender figure fits with the modernist artistic love of form suggestive of movement and speed, and also with its rejection of the 'natural'. In the following chapter I shall discuss the concept of the natural in relation to gender. Fashion commentators have surprisingly often failed to distinguish between sexuality and gender, just as they have too readily assumed that 'femininity' and 'masculinity' are to be equated in a simple and unproblematic way with the erotically desirable. Fashion is as much about the boundaries of gender as it is about direct sexual display, indeed the two, as we shall see, are often very different.

Chapter 6

Gender and Identity

I wish her beauty ...

Something more than
Taffata or Tissew can,
Or rampant feather, or rich fan.

More than the spoyle
Of shop, or silkewormes Toyle,
Or a bought blush, or a set smile.

A face thats best
By its own beauty drest ...

A face made up,
Out of no other shop
Than what natures white hand sets ope ...

A Cheeke where growes
More than a Morning Rose:
Which to no Boxe his being owes ...

Lookes that oppresse
Their richest Tires, but dresse
And cloath their simplest Nakednesse.

Richard Crashaw: *Wishes. To his (supposed) Mistresse*

Fashion is obsessed with gender, defines and redefines the gender
boundary. Until the seventeenth or even the eighteenth century,
sexual difference in dress was not strongly marked. This may seem
an unlikely statement to those whose impression of dress from
the sixteenth to the nineteenth century is of flowing skirts, wide

farthingales and panniers for women, and revealing breeches and hose for men. Yet although the female leg could not be shown, and although the more sculptural forms of dress inaugurated in the later medieval period did more clearly distinguish between the sexes than the loose robes of the early middle ages, in many ways men and women continued to dress alike. For riding and sport women dressed, almost exactly like men, in long robes or heavy cloaks, and boots. Women, like men, carried purses and daggers suspended from their belts (pockets not being invented until the sixteenth century). By the close of the fifteenth century, fashionable dress had become so fantastical and absurd that it was difficult to tell men from women at a distance. Sixty years later Elizabethan moralists voiced outrage because women were dressing like men.[1] The mannerist styles of dress of the sixteenth century made of clothes a 'rigid, abstract shell',[2] bisexual styles in which both men and women appeared flat chested, wore ruffs and appropriated the masculinity of high-crowned hats and simultaneously the androgynous splendour of slashed and jewelled bodices. In the seventeenth century ringletted hair, hats, silk and lace bodices, jackets, muffs, shoes, stockings, frills, lace, earrings and gloves were common to both sexes.

In the eighteenth century increasing privacy, comfort and hygiene led to redefinitions of decency, modesty and 'delicacy'. Although the women of the bourgeoisie, which was growing in strength, were not to be coerced or beaten, subtler forms of restriction confined them to a narrow sphere: henceforth they were to preside over the home, the sphere of privacy and domestic harmony, protected, fragile and above all feminine. The bourgeoisie prided itself on its sobriety, good taste and refinement – by contrast with an aristocracy that often seemed coarse, profligate and immoral. In Germany the very notion of 'civilization' was organized around this sense of superiority by which the educated middle class elevated itself to a sphere that was morally – if not financially – superior to that of the landowning classes.[3]

Yet even at the height of the crinoline epoch, and when middle-class women at least were most stringently kept within a narrow sphere by the invisible bonds of etiquette, women never ceased to borrow male fashions. In 1857 *La France Élégante* commented: 'Our clothes are becoming like men's; we wear round hats, turned down collars, musketeer's cuffs; nothing is missing, not even

French Court Dress, c. 1670: bisexual curls and furbelows.
Reproduced by courtesy of the Mansell Collection.

trousers for many of us.'[4] (This last is a reference to bloomers or 'drawers'.)

In general, however, in the early industrial period gender difference was more firmly marked by dress. Fashion became an important instrument in a heightened consciousness of gendered individuality.

Elegance does not necessarily increase sexual appeal – it may on the contrary be forbidding – and, paradoxically, exaggerated masculinity or femininity may be less sexy than a sexual presence tinged with ambiguity. This is not necessarily the same as androgyny; there is nothing androgynous about Marlene Dietrich or Greta Garbo, for example, it is rather that the mysterious quality of their allure comes in part from a hint of manliness at the very heart of their feminine presence.

Canons of taste which define what is 'sexy' themselves change over time, of course; but what I am suggesting here is that sexual allure – however defined – is not necessarily tied to conventions of what is held to be appropriately 'masculine' or 'feminine'. This opens up a question about the relationship of conventional definitions of gender and sexuality; it becomes possible to separate them.

Although feminist theory has questioned whether gender can be simply mapped onto sexuality, it has sometimes still tended to assume that in the end the two coincide. This is especially true of feminist theories that rely on psychoanalysis, for in Freud's own writings there is an ambiguity about the distinction; he perceives that they are separate, yet defines their drawing together as a prerequisite in particular for the achievement of womanhood.

Freud recognized that the task of becoming feminine was a complicated and difficult one – perhaps never fully achieved. In all women, he suggested, a residue of the masculine survives (and in all men something of the feminine), and, consequently, 'some portion of what we men call "the enigma of women" may perhaps be derived from this expression of bisexuality in women's lives'.[5] Femininity, Freud suggested, remains always to some extent unstable and insecure. In fact, he goes further, and argues that both sexes flee from the passivity that is implied by femininity. This view sheds an ambiguous light on the radical feminist account of the subordination of women, which would perceive fashion as but one

Aunt. "Well, I daresay they're comfortable, but—I suppose I'm old-fashioned—I don't much like them. Why one would think you were a boy."
Niece. "Oh, come, dear old thing, that's absurd. Who ever saw a boy wear earrings?"

Androgyny in the Twenties.
Reproduced by kind permission of the proprietors of Punch.

instance of the way in which men impose punishing restrictions on women, as an instance of patriarchy; men, they might argue, use dress as a way of imprisoning women within the passive feminine, thus locating passivity in 'the Other' and keeping it at a safe distance. Yet at the same time, we would expect, if we follow Freud's line of reasoning, that both women and men would reject any form of dress that emphasized the feminine and passive.

Peter Ackroyd, writing about transvestism, takes an entirely different view, and suggests that what lies behind the social construction of gender is not a fear of passivity, but the fear of and desire for the 'chaos of androgyny', which he says, is sacred:

Cross dressing has often been the sign of an extraordinary destiny. In many shamanistic cultures, transvestites are regarded as sorcerers or visionaries, who, because of their double nature as men dressed as women, are sources of divine authority within the community . . .

It is not surprising that this double nature should be seen as a sign of the sacred, when we consider the androgynous or at least bisexual nature of the deities [that] are worshipped. If, as the Creation myths assert, Chaos – or the unity of undifferentiated sexuality – is the progenitor of all life, then the separate sexes represent a falling off from that original fecundity. Androgyny, in which the two sexes co-exist in one form and which the transvestite priest imitates in his own person, is an original state of power.[6]

(Peter Ackroyd gives no examples from other cultures of women who have dressed as men and thereby taken on sacerdotal powers.)

Today androgyny has ceased to be sacred. Modern fashion *plays* endlessly with the distinction between masculinity and femininity. With it we express our shifting ideas about what masculinity and femininity are. Fashion permits us to flirt with transvestism, precisely to divest it of all its danger and power.

In constructing identity fashion is not, however, concerned only with gender. If, as I suggested earlier, the self in all its aspects appears threatened in modern society, then fashion becomes an important – indeed a vital – medium in the recreation of the lost self or 'decentred subject'. If post-modernism articulates an experience of the world as fragmented, atomized beyond recognition, then the plurality of styles in present day fashion – the end of the single, Paris-dictated 'line' and in its stead a confusion of retro-chic, plagiarism, camp, ethnic chic – reflects this. At the same time, for the individual to lay claim to a particular style may be more than ever a lifeline, a proof that one does at least exist.

Yet while masculine, feminine and the androgynous may become a kind of play, elegance for women has also been a form of gruelling *work*.

In the nineteenth century the bourgeois woman's appearance was an artistic production. To achieve status, each woman must wear the uniform of fashion, yet, in a world that believed in individualized romantic love she must also express the uniqueness of her personality. This necessity of uniqueness within similarity intensified, if it did not originate, in the nineteenth-century marriage market. The bourgeois ideology of a free choice of marriage partner (strictly limited in practice) cemented the socially mobile society of the machine age. Dress was one aspect of social mobility; and the courtship ritual, particularly for women, an important part of that mobility. The niceties of courtship in that society required that marriage be officially the outcome of personal attraction and mutual love, yet actually marriage was an avenue for both sexes to self betterment, and often promoted the economic interests of men and women, and their families; for middle-class women it was the only certain route to economic security.

The dress of the nineteenth-century virgin on the marriage market had therefore subtly to convey family status as well as personal desirability: seductiveness, albeit virginal; along with apparent submissiveness and a willingness to obey, the ability to run a household should be suggested; the ethereal qualities of the Angel in the House must somehow be combined with the suggestion of sufficient health and strength to bear a large family. And in a society, or at least in a class, in which women outnumbered men, the importance for a woman of distinguishing herself from her rivals could not be overestimated.

This ideology extended beyond dress to the home in which the woman reigned. Appearance became more and more mixed up with identity. It was the beginnings of the idea of the Self as a Work of Art, the 'personality' as something that extended to dress, scent and surroundings, all of which made an essential contribution to the formation of 'self' – at least for women. Frances Power Cobbe, a nineteenth-century feminist, seems to have recognized the strangeness of this ideal, and wrote in the 1860s:

> The more womanly a woman is, the more she is sure to throw her personality over the home, and transform it, from a mere eating and sleeping place, or an upholsterer's showroom, into a sort of outermost garment of her soul; harmonized with all her nature as her robe and the flower in her hair are harmonized with her bodily beauty.[7]

By the mid twentieth century, a special emphasis on what was called 'the art of being a woman' reached its zenith. The women's magazines urged every woman to discover her 'type' and yet to dress to 'be herself': the paradox of artificially created spontaneity. To reconcile the desire to look 'different' with the simultaneous yet conflicting compulsion to conform was the tightrope along which millions of women teetered. Women who wanted to look smart for many years faced a problem similar to that of the teenage girl of the fifties in relation to petting: how far to go? There was risk and daring in the length of a hemline, and a woman could outrage equally by conforming in too slavish a way to fashion or by flouting its 'dictates' too arrogantly.

As the mass market developed, so did the sizing of garments. This was equally contradictory, for it aimed to individualize garments, yet sorted individuals into groups, and as such could also be seen as part of the increasing uniformity of mass society. After sizing came more refined consumer typologies that tried to classify women according to personality. In the 1920s, Bullock's department store in Los Angeles had divided customers into six personality types. These were the Romantic; the Statuesque; the Artistic; the Picturesque; the Modern; and the Conventional. The store's promotional material attempted a description of each, trying to match them to the kinds of clothes they were likely to buy. For example, the Artistic Type was described as,

> A bit enigmatic. Usually with a suggestion of the foreign. Usually dark-haired, dark-eyed. A type that may accept vivid colors, bizarre embroideries, eccentric jewellery. The artistic type welcomes the revivals of Egyptian, Russian and Chinese motifs and colorings. Peasant necklines. Berets. Hand-loomed fabrics.

The Modern Type on the other hand was:

> The fashionable type. The woman who can fit herself into the latest mould without discomfort. Just now shingle-bobbed. Boyish. Sleek. Skirts short when they are so. And longer than anybody's when they are so.[8]

In 1945, an American self-help manual aimed to help women to dress to type, each type exemplified by a film star. Again, there are six major types:

The Exotic Woman — Ilona Massey
The Outdoor Woman — Katharine Hepburn
The Sophisticate — Merle Oberon
The Womanly Woman — Greer Garson
The Aristocrat — Joan Fontaine
The Gamine — Betty Hutton[9]

Throughout the late 1940s and the 1950s, popular women's magazines regularly ran quizzes to help the reader decide her type, together with advice on how to enhance it. As late as 1958 *Vogue* (mid September, 1958) was advising its audience: 'Dress to your type is one of the basic fashion maxims. . . . We present four types, one of which must be you.' The four types turn out to be caricatures of different styles of looks and taste: the sporty; the clothes-horse; the ultra-glamorous and the pretty.

The appeal of this kind of typology is rather like that of astrology. There's a strange psychological reassurance in the idea that one *can* be categorized, the thrill of self-recognition in saying 'I'm a typical Leo', or 'I'm the Artistic Type'. For there is then the further assurance that by adherence to certain rules – whether celestial or sartorial – one can make everything somehow all right. The last fifteen or twenty years has undermined this ideology of the relationship between elegance and essence, and *Vogue*'s 1984 advice expressed a very different ideology: 'Change characters. How many fashions can *you* play? As style's horizons change, no one need be pinned inside a single fashion character' (*Vogue*, March 1984, p. 264). But for decades the idea that each woman expressed the uniqueness of her personality via her taste and preferences in dress influenced the way we all thought about fashion.

It was during the early part of the post-war epoch that Simone de Beauvoir wrote feelingly about the bondage of elegance:

> Elegance is really just like housework: by means of it the woman who is deprived of *doing* anything feels that she expresses what she *is*. To care for her beauty, to dress up, is a kind of work that enables her to take possession of her person as she takes possession of her home through housework; her ego then seems chosen and recreated by herself.[10]

Yet at the same time the woman engaged in this work is turning herself into something else: a jewel or a flower. To say that foundation garments, dress and make-up improve and disguise the body does not adequately explain what really happens, the becoming something other than and more stable than one's fluctuating and moody self:

> The least sophisticated of women, once she is 'dressed', does not present *herself* to observation; she is, like the picture or statue, or the actor on the stage, an agent through which is suggested someone not there – that is, the character she represents, but is not. It is this identification with something unreal, fixed, perfect . . . that gratifies her; she strives to identify herself with this figure and thus to seem to herself to be stabilized, justified in her splendour.[11]

But the problem is that – except on celluloid – the attempt to achieve an absolute, petrified state can never succeed. For one thing it is a losing battle against the inevitable deterioration of the body, just as housework is the endless struggle to control dirt, that 'matter' that is always 'out of place'; and so the 'drudgery' of beauty care becomes a struggle against life itself, for

> good meals spoil the figure, wine injures the complexion, too much smiling brings wrinkles, the sun damages the skin, sleep makes one dull, work wears one out, love puts rings under the eyes, kisses redden the cheeks, caresses deform the breasts, embraces wither the flesh, maternity disfigures face and body.[12]

Just as with housework, moreover, catastrophe is ever imminent:

> Accidents will happen; wine is spilled on her dress, a cigarette burns it; this marks the disappearance of the luxurious and festive creature who bore herself with smiling pride into the ballroom, for she now assumes the serious and severe look of the housekeeper; it becomes all at once evident that her toilette was not a set piece like fireworks, a transient burst of splendour, intended for the lavish illumination of a moment. It is rather a rich possession, capital goods, an investment; it has meant sacrifice; its loss is a real disaster. Spots, tears, botched dressmaking, bad hair-dos are catastrophes still more serious than a burnt roast or a broken vase, for not only does the woman of fashion project herself into things, she has chosen to make herself a thing.[13]

And Simone de Beauvoir ends with the sinister comment that 'the best examples of this magical appropriation of the universe are found in asylums for the insane'.

They are found in Hollywood too, once the dream factory that did turn a few women – the stars – into permanent works of art (whilst often destroying them as women). On the streets of Los Angeles and Hollywood today the passer-by encounters walking embodiments of the failed dream, women now in their sixties and seventies who must have arrived on the Pacific coast in the 1930s. Maybe Cecil Beaton glimpsed one or two of them among the 'desperate blondes in black satin, osprey and furs' he described then:

> It is as if the whole race of gods had come to California ... I see classic oval faces that might have sat to Praxiteles. The girls are all bleached and

painted with sunburn enamel. They are the would-be stars who come to Hollywood from every part of America ... The diehards hang on, buoyed by empty prospects and promises, eking out a piecemeal existence by working at 'drive in' quick-lunch counters or as shoe shiners.[14]

Some stayed there forever, and today still haunt the scene of their youthful failure. Even when the temperature stands at 104° Fahrenheit they still parade in their evening gowns and furs. Their bedraggled lace and satin defy reality; kohl and lipstick vein their sunken faces. They have *become* their dreams, and as they trail along the seething sidewalks of downtown LA an obsessive, vengeful muttered dialogue keeps them going, halfway between the strutting call girls of the plush hotels, and the moribund alkies and bums dumped in doorways along with the garbage. These old women are 'mad' because they have revenged themselves on a world of lost hopes by becoming their own illusions; a nightmare instead of a dream. What could be worse bondage than elegance as domestic labour or elegance as insanity?

The Hollywood dream factories created ideals of beauty that in retrospect seem haunting, strange, exaggerated and 'ugly', demonstrating the extent to which ideals of beauty are arbitrary and changing, even within the space of a few decades. And, if, on the whole, the Hollywood styles seem magnificently unnatural, they are surely part of the long-running dialogue between the artificial and the natural in western industrial society.

It was not simply morals or health that caused the nineteenth-century bourgeoisie to reject cosmetics. They, the first generation to be penned up in the new industrial towns, mourned and admired nature. Their aesthetic often revolved round the imitation of nature, but this was now a city dweller's memory or dream of nature. The poets and novelists of the industrial city, such as Baudelaire and Dickens, found in the very ugliness and squalor of those cities a melancholy, perverse beauty and eroticism. The great cities of the nineteenth century indeed gave birth to new ideas about beauty. Beauty was found in 'ugliness'; the link between beauty and 'the natural' was severed. What was 'unnatural', exaggerated, even deformed could, according to these new, industrial canons of taste, become 'beautiful'.

To say this is, of course, to make a generalization. We can say that the gothic or mannerist taste in beauty was equally arbitrary and 'ugly' in the sense that they deviated from Grecian standards of symmetry that, as we shall see later, the Victorians themselves attempted to reintroduce into their art and into female dress.

There was, nevertheless a sense at the time that the city produced a new aesthetic. The masculinity in dress mentioned earlier sometimes hinted at sexual ambiguity. Since nature was altogether overturned in the city, a new form of beauty and new forms of sexuality were appropriate for its iron landscape, a form that combined masculine grandeur and strength with feminine allure. 'The lesbian is the heroine of modernism,' asserted Walter Benjamin. Her new beauty arose inevitably, he argued, out of the new conditions of life:

> The nineteenth century began to use women without reservation in the production process outside the home. It did so primarily in a primitive fashion by putting them in factories. Consequently, in the course of time masculine traits were bound to manifest themselves in these women. These were caused particularly by disfiguring factory work. Higher forms of production as well as the political struggle as such were able to promote masculine features of a more refined nature.[15]

Walter Benjamin is writing here of Charles Baudelaire's Paris of the 1850s, and there is certainly present in Baudelaire's poems about lesbians the idea that their 'unnaturalness' is in some sense sterile. Benjamin twists this round so that it becomes admirable.

An English commentator on taste and fashion, writing in the 1870s, makes a similar point (although with none of the sexual implications) about the work of the pre-Raphaelite painters (whose influence will be discussed later). There is a new type of good looks:

> Morris, Burne-Jones and others have made certain types of face and figure once literally hated actually the fashion. Red hair – once to say a woman had red hair was social assassination – is the rage. A pallid face

The Pre-Raphaelites invent the Aesthetic of the Ugly: 'La Donna della Finestra' by Dante Gabriel Rossetti 1870 (detail).
Reproduced by courtesy of the Mansell Collection.

with a protruding lip is highly esteemed. Green eyes, a squint, square eyebrows, whitey-brown complexions are not left out in the cold. In fact the pink cheeked dolls are nowhere; they are said to have 'no character' ... Now is the time for plain women.[16]

Beauty and nature ceased to be synonymous. A machine could be beautiful, there could be beauty in the harsh vistas of the city, beauty found itself in garish colours, in exaggeration and distortion, in the flickering cadaverous images of the screen, in the black and white contrasts of photography, in the discords of both jazz and atonal music.

This modernist aesthetic of ugliness infiltrated received standards of 'good looks', as *Vogue* already recognized in the 1920s:

> The much admired woman of today ... isn't in fact the beautiful woman. Look at the international 'beauties' of today and you will see features that never were lovely, individual, unusual faces, faces that a passed [sic] generation might even have called ugly but which today are universally admired for their chic.   (*Vogue*, 21 August 1929)

Only two years later, however, *Vogue* claimed that naturalism was returning:

> What now is the justification for that makeup developed during those ten years ... eyebrows plucked to nothingness, green and crimson finger nails, shouting mouths and strangely shadowed eyes – with shingled heads and flat breasts they must go. The exaggerated, almost masculine simplicity and severity have been replaced by a more feminine, a more natural mode.   (*Vogue*, 15 April 1931)

Modern tastes in looks do seem to oscillate between naturalism and artificial exaggeration – what I have termed the 'aesthetic of the ugly'. The late 1960s and early 1970s, for example, were another period in which a naturalism that came from the hippie counterculture became fashionable – although the 'naturalness' was itself often simulated, and in any case even the natural may easily be a pose, consciously manipulated, as Michèle Roberts recognizes:

> She looks critically into the mirror at the tight, worried lines of her face. If she applies mascara and kohl, then she won't be able to cry, because they'll run and smear. Her hands hesitates [sic] on the zip of her bag. Warpaint to make her feel brave and frighten George with a hissing, glistening Medusa face. Or naked skin worn as a mask of babyhood,

vulnerability. She compromises by washing her face and brushing her hair.[17]

The twentieth-century fashion for the tan is perhaps one of the best examples of a *confusion* between the natural and the artificial, and is a good example of the aesthetic of the 'ugly'. The tan had always been the sign of a worker, and therefore abhorred by those with pretensions to refinement, but in the 1920s the tan became the visible sign of those who could afford foreign travel. The Americans who discovered the Riviera invented the photographic negative look – bleached hair and dark skin: 'Her bathing suit was pulled off her shoulders and her back, a ruddy, orange brown, set off by a string of creamy pearls, shone in the sun.'[18]

In its time the tan was the skin colour of modernism, beautiful because extreme:

> The personification of a new type of woman was the Duchess of Penaranda, a Spanish beauty who appeared wearing a short white tunic with a deep scooped neckline and a skirt that stretched hardly to the knees. She wore sunburn stockings with white satin shoes whose Spanish spike heels were fully six inches high. Her hair brilliantined to a satin brilliance, was drawn back tightly as a bull fighter's. The Duchess's complexion matched her stockings, for she was burned by the sun to a deep shade of iodine. Two enormous rows of pearl teeth were bared in a white, vital grin, complementing the half a dozen rows of pearls as large as pigeon's eggs that hung about her neck.[19]

A tan symbolized health as well as wealth in the 1930s. Recently its carcinogenic dangers have become known, and in any case it is no longer truly chic because too many people can afford holidays in the sun. But it is not primarily for those rational or at least simple reasons that it has begun to lose its appeal.

It is no longer sufficiently extreme. It looks too healthy. The white-faced punk has made the compulsively healthy glow of the open-air freak look a little mad and very dated. Tan is being abandoned because of visual boredom with a beauty style that has lost its novelty. The white face won't now be the sign of a woman confined to the shrouded half light of the Victorian parlour, or even locked in a Manhattan penthouse for fear of the violence on the streets, but of a different aesthetic of artificiality – the neon-bleached beauty of the subway, the disco, the bar.

It has even been suggested that the 'aesthetic of the ugly' is fundamental to the modern sensibility:

> Our literature adopts an aesthetic that aims to reveal the ugly as the true, and it often uses the sexual libido, which our culture has turned into a species of the ugly, as part of its rhetoric ... the ugly becomes an ironic figure of revelation, exposing an implacable universe unrelieved by spiritual or moral design. Sartre's concept of *slime* and *nausea* are eloquent statements of an aesthetic of the ugly.[20]

The example the author uses from Sartre of slime and nausea appears in a discussion by Sartre of the horror of the ambiguous.[21] Mary Douglas, in her discussion of the ambiguity of boundaries (which I mentioned in Chapter One) uses the same passage from Sartre to illustrate her thesis that boundaries have to be ritually strengthened because their uncertainty gives rise to the anxiety that necessitates taboos and magic. Fashion in its 'modernist' mood flirts with these dangers of the boundary, not only the boundary of androgyny, but also the boundaries of decency, good taste and sanity.

Secondly, if it is true that western culture does perceive the sexual as a species of ugliness, then this must complicate any relationship between fashion and the way in which it constructs 'the beautiful'. And in fact contemporary fashion does call into question its own basis in canons of taste and charm.

Jean Paul Gaultier, a punk-influenced Paris couturier of the early 1980s, dressed his models in 'a motley fusion of punk pilferings, slattern sophistication and B-movie anecdotes: his mannequins interspersed with "real" girls of all shapes and sizes' (*Vogue*, November 1983). He showed 1950s corsetry as outerwear, put together everything that doesn't 'go', subverted the whole idea of a fashion showing:

> The antics of stick-thin models shimmying in parodies of femininity guarantee roars of approval; tawdry transparent white blouses over black bras are greeted as great innovations; a dwarf and a fat girl parade the catwalk to catcalls and hoots of derisory laughter. (*Observer*, 30 November 1983)

And in an interview with *The Face* (February 1984) Gaultier enunciated the classic contradiction of the aesthetic of the ugly: 'It's always the badly-dressed people who are the most interesting.' This is truly the absurdist notion of fashion.

Gaultier derived his inspiration from British punk, and the street fashions of the late 1970s and the 1980s certainly challenged norms of what is 'beautiful', as I shall discuss in Chapter Nine. In doing so, they have used, perhaps unconsciously, the feminist critique of imposed standards of beauty.

What the feminist critique misses is the importance of exaggeration and of the extreme in contemporary standards of beauty. This element of exaggeration is due at least in part to the nature of city life, for in the rushing metropolis it is the strange that most catches the eye.

Chapter 7

Fashion and City Life

The streets belong to everybody, I repeated to myself.
  Marcel Proust: *The Guermantes Way*

As Paris was 'capital of the nineteenth century', so New York is the capital of the twentieth century. In New York the future inhabits the present. A surreal future is made concrete, material and immediate. This is a world in which the necessities and rhythms of nature have been abolished: yet at the same time the man-made landscape comes to resemble a freak of nature, and to have a life of its own that takes it outside the control of human agency. Just as Marcel Proust likened Venice to a crystalline formation, so New York, with its canyons and its sandstone heights, the crenellated cliffs of its skyscrapers and its whirlpool speedways, seems less the result of conscious human choice than the inevitable ecological niche for the 'unnatural' dissonance of the new beauty.

In nineteenth-century Paris the leisurely parade, in the Tuileries or in the Bois de Boulogne, was a high point of metropolitan life, and the latest fashions were an absolutely essential part of this parade. Honoré de Balzac, the French writer who most fully chronicled the life of early nineteenth-century Paris, describes his hero, Lucien de Rubempré, suffering 'two hours of torment' soon after his first arrival in the capital, as he compared his provincial appearance with that of the smartly dressed crowd:

This highly sensitive and keen-sighted poet recognized the ugliness of his own apparel, which was fit only for the rag-bag, the out-of-date cut of his coat, its dubious blue, its outrageously ungainly collar and its tails nearly meeting in front through too long usage; the buttons were rusty and there were tell-tale white lines along the creases. Also his waistcoat was too short and so grotesquely provincial in style that he hastily buttoned up his coat in order to hide it. Lastly, only common people were wearing nankeen trousers. Fashionable people were wearing attractively patterned or immaculately white material . . .

'I look just like an apothecary's son, a mere shop assistant!'[1]

What struck those who dwelt in the new or transformed cities of burgeoning industrialism were the dreamlike anonymity of the crowds and the inhumanity of a new environment which both fascinated and alarmed. Engels wrote of London:

> The very turmoil of the streets has something repulsive, something against which human nature rebels. The hundreds of thousands of all classes and ranks crowding past each other, are they not all human beings with the same qualities and powers, and with the same interest in being happy? . . . and still they crowd by one another as though they had nothing in common, nothing to do with one another, and their only agreement is the tacit one . . . the brutal indifference, the unfeeling isolation of each in his private interest.[2]

In the novels of Charles Dickens the city, London again, comes to have a life of its own, and indeed to be more alive – with its fogs, its bleak Sundays, its oily riverside darknesses, its alleys and melancholy courts – than the shadowy beings that inhabit it. In Edgar Allen Poe's tale of that name, The Man of the Crowd haunts the metropolis. Guilty of some nameless crime, he can never leave, but only lose himself within its surging, turbulent eddies, ebbs and flows. The city crowd becomes the haven for everything unspeakable, strange, mysterious.

Above all it is the silent gaze that typifies city life:

> Someone who sees without hearing is much more uneasy than someone who hears without seeing . . . Interpersonal relationships in big cities are distinguished by a marked preponderance of the activity of the eye over the activity of the ear. The main reason for this is the public means of transportation. Before the development of buses, railroads, and trams in the nineteenth century, people had never been in a position of having to look at one another for long minutes or even hours without speaking to one another.[3]

There was therefore an eroticism special to the nineteenth-century crowd, an eroticism of the impossible, an eroticism both voyeuristic and romantic, of the stranger who is herself a part of the phantas-magoria. Charles Baudelaire describes such a woman in one of his poems, and his longing for this beautiful passer-by, clothed in deepest mourning, is a form of madness, for the 'sweetness that fascinates, the pleasure that kills', a longing for the impossible, for 'love at last sight'.[4]

In the crowd all sorts of fetishes and 'perversions' are born. Frotteurism, exhibitionism, voyeurism (illicit touching, showing and looking) are sexual aberrations that rejoice in the stealth and irresponsibility of the crowd. In each case a single act out of the many possible components of the sexual act swells into a strange obsession when taken out of context and performed not with a lover but *at* a stranger.

In the great cities of the industrial world eroticism was divorced from nature – from reproduction – and the intensification of mas-culinity and femininity was surreptitiously undermined. Street clothes in the nineteenth century expressed a fetishistic secrecy about the body, and industrialism and the modern city had found its first appropriate style of dress for the street – the discreet and secretive style of the business or professional man. There was often a furtive masculinism in women's street dress too, since out of doors women went veiled, bonneted and cloaked in the dark colours that were necessary because they did not show mud or soot, and also suggested respectability.

Writing of the last decades of the nineteenth century, Marcel Proust recognized the charm of the incognito, when his heroine, the Duchesse de Guermantes, played at being an ordinary person:

> She was now wearing lighter, or at any rate brighter clothes ... The woman whom I could see in the distance, walking, opening her sun-shade, crossing the street, was, in the opinion of those best qualified to judge, the greatest living exponent of the art of performing those movements and of making of them something exquisite ... I watched her adjust her muff, give alms to a beggar, buy a bunch of violets from a flower-seller, with the same curiosity that I should have felt in watching the brush-strokes of a great painter ...
>
> The streets belong to everybody, I repeated to myself ... and marvel-ling that indeed in the crowded street ... the Duchesse de Guermantes

mingled with the public life of the world moments of her secret life, showing herself thus in all her mystery to everyone, jostled by all and sundry, with the splendid gratuitousness of the greatest works of art.[5]

The nineteenth-century urban bourgeoisie, anxious to preserve their distance from the omnipresent gaze in the strangely inquisitive anonymity of the crowd where 'anyone' might see you, developed a discreet style of dress as a protection. Yet paradoxically street dress became full of expressive clues, which subverted its own anonymity, because it was still just as important, or indeed even more important, to let the world know what sort of person you were, and to be able to read off at least some clues from the clothes of other people. It became essential to be able to read character and proclivity from details that were immediately perceived. New and more complicated 'codes of dress' developed, for in the metropolis everyone was in disguise, incognito, and yet at the same time an individual more and more *was* what he wore. For example:

One could always recognise gentlemanly dress because the buttons on the sleeves of a gentleman's coat actually buttoned and unbuttoned, while one recognised gentlemanly behaviour in his keeping the buttons scrupulously fastened, so that his sleeves never called attention to this fact.[6]

As early as 1762 James Boswell, the English diarist, had written 'there is indeed a kind of character perfectly disguised, a perfect made dish, which is often found, both male and female, in London.'[7] The experience of city life was – and still is – of the intensification of contrasts. Extreme wealth and extreme poverty flaunt side by side; shock and collision become mundane; one is constantly both alone and in a crowd, both lost in one's thoughts and exposed to all. In order to survive in this maelstrom the individual had to learn pliability, flexibility and cunning. Part of this technique of survival was in the nineteenth-century metropolis, and still is today, the art of dissimulation and disguise. Behind the public display, whether of a fantasy or of a 'real' self, the secret of the self still lurks. A particular kind of obsession with secrecy and secrets (one of the great themes of the nineteenth-century novel and the twentieth-century thriller) is a further result of the separation of private life from the public realm. Moreover, in modern life the street, where almost all passers-by are strangers, has itself become a peculiar kind of private zone, where appearances hide secrets and tell lies (but what is the 'truth'?).

Georg Simmel, a German sociologist of the later nineteenth century, drew out the relationship between city life, individualism and the rapid development of fashion in the industrial era. A heightened sense of individual personality and ego developed when men and women moved in wider social circles, and the constant friction of self with a barrage of sensations and with other personalities generated, he suggested, a more intense awareness of one's own subjectivity than the old uniform and unwavering rhythm of rural and provincial life. In the city the individual constantly interacts with others who are strangers, and survives by the manipulation of self.

Fashion is one adjunct to this self-presentation and manipulation. It is the imposition of this newly found self on a brutally indifferent and constantly fluctuating environment. This, too, Simmel believes, is a further reason for fashion's association (as suggested in Chapter Two) with the *demi-monde*:

> The fact that the *demi monde* is so frequently a pioneer in matters of fashion is due to its peculiarly uprooted form of life. The pariah existence to which society condemns the *demi monde* produces an open or latent hatred against everything that has the sanction of law, of every permanent institution, a hatred that finds its relatively most innocent and aesthetic striving for ever new forms of appearance. In this continual striving ... there lurks an aesthetic expression of the desire for destruction.[8]

The iconoclasm, the outrage and the defiance of fashion thus come, according to Simmel, from the deviant, the dissident and the outsider. In the bourgeois epoch, the aristocrat could to some extent be included in these categories, and it is clear both in Balzac's and in Proust's descriptions of French society that both high born women and *demi-mondaines* were fashion leaders. Both, for example, were to be seen in the Bois de Boulogne where, far from being incognito, society was on parade.

Proust's description of this in the early years of the twentieth century illustrates his sensitivity to the changes that had taken place in fashionable dress among his contemporaries:

> I wished to ... see ... little women's hats, so low-crowned as to seem no more than garlands. All the hats now were immense, covered with all

manner of fruits and flowers and birds. In place of the beautiful dresses in which Mme Swann walked like a queen, Graeco-Saxon tunics, pleated à la Tanagra, or sometimes in the Directoire style, accentuated Liberty chiffons sprinkled with flowers like wallpaper ... And seeing all these new components of the spectacle ... they passed before me in a ... meaningless fashion, containing in themselves no beauty ... They were just women, in whose elegance I had no faith.[9]

This, the Paul Poiret style, effected a transition between the static styles of the nineteenth century and the modernism of Chanel.

The Chanel suit was seized upon by the American garment makers. In the 1940s, for example, Adrian, formerly a Hollywood designer, became a New York couturier for the masses and designed from Seventh Avenue the ideal suit for the go-anywhere woman of the war years: 'an Adrian suit was the civilian uniform of the American woman during the hectic days of the Second World War, when she needed a style and costume appropriate for all occasions – morning, noon and night'.[10] With Paris out of the contest, American fashion then came into its own. By today's standards, however, the 1940s woman was still dressed *up*:

> The woman was smart, small, lusty. She wore her blonde hair piled high, a black and white silk blouse, a red suit and a fur coat. Heavy bracelets jingled on both arms.

or:

> She looked fresh and brilliant, her black hair piled in a braided crown. Her business dress, cut low in the bodice, was of silk shirred all over in two inch bands, tight in the waist and very short. She had steel studded buckles on her high-heeled shoes and long black kid gloves. She threw her black astrakhan coat on the sofa, with an enormous handbag in calf and gold. She had a wide bracelet of brilliants, much perfume, and no colour in her cheeks but a dark red lipstick which brought out the darkness in her eyes.[11]

These women, characters from a novel about wartime New York by Christina Stead, were on the make, but in a new way. They might have been wearing Adrian suits, black or grey. The jacket would be square cut, waisted, with one or two details designed to feminize – 'interesting cuffs', a side fastening, inserts of material cut diagonally or latticed in a different shade. The formality of the jacket would be set off by a 'lean' skirt. A tilted, veiled hat, a lace blouse, high heels, would give the characteristic allure to this masculine suit that was at the same time so feminine, so sophisticated with its little bunch of artificial violets or single gardenia on the shoulder. This was not androgyny, but the womanly woman, heterosexual as they come, on the streets, but her independence made vulnerable when she unbuttoned her jacket to reveal the bosom of a soft georgette blouse. Wartime New York was a sexual boomtown, a wartime frontier, with servicemen dropping in to meet war widows, permanent or temporary, in search of substitute romance, businessmen in search of a killing and a girl, girls in search of pleasure and profit. Then, the suit could be seductive. The wartime suit was also worn in the British 'shires', was a uniform not only for women in the forces, but also for the provincial ladies who were still having their suits made to measure by local tailors in restrained, asexual men's suitings, with beautiful finishings, and lined in crêpe silk. But as with British men's tailoring, the severity could have a paradoxical allure.

'Adrian' women are still to be seen on the streets of New York City today, a spring hat crowning an office ensemble with a formality strange to the British eye. Their appearance combines the business-like and the womanly. The post-feminist career woman of the 1980s, on the other hand, has eliminated sexuality. In the wake of best sellers John T.Molloy's *The Women's Dress For Success Book* and Mary Fiedorek's *Executive Style*,[12] many American career women appear to have followed the advice these authors give on dressing 'seriously' for work. An army of New York clothes consultants are teaching business and professional women to eliminate not only sexuality but even gender. According to the *New York Herald Tribune* (27 April 1984) John Molloy believes that 'dressing to succeed in business ... and dressing to be sexually attractive are almost mutually exclusive'. That is certainly one way to frighten women out of the career market! 'The look,' reports the *Tribune*, 'is Brooks Brothers rather than Chanel, tailored but not in the style of the currently fashionable European androgynous look, which combines the best of both sexes'.[13] In the worst of all worlds the dress-for-success woman has ruled out ambiguity, and polyester shirt frills hint only at the coif of the nun or hospital matron, the suit articulates only the professional persona.

New York street life nevertheless retains its panache. There is the

New Yorker in her fur, for example. In Knightsbridge furs are just another British uniform, a badge of class, and 600 brown and pastel minks an hour the only reward for those who watch the crowd. But on the Upper East Side a fur is a woman's glove in the ring, her bet on the poker hand of her luck, a badge of individualism, not uniformity. Furs accordingly run the gamut from Rita Hayworth silver fox to strictly tailored sable trench-coats. Such unrepentant, brash display is one way of having the world by the tail − or imagining that you do.

Yet although parts of Manhattan retain all the characteristics of the nineteenth-century city, the brooding gloom of those cities has given way to a kind of hysteria, and if New York may be called the capital of the twentieth century, it is partly because it is different from the Paris of Balzac or Proust. The great cities of the industrial nineteenth century sprang up spontaneously and even ancient cities such as Paris and London altered their character during the period of capital at its most confident. The twentieth-century modernist project for the city was rather different − a plan for the total environment, for the separation of pedestrian and vehicle, for the futuristic skyscrapers of the garden cities pioneered by Le Corbusier, and the thruways of Robert Moses. (Le Corbusier's motto was 'We must kill the street.'[14]) These futurist cities have become the urban nightmare of the 1980s, the gouged out twilight zones, the tower block wastelands, and the motorways carving through the picturesque old city quarters of the South Bronx and North Kensington, creating blitzed zones of despair.

Fredric Jameson suggests that the post-modernist reaction to this − a return in architecture to the populist, the traditional and the pop − nevertheless confronts us with an even more daunting environment, for *this* city

> is above all a space in which people are unable to map (in their minds) either their own positions or the urban totality in which they find themselves: grids such as those of Jersey City, in which none of the traditional markers (monuments, nodes, natural boundaries, built perspectives) obtain.[15]

He argues that the 'play' element in post-modernism is so unreal that it destroys the city we have known, replacing it with unrelated environments, decentred, endless suburbs.

At the sartorial level this is matched by the use of leisure wear in the city. Another figure of New York street life is the woman, like her austerely suited professional sister, costumed for only one thing at a time, but in this case for play. A new dress code, by now almost a cliché of the 1980s, has come into being to signify 'leisure'. The leisure for which the woman in track suit, leotards, leg warmers is costumed is actually both display and 'work'. You have to have already become 'fit' in order to participate adequately in the public ritual of the jogging track or the aerobics class. The bright uniform acts out a lifestyle, as does the elaborate make-up, the artificially flushed cheek and kohl-enlarged eyes of health-made-erotic. The natural signs of exertion on the other hand, such as sweat and glistening forehead, must be rigorously concealed. The correct costume of the fitness freak has its own obsessional details that alter from year to year, and to wear leg warmers drawn too high, or the wrong kind of leotard is to spoil everything. It all mimics casual informality, but is minutely thought out. At the same time, like much twentieth-century fashion, it mimics the worker, in this case the dancer in rehearsal. The woman in dragonfly Lycra plays the role of the creative artist and dedicated interpreter, imitating the glamorous asceticism of singleminded devotion to a skill. It is almost always just a dream, though, and the artistic product is the self, the new guise of training clothes and ballerina wear leading us back to the mirror of narcissism.

It's often said that such costumes represent hedonism and the apothosis of the consumer culture, foster the values of youth, health and overt sexuality, create the illusion of triumph over age and, implicitly, death. According to Christopher Lasch one response to the 'spiritual desolation' of modern life is just this kind of consumerist narcissism:

> To the performing self, the only reality is the identity he can construct out of materials furnished by advertising and mass culture, themes of popular film and fiction, and fragments torn from a vast range of cultural tradition ... In order to perfect the part he has devised ... the new Narcissus gazes at his own reflection, not so much in admiration as in unremitting search of flaws ... Life becomes a work of art ... All of us, actors and spectators alike, live surrounded by mirrors.[16]

The 'aerobics style' has become a code for a certain kind of sophistication; a young woman wearing leg warmers in an advertisement, for whatever product, is an immediate signal of 'modern-mindedness'. The style is about play, about energy, about independence. The woman on display suggests boldness, and mastery both of herself and of her environment.

To that extent the assumption of such an up-front persona is almost a gesture of defiance. In displaying herself so openly she dares the metropolis to take her on. The guise of dancer or runner veils the overt sexuality of the performance. She is as boldly made up as a hooker, but is emphatically not one.

Yet this new woman of the sidewalks achieves her total meaning only in the context of the danger all around her. This flaunting of self knowingly peacocks in the face of misery, pauperism, despair. Not cruelly or consciously exactly; yet the full zest of the performance emerges only in the context of imminent threat, the lightning flicker of aggression and the pall of despair. It's a statement about energy pointed up by those who conspicuously lack it. It's almost witty to flash past the bums who shout their obscenities from their doorways. Ex-patients from closed-down mental hospitals spilled out into the city, they speak the threat of madness and violence against which the dancing girl's 'energy' is revealed as classic hysteria. She can preserve her brightness only because she does not 'see' the danger, but blots it out in hysterical denial.

Both this hysteria, and a vision of New York City as the ultimate modernist nightmare, are explored in Brian de Palma's film, *Dressed to Kill*. De Palma's Manhattan is the mythic capital of the twentieth century, and his heroine is a hooker. Male writers have described the hooker as the ultimate narcissist, the ultimate inhabitant of the modernist city, for she takes the mirror of performance and with it the cash nexus into the very heart of intimacy.

Dressed to Kill is an exploitation movie, and was hated by feminists for its message that women are to be punished for their sexuality. Yet it is also a version, flawed as the culture it reflects, of a *myth* of New York as the nightmare megalopolis where pleasure and danger unite in death. The place of woman, the predatory victim, is necessarily ambiguous. Everything remains unresolved – in 'real life' as well as in Brian de Palma's bad dream. It is not fully established that women have the right to be out there on the street. Yet they are there. How they then present themselves is necessarily contradictory. The persona of the hooker blurs with that of the 'streetwise woman'.

The heroine-villainesses of the 1940s *film noir* expressed this ambiguity in a different way, which is why they still appeal to us today. Mary Astor and Joan Crawford dripped furs over their severe tailor-mades, appeared at one moment in backless, slinky dresses, at the next in trenchcoats and hats that seemed to imitate their male companions, whether lovers, victims or destroyers. Their dilemmas are still ours, although we express them differently, less elegantly, in an even more fragmented way.

This new experience of city life was built upon a new economic order. Life in the nineteenth century was more sharply than before divided between working hours, repaid in wages, and 'leisure' during which wages could be spent. For many, wages barely covered necessities, but there were some for whom they opened a door at least a crack to reveal vistas of freedom and pleasure. The spending of money became a leisure activity in itself, both for the women of the bourgeoisie, and, to a lesser extent, for the better-off workers. Production bred consumption, commerce bred commerce. To cater to this, the capitalist city invented a fantasy world that was neither wholly a public nor quite a private realm: the department store.

There was a revolution in shopping. Before the industrial revolution most country dwellers had had access to goods for purchase only at seasonal fairs and markets, and from travelling pedlars. There were shops in the cities, however, and London is said to have been particularly advanced in this respect. Great bazaars and shops apparently existed in Cheapside and Charing Cross in the early eighteenth century, and the word 'shopping' had come into use by the middle years of the century, although the process of purchase remained a lengthy and anxious one.

The haggling and bargaining that was still widespread in France in the earlier half of the nineteenth century had not persisted to the same extent in the more advanced pre-industrial cities of eighteenth-century England, but to enter a shop still implied a commitment to buy, stocks were limited, and of course there was nothing ready made. Yet already, shopping was a social event. Advances in architecture opened up fresh possibilities in London when the new Regent Street was designed by Nash with an elegant colonnade in the early nineteenth century. It became the mecca of the fashionable shopper, the thoroughfare was a promenade, and society's élite went there at least as much to see and be seen as to shop. It continued to be a fashionable shopping centre, and in 1866 the *Illustrated London News* described how

Regent Street in 1858 – the life of the streets in the nineteenth century.
Reproduced courtesy of the Mary Evans Picture Library.

the fireflies of fashion glance rapidly hither and thither ... the pavements being crowded with fashionable loungers. With what dignified ease the gorgeously bedizened footmen attend to their mistresses or lounge about in attitudes of studied grace.[17]

By night on the other hand the area, along with Haymarket and Cheapside, became one of ill repute and witnessed a different kind of promenade:

On the wide stone pavement the promenaders mingle, beautiful girls in shining dance frocks, pearls braided in their hair, promenaders of all nations ... laughing, whispering, disappearing through the brown mahogany doors of the cafés. ... The night air is impregnated with the scent of patchouli and '*Eau de mille fleurs*'. The trains of satin dresses rustle on the stone, scarves float, rose-coloured ribbons flutter; sparkling eyes, caressing words; there a greeting, here a whisper and a laugh.[18]

In the 1830s and 1840s stores selling 'dry goods' (haberdashery, cloth, cloaks and trimmings) began to appear both in European capitals and in the eastern seaboard cities of North America. The *Bon Marché*, which has usually claimed the title of the first department store, opened as a small left-bank piece goods shop in 1852, but it seems likely that there were small early forms of the department store in the English provinces at least a decade earlier, for Kendal Milne of Manchester – significantly one of the major northern British cities to have been transformed by the industrial revolution – and Bainbridge of Newcastle were open in the 1840s,[19] while Ralph Hower, the historian of Macy's of New York suggests that the first approach to the department store in Europe was the London firm of W. Hitchcock and Co., which was already organized into twelve departments in 1839. He also suggests that although general trading and barter were still much more common in North America, there was increasing specialization of shopping in the cities there as well, and that the department store emerged in both the United States and Europe at about the same time and probably independently.[20]

The two most important innovations in shopping at this time were that goods were offered at marked prices, so that haggling and bargaining were no longer necessary, and that customers were invited into the shops to look round freely with no 'obligation to purchase'.

By 1845 Bainbridge of Newcastle already had ten assistants and stocked a wide variety of merchandise, including dress and furnishing fabrics, fashion accessories, furs and family mourning (a most important item) as well as an early form of ready-to-wear clothing in the shape of made-up muslin dresses. By 1865 Bainbridge owned a stretch of buildings over 500 feet long, and later a four-storey shop was built on the site. In 1883 they began to run their own factories for men's and boy's clothing, and factories for women's clothes; knitted stockings and mattresses came later.[21]

In New York similar developments occurred. A. T. Stewart and Co. was the first big Manhattan store. In 1848 it was a 'marble palace' for the sale of dry goods at the corner of Broadway and Chambers in lower Manhattan, and in 1862 transferred to an even more magnificent building constructed in the revolutionary new method which made use of cast iron so that open spaces, imposing staircases and glass rotundas to let in the light created a spacious and opulent environment. Macy's, which was to become the world's largest department store, opened in 1857, and later became part of the move uptown (although Bloomingdale's was from the beginning located on its present site in midtown Manhattan).[22]

Everywhere, the big department store was the apotheosis of shopping in the second half of the nineteenth century; it was largely the product of the period from 1860 to 1910. The concept was an application in the retail field of the industrial principle of delegation of skill and the breaking down of processes into their component parts. The division of labour that had earlier been brought into being and perfected by the factory system could be applied to sales, thus further accelerating the circulation of capital. At the same time, there was a constant diversification of goods to be sold. The large volume of business in the department store, the separation of merchandise into departments and at the same time the centralizing of many administrative functions went hand in hand with the development of free services such as delivery, alterations, goods on approval and the provision of credit, although cash sales now predominated. There was constant rationalization of marketing processes and administration in the expanding stores.

The workforce in the department store was bureaucratized, disciplined, regimented, the emphasis on obedience and loyalty to the firm, and *Bon Marché*, for example, tried to build up the idea of shop work as a civil service-like career. Formerly, shop employees

LA GALERIE DE LA RUE DE BABYLONE

had been men notorious for their rowdiness and indiscipline. Now, greater refinement was required in those ministering to the clientele of the department store, which was distinctively bourgeois and feminine. Gradually the stores began to employ women workers (they were first introduced as strike breakers at the *Bon Marché* in 1869) although they still formed a minority of the retail workforce.

A new emphasis on respectability lifted the status of these young women above that of factory workers and seamstresses. These proletarian women had always been exposed to the advances both of male fellow workers and of overseers, nor had they been protected from the dangers of the drift into prostitution. They had therefore been experienced as a threat to the propriety of bourgeois society. Here, on the other hand, was an emergent class of white collar workers. To some extent they were protected by the paternalism that was such a marked feature of some of the department stores, certainly of the *Bon Marché* – and of Marks and Spencer, for example, in the twentieth century. There were benevolent funds and pension funds at the *Bon Marché*, forms of private welfare capitalism more characteristic of French than of either British or American industry. There were living-in facilities, canteens, libraries. Marriages were often the outcome of this ritualized commercial life which attempted to recreate the family outside the family. Yet at the same time the women behind the counters aroused moral anxiety because they actually belonged neither quite to the petit bourgeois nor to the working class.

Thus the department stores everywhere created a new type of worker whose obsequious manner and deference to the customer within the store echoed the manner of upper servants within the upper-class household. The clients were overwhelmingly middle class, yet this ambience of service rather than commerce gave an illusion of aristocratic life, and in this way old forms of class and personal relationships persisted in the midst of the new.

In reality, 'the department store was the bourgeoisie's world. It was the world of leisurely women celebrating a new rite of consumption. ... Bourgeois culture was on display.'[23] It not only reflected bourgeois life, however, it also created it, for its displays

The *Bon Marché* in 1880.
Reproduced courtesy of the Mary Evans Picture Library.

depicted the proper household and correct attire, conjured up a vision of what the bourgeois life ought to be, and subtly educated its clientele into new norms of more and different clothes and household items for every conceivable occasion and hour of the day.

In a very real way the department store assisted the freeing of middle-class women from the shackles of the home. It became a place where women could meet their women friends in safety and comfort, unchaperoned, and to which they could repair for refreshment and rest. In the closing decades of the nineteenth century, cloakrooms, lavatories and refreshment rooms became an important feature of the department store.[24] This was a major change at a period when it was improper for a woman to enter an ordinary restaurant unless accompanied by a husband, brother or father. Macy's ladies' lunch room opened in 1878, and by 1903 had become a restaurant catering for 2500. In 1904 a Japanese tearoom was added. Marshall Fields of Chicago was more conservative, but Harry Gordon Selfridge, then employed there, persuaded them to open a small tearoom in 1890, and again by 1902 a restaurant took up one whole floor.[25]

Yet the newly independent women customers caused as much moral anxiety as the salesgirls. A new sin against the spirit of commerce came into being: shoplifting, which the medical profession was to transform into the more respectable 'disease' of kleptomania. Shopping was almost sexualized, fetishistically, as women who had 'fallen' spoke of the irresistible touch of silk and satin, the visual seduction of the displays, and their thirst for possession.[26]

So feverish a response was perhaps appropriate to what was after all ultimately an illusion. The bourgeois clientele were not really aristocrats, nor were the floor walkers real butlers. There was a sense in which it was all a giant performance to magic away the cash nexus around which it all the time revolved. The *Bon Marché* was perhaps only the apotheosis of the department store because of the enormous lengths to which Boucicault, its creator, went in order to sustain the illusion, organizing, like some great impresario, galas,

London shopgirls in the lunchbreak, 1890, by the French illustrator 'Mars': fashion in the street – working girls become smart.
Reproduced courtesy of the Mary Evans Picture Library.

concerts and spectacles of all kinds, which, intended to advertise his store, contributed to the blurring of reality and to the idea of the department store as an adventure in exotic realms rather than anything so mundane as buying and selling.

And, along with exhibitions and museums, the nineteenth-century department store and its concept of shopping as a leisure activity, and as a pleasure rather than a necessity, testifies to the importance of *looking* in capitalist society. Once the colonnade had been removed from Regent Street, and the old fashioned shop window panes replaced with plate glass, window shopping was born, and inside the great store an even more thrilling gluttony of the eye could be experienced.

Gordon Selfridge left Marshall Fields and came to London to open his own department store, which was intended to offer a more streamlined service in the American style to a client group less wealthy than those of Harrods, Whiteleys and Marshall and Snelgrove. Selfridges opened in Oxford Street in 1909, but although it has been extremely successful ever since, the heyday of the department store was already over when it opened.

Between the two world wars the major developments were the modernization of existing stores and the phenomenal growth of chain stores: Sears Roebuck, Montgomery Ward and J. C. Penney and Co. in the United States, and Marks and Spencers, British Home Stores and Littlewoods in Britain. Marks and Spencers is now an international marketing and manufacturing empire; yet it was started by Michael Marks, an itinerant Jewish immigrant pedlar who set up a penny bazaar in Manchester in the 1880s. By the 1920s he and his brother-in-law, later Lord Sieff, had created a large multiple concern, with factories making goods to Marks and Spencer's specifications. Theirs was an optimistic vision in which science and technology continuously improve the quality of human life and make possible the fulfilment of the needs and desires of millions.[27]

In the 1950s the department store began to seem old-fashioned. A youthful, less class-divided clientele disdained the customer services of delivery, telephone ordering and alterations to clothes. One response aiming to cater to the needs of this new group, which collectively had ample cash to spend, and wanted cheap, bright, smart clothes to spend it on, was the 'little shop', rechristened the 'boutique'. Mary Quant's Bazaar in Chelsea seems to have been the

first of the hundreds that sprang up and died. Sometimes department stores copied the idea, and created boutiques within their
stores; although they also foresaw this development and created
'young' fashion departments such as Bergdorf Goodman of New
York's 'Miss Bergdorf' department, opened in 1955. But when
Woollands, for example, then a department store in Knightsbridge,
London, opened its Twenty One shop, it seemed much more
consciously in imitation of the Bazaar concept. In the early 1960s
boutiques appeared everywhere, in England Biba in Kensington
was perhaps the most famous; there was Bus Stop (which had
branches all over Britain at the height of its success around 1970),
Countdown and Top Gear, also in London. All had chaotic mass
changing rooms where 'dolly birds' stripped off to reveal that their
only underwear was tights, there were football scrums to snatch
tiny, cheap dresses off the racks, and throwaway 'fun' accessories
were displayed with crazy inventiveness. Every provincial British
town had its boutique, and the down market chain dress shops, as
well as the big stores (such as Selfridges with its Miss Selfridge
department) were quick to copy their ambience.

In the 1970s, when prices began to rise and the garment industry
to feel the cold wind of the recession, boutique fashion catering to
the young became more outrageous. One saleswoman described the
almost hysterical atmosphere in the shop in which she worked
during the early 1970s. The sales assistants were given new outfits
every four weeks, and were encouraged to dress in the most exaggerated styles and make-up. There was a kind of overkill of style,
and ultimately this generation of boutiques failed, as the young
developed dissident fashions so extreme that only a new generation
of designers could respond to or develop them commercially; while
an intensified emphasis on luxury and on clothes for the successful
career woman took over the upper end of the market.

The formerly down market chain, Marks and Spencer, now sell
garments made from suede, leather and silk; many department
stores have closed; new chains of shops selling 'coordinated ranges'
that speed up selection for the prospective buyer have appeared,[28]
and again it seems as if these have been particularly developed in
Britain. One of the most successful is Next, owned by Hepworths, a
large British mass-production tailoring firm; while in direct response[29] the Burton tailoring group has come up with Principles, a
similar chain. Typically these shops sell men's wear as well as clothes

for women; and typical again is the move made by Jeff Banks of Warehouse, another London chain selling high-fashion, medium-price clothes, who in 1984 opened in the United States, not in Manhattan but in a New Jersey shopping mall.

For the decline of the old department store has to do with the decline of the inner city, and of the railway, while the dissemination of the motor car has brought the development of suburban shopping centres, out of town hypermarkets and, in North America, regional shopping centres. This is a new kind of consumerist dream world for the new 'decentred' concept of city, a shopping nirvana, more completely separated from the rest of the world than the *Bon Marché* ever was, a complete world or city of its own.

The question arises: does this new type of city and this new type of shopping kill fashion? Fashion always set up a radical distinction between the world of the capital city and the world of the provinces. Exclusivity and chic belonged to metropolitan life; dowdiness to the provincial backwaters – from which so many heroes and heroines of nineteenth-century literature longed to escape.

Today, on the other hand, fashion is less about belonging to a select band, and more about the extreme individualism that is one mark of extreme alienation; and it may therefore become less the acknowledgement of some form of *membership* than an insistence on isolation.

Group counter-cultural fashions could, however, arise in the 'provincial' setting; a group might impose its collective norms of outrage on the boredom of small town life. Group styles – counter-cultural fashions – are in a sense a response to boredom. Indeed they often use the supreme boredom of a mad attention to details that are in themselves meaningless (the knot of a tie, the droop of a sleeve) to destroy the surrounding ennui, to create meaning out of emptiness and to impose the imperative of self on the alien, computerized routines of the dominant culture.

Today, this could be true of all fashions, so to that extent all fashion could possibly be said to have become counter-cultural. Before turning to the subject of counter-cultural fashions, however, it is useful to look at the general influence of popular culture – sport, entertainments, dancing – on fashion as a whole.

Chapter 8

Fashion and Popular Culture

'Transformations' are at the heart of the study of popular culture. . . .
Popular culture is neither . . . the popular traditions of resistance to these
processes; nor is it the forms which are superimposed on and over them. It
is the ground on which the transformations are worked.

Stuart Hall: 'Notes on Deconstructing "the popular"'

After the industrial revolution, life was no longer divided according
to the seasonal imperatives of the agricultural calendar. These were
replaced by the mechanical imperatives of industrial time, in which
each day was identical regardless of the time of year, and each hour
of the day or night equally fit to be used up by the machine. The
traditional holidays and festivals persisted in the popular consciousness, but even these were gradually replaced by a new and more
rigid demarcation between 'work' and 'leisure'. Not only was production recognized; so also was consumption. Economic expansion
was the basis for a revolution in customs, beliefs and daily experience; henceforth fashion itself was to become one medium for the
expression of the values of modernity.

There was a move from display to identity. In the nineteenth
century fashion – not uniforms alone – became one of the many,
and one of the most elaborate, forms of classification that bur-
geoned with the triumph of industrial culture. No longer was it
enough to be recognized as a member of a class, caste or calling.
Individuals participated in a process of self-docketing and self
announcement, as dress became the vehicle for the display of the
unique individual personality. At the same time men and women

were drawn back into new forms of anonymity, locked into the impersonal difference of gender more strictly than before. Yet although anonymity was essential to city life, dress subtly subverted it. Dress could act as display *or* mask – or both. The reverse side to the world of display, whether bold or surreptitious, on the street, was the retreat into privacy.

Fashion had never been wholly reserved for the rich. Fernand Braudel[1] has found evidence of a fashionable peasantry in France in the 1690s, although the spread of fashion only really advanced with the raised standards of personal hygiene of the eighteenth century. In the nineteenth century fashion, far from necessarily representing enslavement to a husband's wealth, might mean for the working woman an emancipation and an independence she had never known before, since now the money she earned might be her own, not her family's. The industrial revolution spelt disaster for many, but while it made harder the lot of the married woman dependent on her husband's wages, it represented a step forward for the single woman:

> For the first time working women had the means to gratify a taste for dress, although expenditure under this head was a matter for much adverse criticism. 'I would state as an important fact with which I am well acquainted,' said the Reverend G. S. Bull, in 1832, 'that in many cases the young women employed in factories do not make their own clothes at all; their working clothes they obtain at the slop-shops which abound in the manufacturing districts, where ready-made clothes are to be had; and their Sunday dress is, of course, of a very smart description, wherever they can afford it, and is manufactured by some notable milliner who knows how to set these matters off to the best advantage.' The fact that women were no longer content to contrive for themselves clumsy, ill-fitting garments, was regarded by contemporaries [men, usually] only as a sign of incompetence and deterioration, and they completely overlooked the fact that from the woman's point of view the change betokened some measure of social advance.[2]

In 1862 Ellen Barlee, writing of the north of England, observed:

> The dressmakers ... thrive upon such an occupied female population, for Lancashire lassies rarely make their own dresses. They can, however, pay well to have them done and it is therefore worthwhile for the dressmakers to study fashions and fits; so that on Sundays and holidays

I was told it was quite surprising to see the elegant appearance these girls made ... On Saturday mills are closed at midday and the men and single women make real holiday. Then the town is all alive; it is quite a gala day; the men appearing in good broadcloth and suits, and the girls as smart as wages can make them.[3]

And Hannah Cullwick, a nineteenth-century servant, records a conversation with the photographer who took pictures of her in working clothes, in which he informed her,

there is so very few that care for pictures in their working dress – they all want to be as smart as can be. I ax'd him about pitgirls' likeness, but he said, 'La' bless you, I couldn't get 'em in their right dress – they're as fine as anybody, drest up.'[4]

Fashion became part of the popular consciousness, and the mass manufacture of clothing enabled it to become part of popular culture.

Fashionable dressing as a popular mass phenomenon and as a leisure activity in its own right has been influenced by the other leisure activities of 'the machine age': sport, music, the cinema and television, all of which produced whole new ways of dressing. Journalism, advertising and photography have acted as the mass-communication hinges joining fashion to the popular consciousness.

Since the late nineteenth century, word and image have increasingly propagated style. Images of desire are constantly in circulation; increasingly it has been the image as well as the artefact that the individual has purchased. The young woman of 1900 who bought a cheap Gibson Girl blouse didn't just buy a blouse; she bought a symbol of emancipation, glamour and success.[5]

Fashion is a magical system, and what we see as we leaf through glossy magazines is 'the look'. Like advertising, women's magazines have moved from the didactic to the hallucinatory. Originally their purpose was informational, but what we see today in both popular journalism and advertising is the mirage of a way of being, and what we engage in is no longer only the relatively simple process of direct imitation, but the less conscious one of identification.

It was above all the camera that created a new way of seeing and a new style of beauty for women in the twentieth century. The love affair of black and white photography with fashion *is* the modernist sensibility.

The great promise of photography was that it would tell the 'truth'. Yet the 'truth' of photography is only a more convincing illusion, selection and artifice lurking behind the seeming impartiality of the mechanical eye. Fashion drawings often give more accurate information, yet it is the photographic image that has captured the feel of modern clothes, and in so doing influenced them. Lartigue, who was taking informal photographs of fashionable ladies just before the First World War, Baron de Meyer, who flourished between the wars, and Steichen, whose work continued into the post Second World War period, all took pictures that reproduced the illusion of movement, and so the suggestion of movement became an element essential to fashionable dress. Black and white photography intensified the importance of line, contrast, and abstract, architectural form.[6]

Photography paradoxically enhanced both the mystery and the suggestiveness of fashion – and fashion magazines come on rather like pornography; they indulge the desire of the 'reader' who looks at the pictures, to *be* each perfect being reflected in the pages, while simultaneously engaging erotically with a femininity (and increasingly a masculinity) that is constantly being redefined.

Photography was a new art of the industrial period and particularly of the twentieth century. It was also a new pastime for the general public. The family snapshot, the informal, 'accidental' style, not only influenced professional photographers, but must also have made the individual more self-conscious and ultimately more sophisticated about her or his appearance, self presentation and performance on the daily scene, in which fashion plays so important a part.

In their turn, the performances of popular culture influenced and transformed fashion in the twentieth century. The most recent stage of this interaction between fashion and popular culture has been that since the Second World War, and especially since the 1960s, fashion has become virtually a form of leisure entertainment in itself, while designers have been elevated to the status of pop stars. In recent years fashion cults have themselves become a kind of performance art.

James Laver, as we saw, believed that the changes in men's dress which occurred at the beginning of the industrial period took the form of the adaptation of sports clothes for polite society wear. Chanel, it is said, adapted sports wear to women's dress at the beginning of the twentieth century.

i) Motoring wear by Burberry in the
first decade of the twentieth century.

ii) Sportswear in the 1920s.
Reproduced by kind permission of Burberry's Ltd.

It was in the late nineteenth and early twentieth century that women's sport began to advance rapidly. Ladies had engaged in archery, riding and croquet throughout the nineteenth century. Victorian women were by no means so passive nor so hampered by their claustrophic clothing as might have been expected. In any case, waterproof clothing was developed in the early nineteenth century and evolved as comfortable and protective outerwear. In the eighteenth century a fashionably dressed woman could not have exposed herself to rain, wind or sleet, whereas in the nineteenth century bourgeois women took to the streets of the great cities in all weathers, and country walks became a favourite pastime.

Protective clothing by Burberry and Aquascutum was given a further boost by the arrival of the motor car in the late nineteenth century and the fashion for motoring in the early 1900s. Driving was at first a hazardous enterprise, as well as an aristocratic and glamorous one. You rode 'on' not 'in' an automobile, and required dust coats, capes, gloves, goggles, a hat or cap and a motoring veil to protect you from the dust raised by the 'iron steed'. One firm advertised leather motoring knickers with a detachable flannel lining, and leather coats and skirts were also worn. Burberry's catalogues referred to motoring as a branch of sport, and its special clothing could be made in a variety of materials according to the weather. Some of the adjustable veils must have made their wearers look like beekeepers, or as if tied up in an old-fashioned 'meat safe' or wire mesh cupboard; some even had little doors at the front. The normal cruising rate for a motor car was then about twelve miles per hour, although Dorothy Levitt, an early 'motoriste', set a record of ninety-one m.p.h. in 1906. She wrote a book of advice for lady drivers; one of her tips was always to have a vanity mirror at hand, not only for morale and good looks, but also to use as a driving mirror.[7]

Lawn tennis was the first 'modern' sport to attract widespread (middle-class) participation by women in the 1870s. It was at first played in bustles, long skirts and corsets. These clothes were only modified in accordance with changes in mainstream fashion, and it was not until 1920 that Suzanne Lenglen, the French champion

Top: Women's tennis dress at Wimbledon 1887.
Bottom: The transformation of tennis dress: Sem drawing of Suzanne Lenglen 1922.
Reproduced courtesy of the Mary Evans Picture Library.

and supreme tennis star of the 1920s, shocked post-war Wimbledon with her revolutionary court wear. She bounded on to the court minus stockings, petticoat and sleeves; but before long women dressed like this all the time; Lenglen's clothes in the mid-1920s – designed by Patou – were much the same off court as on, and consisted of little pleated skirts, straight cardigans and vests or short-sleeved blouses.

It was in the 1890s that women's sport made its most striking advances. The first ladies' cricketers' club was formed in 1890, the ladies' golf union in 1893, and the first ladies' international hockey match took place in 1897. Fashion was not always immediately modified to suit this new activity. The V-neck, for example, was not introduced into fashion until just before the First World War (many people thought it totally indecent) so for ten or twenty years women were playing strenuous games with even their necks muffled up and constricted in whalebone and cambric. But bicycling – far more widespread than motoring, and not, as motoring was, restricted to a few aristocratic women who could afford to defy convention – did mean the advent of new costumes. At first it was considered 'fast', but it soon made the long-ridiculed bloomers[8] respectable, and it was the sporting crazes of the late nineteenth and early twentieth century that made trousers popular wear for women.

It is possible that the advance of the trouser for women is the most significant fashion change of the twentieth century. For centuries, western women's legs had been concealed, trousers and pantaloons worn only by actresses, acrobats and others of dubious morality. Paradoxically, in Islamic cultures women wear trousers and men robes, but in the western world until the 1900s only working women, and then usually only those engaged in the coarsest labour, and entertainers, wore trousers or showed their legs, and when they did so their morality was impugned. Women in the mines, the girls who scavenged along the Yorkshire sea shore, and many female agricultural workers wore trousers; those in the roaming field gangs, for example, were particularly suspected of immorality:

> These gangs will sometimes travel many miles from their own village,
> they are to be met morning and evening on the roads, dressed in short
> petticoats with suitable coats and boots, and sometimes trousers, look-
> ing wonderfully strong and healthy, but tainted with a customary

Trousers for women: 'Females as they work at the pit banks' from Transactions and Results of the National Association of Coal, Lime and Ironstone Miners of Great Britain, held at Leeds 9–14 November 1863.
James Klugman Collection. Reproduced by kind permission of the Marx Memorial Library.

immorality and heedless of the fatal result which their love of this busy and independent life is bringing on their unfortunate offspring who are pining at home.[9]

Lady Rhondda, a prominent feminist between the two world wars, commented in her autobiography on the extent to which the desire to be 'feminine' persisted even in the wilds of western Canada before the First World War:

One would expect that the further out one moved from the centres of civilization the more practical and the less conventionally feminine would the dress and demeanour of women become. But up to a point this is not so. In Peace River Crossing, for example, the women walked through the muddy roads and along the rickety half-made sidewalks in the highest of pin-pointed heels, in the most exaggerated if not quite the latest of fashionable clothes, and round their bepowdered necks hung huge pearl necklaces ...

Further out the thing is reversed and one sees what one would expect. You cannot run a farm and six babies in the wilderness on pin heels and powder. The women up and down the river are practical and not dressy. Many wear brown trouser overalls much like the men.[10]

Trousers were, however, respectable wear for women only on the beach, on the sports field or for leisure until well after the Second World War. In the 1920s the members of the famous Paris coterie of lesbians, which included Radclyffe Hall, Romaine Brooks and Natalie Clifford Barney, as well as a number of other artists and writers, wore skirts with their men's jackets and waistcoats, ties and monocles, although by the 1930s Brassai's photographs of Paris night life show couples at the Montparnasse lesbian club, *Le Monocle*, the 'male' partner in full drag.

Theodora Fitzgibbon recalled[11] that during the Second World War it was still not usual for women civilians to wear trousers, but she herself wore old jodphurs and riding jacket in London as a protection against the cold, and the usefulness of 'slacks' as they were then called was much discussed in the pages of fashion magazines. Women mobilized into munitions and other factories during the war became accustomed to wearing dungarees and trousers for work, so they certainly lost their capacity to outrage, and Nancy Mitford pokes fun at one of her characters in *The Pursuit of Love*, written in 1945, who

> was curiously dated in her manner, and seemed still to be living in the 1920s. It was as though, at the age of thirty five, having refused to grow any older, she had pickled herself ... She had a short, canary-coloured shingle ... and wore trousers with the air of one still flouting the conventions, ignorant that every suburban shopgirl was doing the same.[12]

In the 1950s trousers, and particularly jeans, became a symbol of youth, but although one attraction of trousers for women was their association with youth and leisure, it was the more formal trouser suit of the 1960s, introduced by André Courrèges, star of Parisian *haute couture* in the early 1960s, that seems to have prefigured their much greater acceptability today. Trousered women were not allowed into the Royal Enclosure at Ascot until 1970 (divorcées were admitted during the same period) and it is still the case that in some professions, in banking and business and on very formal social occasions women may not wear trousers. Nevertheless, the acceptance in principle of trousers for women has been a more significant change than the ups and downs of hemlines in the years after 1945.

The easiest way of explaining this change is in simple evolutionary terms, as an index of the advancing freedom of women, and their equality with men. This is not entirely satisfactory. For one thing, women remain unequal, so while the trouser for women might symbolize a myth in western societies that women have achieved emancipation, it can hardly be interpreted as unproblematic of their status. If it were interpreted in this literal way it would certainly lead us to believe what many feminists believe *is* the case, that in so far as women have made progress in the public sphere of paid work, this has been on male terms and within the parameter of masculine values. This partial emancipation has also occurred in a culture (speaking generally of the West) that is positively phobic about 'effeminacy'. In these 'liberated' times a man in a skirt causes considerable anxiety and hostility. The counter-culture of the late sixties flirted with the idea (Mick Jagger once wore a kind of minidress, but only over trousers, to give a concert, and some men wore caftans occasionally), but in general in order to wear a skirt a man has to define himself as a transvestite, that is, a sexual deviant.

A second argument brought forward to explain women's adoption of trousers is a functionalist one: that they are more comfortable and practical than skirts. In many ways this is true. Yet I have argued that fashion cannot be explained in functional terms. Anne Hollander's explanation in terms of aesthetic styles is (although she is speaking of bare legs rather than trousered ones) that in the twentieth century the female leg has symbolized movement, and that movement is an important feature of modernism. All of these explanations probably contain some truth, although each seems insufficient on its own.

The elevation of sport, with its ethos of physical health and streamlined efficiency, into a dominant feature of western culture must also have played a part, so that trousers become one means whereby women express an aspiration towards an athlete's body. For similar reasons both sexes have adopted jogging suits, T-shirts and running shoes for daily wear. But although sport has been possibly the most important twentieth-century influence on fashion, dancing has perhaps had a more persistent long-term effect on the evolution of dress.

According to David Kunzle fashion is 'always closely linked with current dance styles', the dancer, the dance and the clothes invariably fused to create one unified effect. For example:

> Rococo stays, tightly moulding and lengthening the torso but cut away over the hips at the side determined in part – or was determined by – the character of the dance, which in the early eighteenth century became very sophisticated technically and very important socially ... twisting and tilting the upper torso from side to side ... From the restrictions imposed by the structure of corsets a manner of holding and using the upper torso, arms and head evolved, and affected conventions around the stylistic execution of steps and patterns of movement.[13]

The waltz took upper-class ballrooms by storm in 1812. Some hostesses refused to allow it, for it involved close physical contact between male and female partner, a thing hitherto unheard of, and it was said to induce a dangerous state of arousal and exhilaration, conducive to immorality. It was of a piece with the 'indecent', close-fitting clothes of the period, yet it became a permanent feature of nineteenth-century ballrooms, and had achieved a quite staid respectability by the time a new set of daring dance crazes emerged 100 years later.

During the second half of the nineteenth century graceful forms of exercise for women – callisthenics, the Dalcroze method and later the aesthetic, lightly clad, free movement dancing of Isadora Duncan, eurythmics – all became increasingly popular. But the dances that became popular immediately before the First World War were purely hedonistic, and made few claims to health or artistry. They were fun – 'Take up the rugs and let's trot' – was the after-dinner slogan of middle-class America in the decade before 1914.

At the same period Irene and Vernon Castle, who became inter-

nationally famous before Vernon Castle's early death in 1918, made
ballroom dancing an entertainment spectacle. Irene Castle was one
of the first women to express the twentieth-century look and way of
moving. Like Gabrielle Chanel – and others – she claimed to be, or
was thought to have been, the first woman to bob her hair (actually
this fashion had begun in bohemian circles some years earlier). She
was certainly the personification of modernity according to Cecil
Beaton:

> There was something terrifically healthy and clean about her ... Her
> marvellous balance of femininity and boyish simplicity was congruent
> to the latest ideal that women had created for themselves ...
> The Castles ... sped modernism on its way. The dance craze they
> symbolised promoted a freer, less restricted social exchange between
> men and women.[14]

The jazz craze that hit America just before the First World War
came out of Harlem and black New York culture, although jazz
itself, of course, had first developed elsewhere. Harlem culture was
contradictory; it had its wild and unrestrained side, but it also had
its own social strata and an upper class that aspired to, and indeed
achieved, a style of life as 'gracious' as white Manhattan. There were
saloons and cafés, but there were also tango tea dances – and
Harlem was just as 'infatuated' with the modern dances popularized
by the Castles as white New York.

> But among the masses of Harlem the tango was more of a fad – a
> fashionable diversion, or classy respite, from such animated and risqué
> rhythms of the popular dance floor as the black bottom, the grizzly
> bear, the eagle rock, the turkey trot, the bunny hug, the Texas Tommy,
> scratchin' the gravel, and ballin' the jack. It was to these that the
> decorous white citizens of Harlem were referring when they used the
> term 'nigger' dances ... The masses of Harlem took to the tango partly
> because it was new, partly because they liked its association with high
> society, partly because they realised that black musicians had con-
> tributed something to its development and popularity.[15]

(The Texas Tommy seems to have prefigured the Lindy Hop, one
of the most famous Harlem dances of the late twenties and the
1930s; both seem to have been similar to the jitterbugging of the
1940s.)
The new dance movement was associated, in the minds of com-

mentators of the period, with a revolution in feminine attire and, however inaccurately, with a new morality of licentiousness. In the 'jazz age' of the 1920s dance meant a whole new syncopated style of movement and the radical modification of constricting clothes. Its jerky rhythms expressed a machine consciousness. Yet the culture within which western technology developed, and which adapted a form of dance invented by one of its most exploited groups, still repressed the body. Modernism romanticized technology and the city, romanticized also what it perceived as 'primitive'. But this was not a relaxed acceptance of the body, for the Judaeo-Christian cultures of the West are still tainted with asceticism and a suspicion of the body. Through the medium of the dance, however, we may recover our relationship to the body in a magical and pre-scientific way, and it is for this reason that dance has gained a 'peculiar prestige'.[16]

In fashion showings since the 1960s music and dance have more and more been used to transform commercial display into entertainment. This however is not new – in the nineteenth century the theatre was a fashion spectacle, and both serious plays and the variety show or music hall the excuse for displays of fashionable dress. Many men and women went to the theatre partly to see the stars wearing exclusive gowns, and the stars in turn influenced fashions in both dress and styles of beauty.

The cinema, with its much larger audience, was correspondingly even more influential in creating new ways for men and women to move, dance, dress, make love, *be*. The cinema in the United States began as a proletarian entertainment, but the move to Hollywood began the process of glamorization. In the silent movies stylization of both gesture and looks was necessary for narrative, and promoted not only new ways of walking, sitting and using the hands, but also the development of styles to suit personalities. Theda Bara incarnated the vamp, Lillian Gish the pure virgin, Louise Brooks the more independent, even tomboyish girl with a capacity for survival, the forerunner of the 'business woman'. Fashions of the twenties were influenced by the office dresses and simple suits she wore; although curiously enough Chanel, enticed out to the Pacific coast to design for the movies, was not a great success, since her clothes were *too* understated to work on the screen.

The 1930s are usually thought of as the 'great' period of Hollywood dressing. The glamour and exaggeration of the costume displays were the mass media equivalent of the spectacle of the courts of the *ancien régime*. The making of the clothes was itself costly and extravagant, but, as elsewhere, the Hollywood cutters and seamstresses were very poorly paid.[17] Although the dresses were not always well finished off, 'real' materials were always used, and big stars could insist on such luxuries as real silk underwear with hand embroidery and monograms – although none of this would ever be seen by the audience. Elaborate and costly ornamentation was used. Eleanor Powell's bugle-beaded dress for *Broadway Melody of 1936*, for example, weighed nearly twenty-five pounds. (Beaded dresses could not be hung up, for the weight of the beads would cause the fragile material to which they were hand-stitched to tear.) In the making of historical costumes months of research was spent. Adrian, MGM's top designer, went to France to study original eighteenth-century costumes and materials before designing Norma Shearer's clothes for *Marie Antoinette* (1938), and real silks, satins, brocades and precious stones were used in their making. Oliver Messel, an English authority on sixteenth-century Renaissance Italian costume, was brought to Hollywood to design the costumes, also for Norma Shearer, for *Romeo and Juliet* (1936). But in the end the star preferred Adrian's designs; and usually the ultimate effect of period costume in films was not historical accuracy, nor were the clothes in fact accurate, for they were always modified to suit contemporary taste. 'Authenticity', 'flavour' and 'suggestion' were held to be the correct way to costume historical films. Anne Hollander even maintains that 'a whole fake history of costume, almost entirely composed of stage conventions, has come to exist, if rather nebulously, in the public awareness'; consequently costume in film or on stage is, she suggests, primarily a series of signals whereby 'powdered hair' equals the eighteenth century, 'a ruff' the Elizabethan period and a 'Juliet cap' Renaissance Italy (although the latter garment was invented for Theda Bara in 1916 and did not even exist in the sixteenth century).

That films were made in black and white contributed to the characteristic art deco aesthetic of the period:

Colour drained out of elegance ... draped lamé and sequined satin offered rivulets of light to the eye as they flowed and slithered over the shifting flanks and thighs of Garbo, Dietrich, Harlow and Lombard. These visions were built on the newly powerful sensuality of colourless texture in motion ... sequins, marabou, white net and black lace developed a fresh intensity of sexual meaning in the world of colourless fantasy.[18]

Hollywood, however, did not restrict itself to the glamorous and the spectacular. Hollywood styles also influenced mass-produced fashions and the woman in the street.

'Fan magazines and studio publicity photos helped to spread an indigenous Hollywood "outdoors" style.' Sports and leisure wear were transformed by the promotion of backless bathing suits, slacks, halter tops and sweaters – all styles created in Paris in the twenties but now translated for the Californian beaches and even for American small town life. The west coast fashion industry took off in the late twenties and became, as it has remained, a centre of sports and casual wear. Films themselves also acted as showcases for chic and avant-garde clothes and interiors, and there was a preference for movies in which the settings could be in department stores, beauty salons or glamorous homes. Certain stars – Joan Crawford is the example usually cited – were promoted as 'clothes horses' so that the clothes they wore became a vital feature of the film and directly influenced retail fashion. Fashions became part of a mammoth tie-up between the cinema and big business, and it has been suggested that Hollywood movies contributed in a major way to the 'consumerism' that developed in America. 'A virulent form of movie mania'[19] was exploited to sell clothes such as Miriam Hopkins pyjamas, Joan Crawford suits, or the same star's famous 'Letty Lynton' dress. This white organza dress had dramatically built up shoulders and short sleeves made of ruffles, and when Joan Crawford stood framed in a doorway the sleeves stood out like twin powder puffs or embryo wings. Adrian designed many outfits for Crawford in which built up shoulders were intended to balance her figure, and the star is credited with the wide popularization of this style. Yet Schiaparelli in Paris was beginning to bring back wide shoulders at the same time – visual tastes change and a general line develops in a way that is never the outcome of one individual or of a single, widely publicized dress.

Films and filmstars as celebrities of course continued to influence fashion. When Brigitte Bardot in the late fifties got married in check gingham and broderie anglaise, these became instantly fashionable materials. When she and Jeanne Moreau appeared in Edwardian dress in *Viva Maria* this also caused a season of imitation looks, although the two stars themselves interpreted the flounced skirts, rich blouses and laced up boots very differently; Moreau wore tight-laced corsets in order to get the correct walk and stance, whereas Bardot strode along in sixties style. In the early sixties Jeanne Moreau had popularized twenties styles in *Jules et Jim*; although the sack dresses, sailor styles, men's style cardigans and wire spectacles were consistent with the Givenchy/Cardin waistless look of the time. In 1967 *Bonnie and Clyde* set going the thirties look of berets and long, lanky skirts with 'old-fashioned' jumpers – although Faye Dunaway's hair remained relentlessly straight and sixties.

Television has been particularly influential in popularizing 'retro-chic' – period clothes, but from the recent past. Dramatizations of novels, documentaries and plays popularized every recent mode from the twenties to (in the early 1980s) the hippies' fashions of a decade earlier as a 'period' style. Hairdressers reinvented 'ear-phones' (plaits coiled round over the ears like small raffia place mats), Betty Grable upswept styles, and the studied dowdiness of hair in a roll round the back of the neck which went so perfectly with the forties print 'frocks' that returned to fashion in the 1970s. *Brideshead Revisited* is only one of the more recent and most widely distributed of a long procession of 'modern' yet 'period' dramas (*The Jewel in the Crown* is another) whose fashions can easily be recycled – although this time around the Brideshead look of cricket trousers, fairisle sweaters and short floppy hair was for women as well as men.

This obsession with pastiche, this 'nostalgia mode' is related to the way in which the dictatorship of *haute couture* broke down in the 1960s and 1970s. A single style can no longer dominate in the post-modern period. Instead there is a constant attempt to recreate atmosphere. In the fantasy culture of the 1980s there is no real history, no real past; it is replaced by an instant, magical nostalgia, a strangely *unmotivated* appropriation of the past:

> Pastiche, is, like parody, the imitation of a peculiar mask, speech in a dead language; but it is a neutral practice of such mimicry, without any of parody's ulterior motives . . . devoid of laughter and of any conviction that alongside the abnormal tongue you have momentarily borrowed,

some healthy linguistic normality still exists. Pastiche is thus blank parody, a statue with blind eyeballs.[20]

This pastiche is related to the more general appropriation of popular culture which I have already mentioned. 'Feminist' and 'progressive' reworkings of popular forms at times, instead of achieving the appropriation of these forms, come close to simply celebrating – even if in a camp way – the kitsch, the degraded and the trite. Fashion can do this with particular panache. Fashionable chic itself, indeed, even becomes a pastiche.

In America the Preppy style, in Britain the Sloane Ranger way of dressing (named after the Sloane Square area in London SW1 where these debs and Hooray Henrys live when in town) have become virtually self imitations. Once such styles would have been invisible within the general category of 'classic chic'; there was a standard of fashion normality – like Standard English – and bohemian and other deviant ways of dressing related implicitly to a common language of chic dress. Classic chic itself was a contradiction; it was always defined in such a way as to suggest that the *truly* fashionable way to look is to transcend passing fashions in order to attain some eternal realm where chic approximates an ideal state. Today, the way in which such fashions have been satirized has undermined the very notion that there is any longer a dominant mode of dress. This is what journalists mean, presumably, when they talk of fashion anarchy: that 'classic chic' no longer exists. Something else, however, exists in its place: parodies of chic, the camping up of style. Even the city stockbroker dressed in his bespoke Jermyn Street uniform can no longer be unselfconscious about it. All styles are now self-caricatures. It is no longer possible unreflectively to *be* the perfectly dressed gentleman whose dress never calls attention to itself; we have all become so sophisticated about performance that we slily recognize the attempted sleight of hand that aimed to suggest the absence of effort or impression-creation. No longer do *any* fashions seem normal or 'natural'.

The beginnings of the breaking down of the dominance of Parisian *haute couture* does, however, pre-date the current craze for pastiche, for already in the 1950s American leisure and teenage fashions captivated the 'Affluent Society' as a new youth market was identified. This youth market came to be equated with rebellion : 'the idea that anybody had the right to be anywhere and do anything, no matter who they were and how they were dressed, was a big thing in the sixties.'[21]

Both *haute couture* and mass-produced fashion were quick to adapt the youth cult to mainstream fashion. This trend began – surprisingly in view of the British reputation on the one hand for dowdiness, on the other for 'classic' clothes that had little to do with high fashion – in London. Janey Ironside, who was Professor of Fashion at the Royal College of Art during the crucial period from 1956 to the late 1960s, explained its origins in terms of the British welfare state and the British 'social revolution' after the Second World War. Local government education grants made it possible for many whose talents would have been wasted in a previous era to go to college. In addition there was British eccentricity.[22]

Already in the late 1950s, fashion journalists such as Ernestine Carter of the *Sunday Times* and Iris Ashley of the *Daily Express*, as well as Clare Rendlesham when she was at *Vogue* and later when she worked for *Queen* – which for a time was *the* 1960s trendy magazine – were influential in giving publicity and support to Mary Quant and other young British designers. Clare Rendlesham concurs in the general judgment of the 1960s as a convention shattering period:

> 'I was Young Idea editor [for *Vogue*] and all those exciting people like Quant and Tuffin and Foale in London and Emmanuelle Khan, Ili Jacobson and Michel Rosier in Paris were producing fresh, youthful clothes. Everyone else on *Vogue* thought I was very peculiar indeed because I thought these clothes were wonderful.' ...
>
> As fashion editor of *Queen* magazine ... Clare Rendlesham made her point most emphatically. On a black-bordered page, she announced the demise of couture and ran a 'premature' obituary of Balenciaga and of his disciple, Givenchy.   (*Guardian*, 9 February 1984)

Under the direction of Janey Ironside the RCA produced some of the key designers of the sixties, such as Ossie Clark and Sally Tuffin. Mary Quant, on the other hand, came from Goldsmiths College in South London, where she met her future husband and backer, Alexander Plunket Green. His was the upper class eccentric style:

> He seemed to have no clothes of his own. He wore his mother's pyjama tops as shirts, generally in that colour known as 'old gold' which usually comes in shantung. His trousers also came out of his mother's ward-

robe. Beautifully cut and sleek fitting, the zip was at the side, and they were in weird and wonderful variations of purple, prune, crimson and putty ... They came to a stop half way down the calf ... I found out later that the dramatic effect his appearance created ... was absolutely unintentional.[23]

They opened the first 'boutique', Bazaar, in the Kings Road, Chelsea, in 1955. George Melly calls this 'the one true pop manifestation in the years between Rock and the Beatles'. It was important that they were well-connected socially and could capitalize on being members of the 'Chelsea Set', 'whose parties and general way of carrying on had won the total attention of the gossip writers of the period'. Many of these new Bright Young Things, though, however well-connected, had to work, and they tended to go in for small crafts and businesses connected with the arts. So to open a fashion boutique was 'a very Chelsea Set thing to do'.[24]

George Melly rightly describes the phenomenon as apolitical, even if Mary Quant herself described it in the rhetoric of democracy:

> Once only the Rich, the Establishment set the fashion. Now it is the inexpensive little dress seen on the girls in the High Street. These girls ... are alive ... looking, listening, ready to try anything new ... They may be dukes' daughters, doctors' daughters, dockers' daughters. They are not interested in status symbols. They don't worry about accents or class ... They represent the whole new spirit that is present day Britain – a classless spirit that has grown up out of the second world war ... They are the mods.[25]

The significance of Mary Quant and Plunket Green was that they were able to transform themselves from 'zany' students whose boutique was a kind of permanent party for their friends, into business tycoons who married their own flair for style to the most modern American methods of sizing and mass marketing. And, as George Melly says:

> Mary Quant affected fashion from a comparatively traditional position, that of the couturier of genius able to translate the flavour of a particular era into colour, shape and texture ...
>
> Male pop fashion was a different case ... at the beginning it was more of a genuine pop manifestation, a general upsurge rather than the work of any one man.[26]

Another influence on sixties fashion was the Parisian designer, Courrèges, who operated in the old system, but whose clothes seemed to prefigure the space age. His first two collections in 1964 'shattered' the fashion world, said Janey Ironside, and it was he rather than Mary Quant who set the mini-skirt in orbit and who made trouser suits high fashion.

Sixties clothes were influenced by the return to fashion of the twenties as a period. They were also influenced by 'op art' and 'pop art'. In imitation of the painter Mondrian, they were hard-edged, brightly coloured or black and white, and squared-off, two-dimensional. Yet the style was not modernistic as the twenties style had been. The futurism of the clothes designed by Courrèges, by Pierre Cardin and by Paco Rabanne, who used plastic discs and chain mail for his dresses, was an adaptation of the sartorial and visual clichés of science-fiction comics (also influential on pop art); they were almost a kind of literary pastiche, futuristic retro-chic. Fashion in the 1960s repeatedly turned to the past for images of glamour, or adopted the high boots and black leather of Christine Keeler, the call-girl – what were known as 'kinky' styles.

For this was Harold Macmillan's and then Harold Wilson's Britain. The world of 'you never had it so good' (a Conservative Party slogan of the 1950s) became the world of Wilson's 'white hot, technological revolution' (the ticket on which he won the General Election for the Labour Party in 1964). The bright promises hid cynicism; the Profumo affair, in which the Tory Minister of Defence was revealed as having had an affair with Christine Keeler, who had links not only with a Soviet attaché but also allegedly with the underworld, seemed to symbolize the tinselly glamour and the manic frenzy of the end of the boom. 1960s chic did not exclude the dark glamour of a *demi-monde* that brought together gangsters and photographers, pop stars and prostitutes.

Yet the style that Britain pioneered retained a certain innocence. Mary Quant's classless young woman was at least *alert* and looked more like the Madcap of the Upper Fifth than some pop group's collective mistress or a girl at the wrong end of a heroin needle.

The clothing of the 'permissive society' was often described as 'unisex', but in retrospect it doesn't look masculine or boyish. When girls – for all women were girls in those days – wore skirts that rose to the crotch and curtains of hair that descended to meet it, when they exposed nipples in see-through blouses and navels below crocheted tank tops that never met hipster pants, they were looking not like men or boys but like children. It was, as the twenties at times had been, a paederastic period, although to the Christopher Robin look of the twenties the sixties preferred a decadent Lolita image. As personified by the newly famous models of the period, it was the decade of the rag doll, of the waif, of the pre-pubertal Twiggy who shot to fame before she reached the age of consent, the age of the Mary Quant schoolgirl in gym slip and black stockings and of Grace Coddington as Pierrot. The waif became even more decadent in the early 1970s when Ingrid Boulting incarnated her in the sleazy sinuosity of Biba's art nouveau and art deco pastiches.

Across the Atlantic Andy Warhol orchestrated the same aesthetic of the banal in which everything is surface. But transported to New York the manic deadpan, the clown look perfected by Twiggy became the sinister nothingness of Edie Sedgwick, one of Andy Warhol's 'stars':

> Ondine and the Duchess would shoot people up in the crowd ... The kids at the Dom looked really great, glittering and reflecting in vinyl, suede, and feathers, in skirts and boots and bright-coloured mesh tights, and patent leather shoes, and silver and gold hip-riding miniskirts, and the Paco Rabanne thin plastic look with the linked plastic disks in the dresses, and lots of bell-bottoms and poor-boy sweaters, and short, short dresses that flared out at the shoulders and ended way above the knee.
>
> Some of the kids ... looked so young I wondered where they got the money for all those fashionable clothes. I guess they were doing a lot of shoplifting: I'd hear little girls ... say things like 'Why should I *pay* for it – I mean it's going to fall apart tomorrow' ...
>
> The kids could be in the dressing rooms stuffing their bags full, or else their pocketbooks, since the new clothes were so skimpy.[27]

The decadence of the later sixties styles, when Biba fashions made chic the druggy trance, and when pastiche pre-Raphaelite hair-styles, Theda Bara make-up and the bleached-out glamour of the thirties followed hard upon the heels of the space age look, was a sinister bring-down after the hysterical high. The art nouveau nymph, stoned and tubercular, replaced the empty vivacity of the sixties girl who was always having such 'fun'. And with vampiric insatiability fashion photography in the 1970s resuscitated Jean

Harlow film stills, the imagery of forties *films noirs* and, when glamour underwear returned to fashion, the lesbian, the prostitute and a whole imagery of soft porn.

The style of the 1960s was also *about* style – about style as a way of life, style as the self, and yet also style as fun. It did more therefore than merely express the entrepreneurial spirit of the white heat of the boom, when dress designers, hairdressers and fashion models became the new social stars. The 1960s obsession with popular fashion – and it was fashion for the 'ordinary girl on the street' – equated the clothes with the good life, and also with the modern, the convention-breaking and the democratic.

Work, sports and entertainment thus transformed the dress of twentieth-century women and, to a lesser extent, men. Fashion became an end in itself; it also became part of all other popular spectacles and activities. In the 1920s the arrival of mass fashion had been welcomed because it had been seen as both democratic and internationalist. It introduced change and seasonal variation, its supporters argued, into the monotony of American industrial exis-tence. For some puritan radicals, on the other hand, fashion is never more than the 'democracy of the image', a mirage that perverts our 'real' desires by converting them into commodities, and individual-ity into conformity. Mass fashions from this point of view are merely the uniforms of a society in which democracy is just a buzz word, and serve only to mask gross inequalities of wealth and opportunity. Even sartorial revolt, according to such a perspective, is nothing more than a part of this mockery of freedom.

These arguments will be taken up in Chapter Ten. In describing contemporary fashion as a form of 'popular culture', however, I have sought to point to an alternative view. The recent writings on forms of popular culture, as I tried to suggest earlier, have rejected this monolithic view of the popular as a form of mass false con-sciousness. Instead, they have described various kinds of popular entertainment as sites of struggle, as arenas in which the conflicts of society are played out in semi-symbolic forms that may *heighten* rather than *drug* the consciousness of oppression.

Fashion, too, as a collective as well as a highly individualistic enterprise, is a means of expression on a mass scale of solidarity and group identity. So we must now look at the costuming of aliena-tion, deviancy and revolt, at oppositional styles.

Chapter 9

Oppositional Dress

The way the left got locked into a style rhetoric in the sixties and early seventies ... they could die by that particular sword, and it all started with fashion, with the dressing-up urge among grown-up liberals. It seemed harmless. Waiting in the wings, however, was a new generation who didn't have any ambivalent feelings; something aggressively stylish, radical-right and obviously unfair simply looked rather like forbidden fruit.

Peter York: 'Reactionary Chic'

Before the 1960s, 'only tarts or homosexuals wore clothes which reflected what they were'.[1] *Sexual* identities – of course; dandyism, which established more rigid standards of masculinity, and which ushered in a new, modern, city 'uniform' for men, led also in the direction of dress as rebellion. Since the nineteenth century social rebellion has frequently fastened on sexual behaviour and sexual identity, expressed through dress, as an appropriate vehicle.

In earlier times, dress could, of course, signal direct nationalist or political rebellion. In the sixteenth century, for example, the English prohibited the Irish from wearing their traditional dress, and in the eighteenth century after the battle of Culloden and the pacification of the Scottish Highlands, the Highlanders were subjected to the same treatment and forbidden to wear the kilt and the plaid.

In the nineteenth century, however, dress could signify both group and individual dissidence, especially for men, and perhaps partly because ordinary men's clothing became more sober and restricted. The crucial figure in this transformation of men's clothing was the dandy.[2] Nineteenth-century men's wear was an adaptation of eighteenth-century country and sporting wear; it was the dandy who made this style dominant.

Dandyism is sometimes misunderstood to refer to overdressed effeminacy – and in the eighteenth century the 'Macaronis' had been fops whose dress had been an exaggeration of frills and brocade, powder and paint. Their style of dress had actually been a reaction against the English country house style of dress that the dandies were beginning to take up and establish as normal men's wear. Beau Brummell summed up this new style: 'No perfumes ... but very fine linen, plenty of it and country washing. If John Bull turns round to look after you you are not well dressed; but either too stiff, too tight, or too fashionable.'[3]

The role of the dandy implied an intense preoccupation with self and self presentation; image was everything, and the dandy a man who often had no family, no calling, apparently no sexual life, no visible means of financial support. He was the very archetype of the new urban man who came from nowhere and for whom appearance *was* reality. His devotion to an ideal of dress that sanctified understatement inaugurated an epoch not of no fashions for men, but of fashions that put cut and fit before ornament, colour and display. The skin-tight breeches of the dandy were highly erotic; so was his new, unpainted masculinity. The dandy was a narcissist. He did not abandon the pursuit of beauty; he changed the kind of beauty that was admired.

The new style was made possible by the use of woollen cloth instead of the tightly woven silks and satins of the old aristocracy; more pliable, it could be shrunk, stretched and moulded as it was being tailored. English tailors were the first to perfect these new techniques; and the dandies set their seal on a style that was already coming into fashion, a style in which the most important element was fit. Hours were still spent on the dandy's toilette, now not in order to produce a painted and bedizened creature, but on the contrary in scraping, scrubbing and shaving the skin, in polishing boots to perfection and in tying the ultimate cravat to create an

French 'Incroyable' of 1815.
Reproduced by kind permission of the Trustees of the Victoria and Albert Museum.

impression of indifference. The dandies invented Cool; but the blasé pose was of course arresting. There was both revolt and classic chic in the dandy style.

Politically it was a result of the revolutionary upheavals of the late eighteenth century: 'When such solid values as wealth and birth are upset, ephemera such as style and pose are called upon to justify the stratification of society.'[4] Dandyism crossed the English channel, where it was taken up by the *Incroyables*, the avant-garde of French post-revolutionary youth. They transformed it into the counter-uniform of the new republican politics, while the *Merveilleuses*, their female counterparts, pushed Englishwomen's informal, uncorseted muslin dresses towards classical Greek garb: this signalled republican democracy by recalling ancient Athens and Rome.

The dandy was one version of the Romantic hero, in his stance of revolt. Yet although the pose appealed to the republican radical, it spoke equally to the reactionary, the disaffected aristocrat. The dandy was a man both of the past and of the future. Yet although the dandy was a version of the Romantic hero, he was not an artist, but rather the other side of the coin of Artist. Although some of the great novelists and artists of the nineteenth century, for example Dickens and Balzac, inclined towards dandyism, the true dandy did nothing. As Hazlitt said, 'the dandy's achievement is simply to be himself'. His perfection in all the inessentials of life was a kind of performance of aristocracy. The modern aristocrat is always incognito, yet always on show, his manners always exquisite since he treats the humblest individual with the same politeness he would employ in high society. He never goes psychologically 'backstage' – to belch, have a fag or act out of character:

> The aristocratic habit of life ... is one that mobilizes all the minor activities of life that fall outside the serious specialities of other classes and injects into these activities an expression of character, power and rank.[5]

The original dandies, then, neither worked nor raised families. In this they resembled the courtesans who set the fashions of the Second Empire in France, when Worth reigned supreme. A woman who lives by her sexuality distances herself from it. The male dandies did not sell their bodies, but, like courtesans, they lived on their wits, dominated society by sheer force of personality, imposed themselves like social courtesans. These walking symbols of eroticism were above all narcissists; and dandyism, Ellen Moers suggests, was spoilt and vulgarized when, at the end of the nineteenth century, it was more openly associated with homosexuality.

Byron, himself sexually ambiguous, was associated with dandyism and 'modern dress'. Indeed, he is sometimes credited with having finally established trousers in place of breeches and stockings. Literary and romantic hero of London society after the publication of *Childe Harold*, a poem that appealed to the taste of the period for gothic exaggeration, Byron was the first modern pop star, and it is even possible that he was the first to wear jeans:

> Lord Byron at that time wore a very narrow cravat of white sarsnet, with the shirt collar falling over it; a black coat and waistcoat, and very broad white trousers, to hide his lame foot – these were of Russia duck in the morning and jean in the evening.[6]

In the mid nineteenth century, Baudelaire, fascinated by dandyism, wore black in protest against the sartorial vulgarity of French bohemian circles. He saw dandyism as a search for perfection, an exacting and stoical discipline, a form of spirituality and also a social response to 'those transitory epochs when democracy is not yet all powerful, yet aristocracy is only partially dethroned and debased'.[7] Like Balzac, Baudelaire understood the dandy as a rebel, '*déclassé*, disgusted, disenchanted', who attempts to create a new aristocracy of genius, or at least of talent. Yet Baudelaire also saw dandyism as 'the last blaze of heroism within decadence . . . dandyism is a setting sun . . . superb, without warmth and full of melancholy.'[8]

Dandyism was, and is, as contradictory as the society that gave it birth. For, as it happens, this 'transitory epoch' of capitalism is *permanently* transitory, condemned to continual change, repeatedly throwing up ambiguous rebels whose rebellion never is a revolution, but instead a reaffirmation of the Self; the dandy, whether aristocrat, artist or romantic radical, or, as Byron was, all three, was and is above all *anti-bourgeois*.

The style the dandies invented, however, led in two divergent directions. It led to conventional men's wear, and thus to 'anti-fashion'. It also led in the direction of oppositional style. Anti-fashion is that 'true chic' which used to be defined as the elegance that never draws attention to itself, the simplicity that is 'understated', but which for that very reason stands out so startlingly. This cult of understatement was what the Brummells of the Regency period invented for men's clothing. Chanel reinterpreted it for women, as we saw, while the British fashion industry has thrived on the production of anti-fashion classics: Burberries, kilts, tweeds, cashmeres, fairisles and classic men's tailoring. Anti-fashion attempts a timeless style, tries to get the essential element of change out of fashion altogether.

Dandyism also contained the germs of something utterly different, of oppositional style. Oppositional fashions aim to express the dissent or distinctive ideas of a group, or views hostile to the conformist majority. One early nineteenth-century romantic fashion was cropped, unpowdered hair for both sexes. Neckties were worn loosely and casually knotted; an air of dishevelled beauty suggested, paradoxically, a mind above mere dress; and, ever since, untidiness has been used to suggest an artistic or intellectual calling – right down to the jeans, often bought ready patched and 'stone washed' to look old and faded, of the 1968 generation. Yet although the male French bohemians of the 1830s wore the romantic style, their mistresses, the *midinettes*, prostitutes and opera girls of Balzac's Paris still usually aimed at conventional elegance. It was not until the English pre-Raphaelite painters of the 1840s and 1850s that a special mode of alternative dress for women appeared.

The United States had its own bohemia too, in the shape of Greenwich Village, a transplantation of the original Parisian subworld of the men of letters. 'Bohemia,' said one American, 'is Grub Street romanticized, doctrinalized and rendered self-conscious; it is Grub Street on parade.'[9] This, like its French and English counterparts, was a world of journalists, hacks, artists and draughtsmen, whose art was devoted to ephemera, to sketches and vignettes of the passing social scene. They lived around lower Broadway in the 1850s, sixties and seventies; by 1900 they had reached Greenwich Village.

Greenwich Village was a centre of political and social ferment and experimental lifestyles in the first two decades of the twentieth century. Djuna Barnes, a writer and artist who spent most of her twenties there, before and during the First World War, was one of the most striking. In an atmosphere in which 'sophistication was the standard to be raised against everything bourgeois, [Djuna] Barnes was fairly unusual for the way in which she expressed her sophistication in terms of striking fashion on limited means. Most of the other young women disdained cosmetics and tended to wear either masculine clothes or flowing robes.'[10]

At a period when everyone, men and women, invariably wore hats in the street, these bohemians went hatless, bobbed their hair and wore a 'bluestocking uniform' of loose shift and brown socks. Djuna Barnes herself made a black cloak her signature. Her appearance was at times so bizarre that children laughed at her in the street. One of the most extreme women in the Village, who called herself the Baronin von Freytag-von Loringhoven, wore black lipstick, yellow face powder, and shaved her head.[11]

Towards the end of the 1920s, however, many felt that its genuine radicalism had been replaced by what was simply a vaguely 'alternative' consumerism in which the supposed emancipation of women was used largely to sell more goods: 'self expression and paganism encouraged a demand for all sorts of products.'[12] This, the first real consumer culture, was also the first youth culture; in it, the clothes you wore did much to establish your membership of a group within the peer group.

In England 'aesthetic dress' (to be discussed in Chapter Ten, in connection with dress reform) had evolved into a further form of oppositional costume. At the time when Lucile was putting Edwardian ladies into pastel chiffons and seductive silk, Vanessa Bell, Bloomsbury painter and sister of Virginia Woolf, was creating an alternative look as she searched through markets for exotic materials and old costumes:

> Vanessa, tall, a little awkward and dressed in bizarre clothes made from stuffs bought in Italian rag markets ... was derided as a bohemian with a private income, a West End lady imitating the style of Augustus John's women [by] Wyndham Lewis ... There was however nothing self conscious about her unfashionable dress ... She had a liking for strong colours, both in her painting and her dress, favouring rich purples and vermilions.[13]

Throughout the 1920s and 1930s the bohemian 'Chelsea' style was familiar up and down the Kings Road, London, in the shape of imitations of Dorelia as painted by Augustus John, the full peasant dirndl skirts, tight waists, kerchiefs and exotically gipsyish appearance in striking contrast to the modernist flapper style. In the thirties, Janey Ironside remembered 'arty' fashions being touched by a period romanticism:

> At that time it was fashionable in artistic circles to wear one's hair in a

bun on the top of the head and a velvet ribbon round one's throat to match one's lipstick – usually cyclamen or Schiaparelli's new colour shocking pink – and to incorporate Victorian ideas into one's dress.[14]

– although by that time romantic Victorianism was influencing Schiaparelli herself. Romanticism was still fashionable in bohemia in the early days of the war, and when Theodora Fitzgibbon first met Dylan Thomas's wife Caitlin,

> she looked like the embodiment of all the heroines in literature ...
>
> The beautiful head and body were set off by the rose-coloured velvet frock which had old and exquisite écru lace at the neck and cuffs, so that she looked like a rich jewel nestling in a velvet-lined case. It was as though a seventeenth century painting had come to life.[15]

The Chelsea alternative style lingered on into the fifties, when Iris Murdoch's heroine Dora in *The Bell* (1958) was only one of thousands of art students who collected 'big, multi-coloured skirts and jazz records and sandals'. Soon after that the Chelsea look went off in two directions as the beatniks exaggerated the pale lips, straight hair and black clothes into a uniform of revolt, while Mary Quant turned it into the latest fashion. The beatniks' use of black came from the existential fashions of post-war left-bank Paris, although black had long been one signal of anti-bourgeois revolt. Again it was the combined influence of the dandies and the Romantics that made of black a resonant statement of dissent.

The dandy as hero appeared in many English Regency novels. The most famous was Edward Bulwer Lytton's *Pelham* (1828). Lord Lytton himself was a dandy and started the fashion for black clothing, and especially for black and white evening wear for men, since black was the appropriate colour for the 'blighted being' that a modern hero must be, and for the 'century in mourning for itself'.

The existentialism of the late 1940s, was, like Romanticism, an oppositional movement of ideas clad in a dark and casual uniform of student chic. As a philosophy it was serious, although stamped with the same ambiguity as Romanticism; popularized as a morality – or an immorality – of nihilism and despair. Jean-Paul Sartre and Simone de Beauvoir, notorious as the originators of post-war existentialism, always denied that they were existentialists, and Simone de Beauvoir described the phenomenon negatively in her memoirs:

> Sartre's petit bourgeois readers had lost their faith in perpetual peace, in

eternal progress ... they had discovered History in its most terrible form. They needed an ideology which would include such revelations without forcing them to jettison their old excuses.[16]

Anne-Marie Cazalis, a young poet, who opened a left-bank night club, jumped on the existentialist band-wagon:

> She belonged ... both to the literary world of Saint-Germain-des-Prés and to the subterranean world of jazz ... She baptized the clique of which she was the centre, and the young people who prowled between the Tabou [the club she ran] and the Pergola [another night spot] as Existentialists. The press, and particularly *Samedi Soir*, which had a financial interest in her success, gave the Tabou a tremendous amount of publicity ... People also began to be interested in her friend ... a beautiful young girl with long black hair: [Juliette] Gréco ... she wore the new 'Existentialist' uniform. The musicians from the various *caves* and their fans had been down to the *Côte d'Azur* during the summer and brought back the new fashion imported from Capri – itself originally inspired by the Fascist tradition – of black sweaters, black shirts and black trousers.[17]

Juliette Greco was enticed into films by Daryl Zanuck, had her nose straightened and her hair reddened – but she never made it in the movies. It was Audrey Hepburn who played the 'left bank' parts in the fifties, and whose gamine looks, short black hair, doe eyes and ballerina slippers translated an ersatz existentialism on to film.

Here it is relevant to try to link the use of black dress with what was its more familiar use in earlier times: for mourning. The relationship of mourning and rebellion is a strange one. Mourning had been customary in earlier times, although black had not always been the only mourning colour, but the particular emphasis on mourning throughout the nineteenth century may have been because death at any age was no longer taken for granted. The death of a child was still frequent but no longer the norm. Besides, the bourgeoisie was larger and more prosperous than ever before, and the mourning ritual, more than merely yet another example of 'conspicuous consumption' – that overworked idea – expressed both the deep seriousness of the Victorian evangelical sensibility and the generalized hysteria of the culture. Lou Taylor[18] accounts for the exaggerations of widows' weeds in terms of women's position as the property of their husbands, arguing that prolonged, or even sometimes perpetual mourning demonstrated the wealth of the deceased patriarch; and it is true that to be a widow in the nineteenth-century middle class was a less attractive prospect than in earlier times. Then widows had often carried on the joint business and, with the advantage of this situation, were favourably placed to remarry – often to younger men. But in the nineteenth century to be a widow was to inhabit a social limbo, for the widow had no male protector – a dangerous situation – yet she was, of course, respectable. Mourning was as much about sexual reputation as about property and ownership. Many Victorian widows did re-marry, throwing off their crape and jet with unseemly abandon; but for those who were content to remain alone, or who preferred to, widow's crape may have acted as a kindly camouflage, a way of crying quits and leaving the mating game without dishonour.

Mourning was huge business in the nineteenth century, and every department store had its mourning section where clothes could be fitted, in haste if necessary. It ceased to be absolutely demanded after the First World War, when, presumably, so many died that it came to be felt as a kind of mockery. Paris, indeed, during the First World War remained as fashionable as ever:

> Young women now went about all day with tall cylindrical turbans on their heads ... and from a sense of patriotic duty wore Egyptian tunics, straight and dark and very 'war', over very short skirts; they wore thonged footwear ... or else long gaiters recalling those of our dear boys at the front; it was, so they said, because they did not forget that it was their duty to rejoice the eyes of these 'boys at the front', that they still decked themselves of an evening not only in flowing dresses, but in jewellery which suggested the army by its choice of decorative themes ... the fashion now was for rings or bracelets made out of fragments of exploded shells or copper bands from 75 millimetre ammunition ... and it was also because they never stopped thinking of the dear boys, so they said, that when one of their own kin fell they scarcely wore mourning for him, on the pretext that 'their grief was mingled with pride'.[19]

And although mourning lingered on in France and Southern Europe for longer than in the Anglo-Saxon countries, and although the bourgeoisie, who had developed such a cult of mourning, discarded it sooner than either the working class or the aristocracy, today it has almost vanished, as contemporary culture has taken flight from the very idea of death.

Since we have ceased to wear mourning, black has established itself as the colour of anger rather than of sorrow, the signal of aggression and revolt. It has been associated not only with the fascists but with the anarchists too; not only with the existentialists, but with the Dutch and Danish radical 'provos' of the early 1960s, while the continental equivalents of teddy boys were known as '*blousons noirs*'.

Black is dramatic and plays to the gallery, as the costuming of revolt must always do. It is flattering. Associated with age, on the young it takes on a haunting and poignant aspect. It is a colour for the urban environment, 'goes with' the red-brick, granite and glass façades of the city better than the too-bright colours of mass-produced clothes or the elegantly faded, 'natural' tints of Liberty silks, of tweed or wool, which suit soft, indoor lighting or the countryside in northern climes, but which look drab in a brightly lit, or artificial environment.

Black is the colour of bourgeois sobriety, but subverted, perverted, gone kinky. The modern 'aesthetic of the ugly' loves the frisson black gives – and gives more powerfully since fascism eroticized the uniform, created a fetishized ideal, a whole philosophy of domination, cruelty and irrationalism made visible in the image of the blonde Aryan, a male Valkyrie in gleaming black leather and knife edge silhouette.

Existentialism related backwards in time, to the old bohemias of the nineteenth century. In the same post-war forties, there sprang up in London a new kind of sartorial revolt, a rebellion not of students and artists, but of young, working-class men: the teds. The name came from 'Edwardian' and the style was copied from the post-war British upper crust, whose tailors persuaded them into narrow crombie coats with velvet collars, and imposed narrower trousers, more fitted, flared jackets, hard hats and bony rolled umbrellas. This was a Tory reaction to 'austerity' and the welfare state. It was epitomized by the suave Conservative politician, Anthony Eden, who purveyed so glamorous an image of upper-class elegance that he was popularized by the fashion artist, Francis Marshall, into a new archetype of gentlemanly restraint. The teddy boy look combined this with a style drawn from America, from western movies: the city slicker villain's string tie, sideburns and frock coat;[20] the result was curiously appropriate to a country locked in cultural conservatism, so that American culture seemed both rebellious and forward-looking by contrast.

After the Second World War many writers and sociologists[21] succumbed to an intense fear that the British 'way of life' would be swamped by American culture (similar fears were expressed in other European countries). Yet in using American cultural icons to create a youth culture that expressed dissent from prevailing values, the British ted gave it an indigenous cast. The new ingredient was class. The ted was a new kind of member of the working class, relatively well fed, compulsorily educated, offered a wage that was generous by pre-war standards; yet living in a world that made no social provision for the working-class young, a world in which old working-class communities were changing and even breaking down, but with nothing much but a concrete 'subtopia' to replace them; a world which – very different from America – was culturally dominated by high bourgeois styles and values; and finally it was cramped on a tiny island, with none of the wide open spaces to which the rebels of America could escape.

Most sociologists have explained the astonishing variety and specificity of British youth styles by reference to the British obsession with class.[22] The styles have been a form of resistance to the straitjacket of snobbery, but they may be experienced subjectively by those who flaunt them less as a class rebellion than as an assertion of youth against age, or the hip versus the straight:

> To have a job like mine means that I don't belong to the great community of the mugs: the vast majority of squares who are exploited. It seems to me this being a mug or a non-mug is a thing that splits humanity up into two sections absolutely. It's nothing to do with age or sex or class or colour – either you're born a mug or born a non-mug, and me, I sincerely trust I'm born the latter,[23]

says Colin MacInnes's 1959 teenage photographer hero in *Absolute Beginners*. Already dressed in a bum-freezing Italianate jacket, he knows that style is on the turn, that the teds are being elbowed aside by something new:

> Take first the Misery Kid and his trad. drag. Long, brushless hair, white stiff-starched collar (rather grubby), striped shirt, tie of all one colour ... short jacket but an old one ... very, very tight, tight trousers with wide stripe, no sox, short *boots*. Now observe the Dean in the modernist number's version. College-boy smooth crop hair with burned-in parting, neat white Italian rounded-collared shirt, short Roman jacket *very*

tailored (two little vents, three buttons), no-turn-up narrow trousers with 17-inch bottoms absolute maximum, pointed-toe shoes, and a white mac lying folded by his side . . .

I would add that their chicks, if present, would match them up with: trad. boy's girl – long hair, untidy with long fringes, maybe jeans and a big floppy sweater, maybe bright-coloured, never-floralled, never-pretty dress . . . smudged-looking's the objective. Modern jazz boy's girl – short hemlines, seamless stockings, pointed-toed high-heeled stiletto shoes, crêpe nylon rattling petticoat, short blazer jacket, hair done up into the elfin style. Face pale – corpse colour with a dash of mauve, plenty of mascara.[24]

The mods: like the teds they had their own music; like the teds they had their own way of life. There had been a certain 'homosexual-ism'[25] about the teds – the narcissism of all-male groups that dressed for one another's admiration and not for the girls who were always on the periphery. The mods took narcissism further. George Melly suggests there was a 'strong homosexual element' – yet that too was really narcissism: 'girls were irrelevant. The little Mods used each other as looking glasses. They were as cool as ice-cubes.'[26] They caricatured neatness, and went beyond that into make-up and hair lacquer:

The mods seemed to have a secret that made adults irrelevant . . . arrogant and narcissistic, cynical and tense; they came on like winners, and consumption was, for them, as much a playground as a last resort; the urge was movement – from shop to shop, club to club – speeding on pills, on dance floors, on the latest fashion coup. The mods became, indeed, the 1960s symbol of consumption generally. Mod style was exploited to transform shopping (the rise of the boutique), listening (the rise of pirate radio), and dancing (the triumph of soul music).[27]

Simon Frith traces the roots of the mods to 'a few petit-bourgeois kids, clothes-conscious children of Jewish rag trade families' who mingled with semi-beatniks in the Soho coffee houses of the late fifties, and in their eagerness to distinguish themselves from the mass, looked to America for their styles.

What is sometimes missed from the analysis of youth opposi-tional or fad styles is their surprising closeness, very often, to the latest mainstream fashions. The mod style was sharp, boxy, spare: like the Chanel and Cardin-inspired fashions for women popular in the early sixties. By the mid sixties these styles were on the wane. Mod ties for men were narrow, but by 1964 there were already variations of these made from Liberty flower-printed cotton, and soon these flowery ties got wider and longer, as trousers likewise flared and hair lengthened.

The first American hippies adopted a naturalistic, flowing style, apparently in total opposition to the mainstream styles; yet, like the pre-Raphaelite style, it turned out to be evolutionary rather than revolutionary, a prefiguration of the way all dress was evolving. Hippie fashion in the late 1960s swung the pendulum against the rectilinear and the straight, for it was a walking adaptation of the fashionable art-nouveau spirals. Hair, which had been short, lacquered and straight, became long and curly, for both sexes. Sleeves which had been tight and shortish became long, gathered, flowing. Bell-bottomed trousers widened until they looked like skirts, and skirts which had been short and straight sank to the floor. Jackets were suddenly flowery, eighteenth-century, and brocade and velvet bloomed. Scarves, a garment unknown either to the mods or Mary Quant, were festooned in twos, threes, fours around the throat, to sink floating to the knees. Collars got larger and longer, like rabbits' ears. Make-up became first naturalistic, then vampishly exaggerated as Biba popularized the thirties style. Model girls – and Brigitte Bardot – took up the cause of cruelty to animals and refused to wear coats made from endangered species; and a demand for 'natural' home remedies for skin and hair was catered to by commercial cosmetic firms which introduced new lines in which herbal and vegetable ingredients figured.

Biba's was an interesting transitional style, which spanned a decade from the mods of the early sixties to the glam-rock of the early seventies. Barbara Hulanicki started Biba as a mail order firm selling low-priced little mod dresses. The success of her venture was such that she and her husband soon branched out into one of the first boutiques of the sixties, twice moved to larger premises, and finally took over what had been a large Kensington department store, Derry and Toms. They preserved its beautiful thirties style furnishings (subsequently ripped out in an insensitive act of vandalism) as an appropriate setting for the Biba style – but the style was simply not sufficiently substantial to stock a whole store (how many people really wanted an aubergine-coloured fridge, or baked beans with a Biba label?); and in 1975 the store closed.

The Biba style managed to link the 'mod' and the 'hippie'; it linked the highly and transiently fashionable to the alternative culture. It did this by being both pared down and exaggerated, especially in the use of distinctive accessories and colours that were always over the top. Already by 1966 Biba was introducing big, cartwheel felt hats, brightly coloured feather boas, floor length vest dresses, and she was soon – like Mary Quant – using 'old-fashioned' materials such as crêpe and lingerie satin. Her clothes had certain stylistic features peculiar to themselves: the very narrow sleeves set into narrow shoulders were pure Biba, as were the canvas summer boots, and – perhaps above all – the 'off' 'greenery yallery' colours she made her own – prune, aubergine, sage, dull duck egg blue, dirty cyclamen, sepia, cream, brick dust and *bois de rose*.

Her clothes were consistent with the hippie sensibility. They had the same kitsch touches as the secondhand little 'frocks' for which long and painstaking searches were beginning to be made in jumble sales and Oxfam shops, and the same dangling, drooping look as the ethnic bits and pieces – ponchos, Hiawatha fringes, macramé belts, feather chokers, Liberty scarves – that were assembled into the hippie look. Then, in the seventies, the 'ethnic' look became mainstream fashion. Many Parisian designers introduced layers, folk fashions and assorted exotica into their collections.

The word hippie came from the United States, where the hippies and their rock music originated in the student counter-culture and the student campus rebellions of the anti-Vietnam war 1960s. In Britain the hippie style meant something different from its transatlantic counterpart, although both were related to student radicalism. The British variant bore a message that was anti-capitalist in the sense that to create a unique appearance out of a bricolage of secondhand clothes, craft work and army surplus was to protest sartorially against the wastefulness of the consumer society. You rejected the mass-produced road, and simultaneously wasteful luxury, and produced your own completely original look. Yet although this was undertaken in a spirit of anti-consumerism, it did involve the expenditure of much time if not money, and reintroduced the snobbery of uniqueness, since there was, necessarily, only *one* of the 'frock' you had found – just as much as if you'd bought a Dior original.

The aesthetic was dreamy and druggy instead of bright and sharp. The Biba girl was wafted in a hash trance instead of bouncing on uppers. At the same period Lee Bender launched her chain of Bus Stop shops – and a more forties look with big, padded shoulders, clashing colours, and daring use of 'cheap' materials that slithered, shone and glittered. Like 'glam rock' many of the looks of the early seventies flirted – or more – with the outrageousness of abandoning all pretence to good taste, and as ethno-chic and retro-chic mingled the whole tone first of counter-cultural fashion and then of mainstream became garishly camp.

Camp welcomes artificiality, recognizing the element of deliberate self presentation in all consciously fashionable dressing – and then caricaturing it. The essence of hippie style on the other hand was its opposite: a belief in the natural, the authentic. Out of the hippie 'moment' though, these two opposed styles could spring: the one a development of the pastiche and artificiality latent in the ransacking of old clothes for new styles; the other the cult of the authentic that lay in the rejection of the fashions imposed by the fashion industry, but which, like camp styles, could be and was commercially reproduced (especially by the firm of Laura Ashley).

British hippies were urban nomads; the Americans (as recorded, for example, in the film of *Woodstock*) were living a wholly other dream from the dream of little frocks and squats in the twilight zones of every British city. Chelsea hippies were the spiritual descendants of the Chelsea art students of earlier decades. The Americans were pioneers. To a 1980s audience the Woodstock rock fans of 1970 look like the settlers of the Old West and it's possible to see now with a clarity that couldn't be there at the time (when the eye was distracted by the paraphernalia of beads, nudity and body make-up that went towards the flower power style) how deeply conservative this image was – of women in long hair and long skirts, naturally lovely and winsome, and of men whose hair was long in a manly way that went with beards, levis and widebrimmed stetsons. Even nudity in the American hippie ethic meant a return to nature in the manner of Thoreau or Walt Whitman – no whiff of English decadence there. For the radical counter-culture of the United States was infused more deeply than the British could ever be with a rejection of the world of the city, and took its inspiration from the existence of the enormous wide-open spaces of the American hinterland. In crowded Britain a commune meant just another urban squat, or at most a country farm house; in the States it could really mean a life in the wilds. The American hippie idiom had available to it a counter-imagery of human unification with nature simply not present in British culture.

It is in the United States, too, more than in any western European country that time has embalmed the hippie style, for it is still possible to find West Coast communities where the hippies live on. The growing of marijuana up in the empty Californian hills has in some cases become a business, but the growers are still hippies too; and with their long print dresses and big western hats, their long hair and sunburned faces and hordes of naked children, they now look less like campus radicals than like the Amish communities of Pennsylvania, where whole towns still wear the long dresses, suits and sunbonnets of their nineteenth-century German immigrant forbears.

British hippiedom, by contrast, could mutate without too much difficulty into punk. Punk took to the London streets in the long hot summer of 1976, and took modernism much further than the mods had done. This really was the fashion equivalent of modernism in art:

> Like [Marcel] Duchamp's 'ready mades' – manufactured objects which qualified as art because he chose to call them such – the most unremarkable and inappropriate items – a pin, a plastic clothes peg, a television component, a razor blade, a tampon – could be brought within the province of punk (un)fashion.[28]

This 'confrontation dressing' aimed to shock – but also to 'make strange', which is precisely what the modernist artists of the early twentieth century (the Russian formalists, for example) had also tried to do – to look at the everyday world in a new way, and force others to do so:

> Objects borrowed from the most sordid of contexts found a place in the punks' ensembles: lavatory chains were draped in graceful arcs across chests encased in plastic bin-liners. Safety pins were taken out of their domestic 'utility' context and worn as gruesome ornaments through the cheek, ear or lip. 'Cheap' trashy fabrics (PVC, plastic, lurex etc) in vulgar designs (eg mock leopard skin) and 'nasty' colours ... were salvaged by the punks and turned into garments (flyboy drainpipes, 'common' miniskirts) which offered self-conscious commentaries on the notions of modernity and taste.[29]

What was important was that nothing should look natural. In this sense punk was the opposite of mainstream fashion which always attempts to naturalize the strange rather than the other way about. This is the sophistication of punk, its surrealism and its modernism in the true sense: it radically questions its own terms of reference, questions what fashion *is*, what style *is*, making mincemeat of received notions of beauty and trashing the very idea of 'charm' or 'taste'.

As a counter-cultural style punk soon lost its hard, working-class edge; in the early eighties a pink, yellow or green flash in short, spiky hair was more likely to be the hallmark of a middle class radical feminist or post-neo-Marxist student. A lot of zips on a jump suit or two earrings in one ear became mainstream fashions. At the same time there remain those who do still identify as punks – just as there remain those of an earlier generation who have gone on being teds.

Because of the doomy, freaked-out feel of punk – shaved heads, green hair and slashed clothes are reminiscent of a band of medieval pilgrims on a penitential journey, or at least of a band of film extras done up to look like pilgrims – there's been a tendency to read it simplistically as an expression of angst about nuclear war and dread of the futility of post-industrial, post-modernist life, a general nihilism – and maybe the kids of the eighties are the secular equivalents of the witches and the dances of death of the later middle ages, another period when Armageddon was thought to be just around the corner. Yet to see punk in this light misses the possibility that to create one's identity in a shocking and deviant way that is none the less well supported within a sub-culture may actually contribute to the building of self confidence, a sense of self and even optimism, albeit within a generalized pessimism.

Punk was followed by a plethora of put-together styles and youth fashion crazes. So much did dressing up become the rage that even *Vogue* ran a feature on it (August 1983). Any and every style could be brought into play. Most were still hitched to a style of music or a single band or star, and some of them recycled previous youth styles. There were the neo-mods who surfaced in the wake of *Quadrophenia*, a film made by one of the original mod bands, The Who. Singers took androgyny even further than David Bowie in his Ziggy Stardust days. There have for years been audiences of fans whose aim has been to reproduce exactly the appearance of 'their' star, but Boy George, best known androgynous pop star yet, who contrived a style of dress from a mélange of sources – Hasidic Jewish black hat, plaited dreadlocks tied with curl rags, shapeless Japanese style tunic and trousers, and masses of make-up – had a following of *girls* who copied exactly this un-masculine male star.

Then there were the 'new romantics' who created a style of big, floppy collars (also incorporated in the Princess Di style) black velvet and exaggerated make-up. There were weird 'horror movie' and 'vampire' styles, all of which were essentially variants of romanticism-decadence, related ultimately to glam-rock, and using artifice of every kind, especially make-up. They are the theatrical, performance orientated fashions.

Slightly different were the styles associated with football club followers, although Kevin Sampson and David Rimmer, writing in *The Face*, suggested that 'high street fashion' of this kind started with a style based on a mixture of David Bowie and punk in 1977: 'mohairs worn with straights and plastic sandals, complemented by duffel coats', and a 'wedge' haircut from 'the last great depression'. At first another cult music club style, it was taken up by football fans, and fad followed fad culminating in a bizarre parody of classic anti-fashions with an emphasis on labels fashion. This look was:

> an incongruous mixture of Nike trainers, frayed Lois jeans and Lacoste shirts, worn with cashmere scarves and jumpers, topped with long Burberry raincoats.[30]

This was 'football chic'. The school children and kids on the dole who longed for these expensive clothes would do anything to get hold of them; and Kevin Sampson recounts the desperation of Lacoste in the face of complaints from British retailers of an epidemic of shoplifting, smash and grab raids and assaults on garments: 'they even cut the crocodiles off with razor blades, tearing *great holes* in the shirts'.

Dick Hebdige argues that the styles are neither arbitrary nor necessarily a substitute for politics or engagement with the 'real world'. Sub-cultural styles reinterpret conflicts of the wider society: in the case of punks and skinheads, it is racism. Punks really did aspire to be outsiders alongside blacks – 'we're niggers'; while the racism of the skinheads who wear their heads almost shaved, and caricature traditional working-class clothes in the shape of old-fashioned shirts, braces with shrunken trousers and heavy 'bovver boots', seemed 'to represent a conservative proletarian backlash to the radical "working class" posturings of the new wave'.

Blacks, and other ethnic minorities, have also developed their own oppositional styles, but these have usually had a conscious and deliberate message. With the expansion of Harlem in the early twentieth century came many, often exaggerated versions of fashionable wear. By the 1940s the young urban blacks had evolved a highly distinctive style: the zoot suit. This had exaggerated, padded shoulders and peg top trousers narrowing to the ankle, and both jacket and trousers were lavishly draped. The word 'zoot' came from the urban jazz culture of the 1930s, but the origins of the style itself are uncertain, and several explanations have been suggested, but it seems possible that the style was first developed by the second-generation children of migrant Mexican workers.

During the war, in 1943, zoot suits led to serious riots, for gangs of predominantly Mexican and black youths in suits that flouted rationing regulations outraged the servicemen stationed in Pacific ports. What were essentially race riots flared first in Los Angeles and then spread along the West Coast. According to one interpretation – unsurprisingly, the most popular explanation at the time – the zoot suiters came from the underworld of petty criminals, evading the draft (although many turned out to have medical exemption) and indulging in a traditional machismo.

Yet not all zoot suiters were men. At least two female gangs, the Slick Chicks and the Black Widows, were reported, the latter so named on account of their black uniforms of zoot suit jackets, short skirts and fishnet stockings. The active and aggressive role that these young women played suggests that the riots expressed something potentially more radical than juvenile deviance: social rebellion against poverty, against the alienation of American city life, especially for the ethnic minorities. They were also bred of the disruptions of wartime and women's rapidly changing role.

The zoot suit is an especially clear example of a symbolic counter-cultural style that caused a moral panic and led to actual violence in the streets. The zoot suit was defiance, a statement of ethnic pride and a refusal of subservience.[31]

Malcolm X, himself a zoot suiter in his youth, when he did live by petty crime, pimping and drugs, was later to reject any positive connotations of the style. His condemnation gestures to the ambivalence, perhaps, of any attempt to defy by stylistic means:

I'd go through that Grand Central Station afternoon rush-hour crowd, and many white people simply stopped in their tracks to watch me pass. The drape and the cut of the zoot suit showed to the best advantage if you were tall – and I was over six feet. My conk was fire red. I was really a clown, but my ignorance made me think I was 'sharp'. My knob-toed, orange coloured 'kick up' shoes were nothing but Florsheim's, the ghetto's Cadillac of shoes in those days.

The 'conk' was hair straightened at home by a method of using lye, which burned the scalp:

> When Shorty let me stand up and see in the mirror, my hair hung down in limp, damp strings. My scalp still flamed ... My first view in the mirror blotted out the hurting. I'd seen some pretty conks, but when it's the first time, on your *own* head, the transformation, after the lifetime of kinks, is staggering ... on top of my head was this thick, smooth sheen of shining red hair – real red – as straight as any white man's ...
> This was my first really big step towards self-degradation.[32]

Later, Malcolm X went to prison. There he became a Black Muslim, and, after his release, a black political leader until his assassination in 1965. Then, rebellion and a refusal of the dominant, white culture, took a more conscious and more explicit form. The natural, Afro hair and the slogan 'Black is Beautiful' were a much more openly ideological reassertion of the distinctive nature of the black experience. Before the 1960s, the majority of black women and men in the west had had only white models of beauty on which to base their own looks. Music stars such as the Supremes and Shirley Bassey had straightened hair, or wore wigs.

Yet although in the glass of fashion ethnic diversity was allowable, this was usually still – as in the 1920s – because it was 'exotic'. Indeed, Donyale Luna, who was the first internationally famous black fashion model, in the 1960s, was marketed not just as exotic, but even as freakish ('Is it a plane? No. Is it a bird? Yes ... it's Donyale Luna') and she herself did not survive this objectification.[33]

Nevertheless, in the 1960s, 1970s and 1980s a variety of distinctively black styles developed, some wholly oppositional, some combining styles adapted, for example, from Africa, with western fashions. In Britain, Rastafarian men wear long, twisted dreadlocks beneath high crowned hats or knitted caps of red, gold and green. The style is an open and deliberate sign of affiliation and both friends and foes recognize it as such. It often leads to harassment on the streets and in prison, where dreadlocks may be forcibly cut off. Similarly Sikh men, who wear their hair long beneath a turban, are sometimes or have been until recently penalized, for example by being prosecuted for not wearing a safety helmet when riding a motorbike. (And of course white men with long hair have also been ritually punished: when two members of the editorial group of *Oz* were sent to prison in the early 1970s in London, their shorn hair made the national news headlines.)

The symbolic significance of long hair on men – in contemporary western culture at least – takes us beyond fashion and its use and subversion by black minority groups. In women's fashions, especially, fashion and dissidence may combine. The Afro-Caribbean fashion for beaded and plaited hairstyles originated in adaptations of African styles and asserted a pride in African descent; they may also reinterpret western styles, for example when a head of narrow plaits is then pinned into a 1940s sideswept roll, or recreated as a twenties bob.

Perhaps what is distinctive about counter-cultural, oppositional dressing as opposed to the direct statement of black identity made by the original Afro style, or the adoption of politically or religiously committed groups of what becomes virtually a uniform, is the ambiguity of the former. In the early days of the Harlem expansion, ghetto fashions seem to have expressed the desire of a particularly oppressed urban multitude for some joy and glamour in their lives, and counter-cultural dressing is usually most distinctive when it expressed hedonism and rebellion simultaneously.

Yet outrage dressing, ambiguous as it is, may on occasion express simply – ambiguity. At first glance the androgyny of rock stars such as David Bowie shocks. New boundaries of boldness have surely been set when a man wears make-up, or a woman shaves her head. Not necessarily; these styles may turn out to be little more than new forms of dandyism. Dandyism expresses difference and disengagement as much as rebellion. The dandyism of the American ghettoes of the 1950s, which was greatly to affect emergent music styles, suggested a sense of élitism rather than identification with a group:

> The hipster was [a] typical lower class dandy, dressed up like a pimp, affecting a very cool, cerebral tone – to distinguish him from the gross impulsive types that surrounded him in the ghetto – and aspiring to the finer things in life.[34]

Moreover there is nothing more secretive than dandyism, nothing more coy than androgyny. They are the opposite of open affiliation. So it was significant that none of the male androgynous stars of the early 1980s 'came out' as gay. They played hard to get, hinted at bisexuality, oracularly suggested that 'love takes many forms'. During a big promotion in late 1983, Boy George, lead singer with the group Culture Club, played down or even refuted any idea of either a homosexual identity or a 'gay life' at the social level. He admitted to having slept with men in the past, but now: 'I'd rather have a cup of tea' (*Woman*, 8 October 1983). He claimed – correctly – to be in the British grand eccentric tradition; and is also in the time-honoured tradition of the British drag artist.

It's as if gender, on the surface so outraged, is for that very reason divorced from a sexuality that remains opaque, a carefully guarded arena of privacy. Yet perhaps this impenetrable ambiguity represents a fidelity to the most fashionable of all sexual 'truths' of the seventies: that gender and desire are ultimately unstable. The rigid sexual identities we cultivate, and which are popularly experienced as 'natural' and given at birth, are really fictions elaborated by the nineteenth-century sexologists; they merely imprison the wayward-ness of lust, constraining us in sexual and social roles.

In the 1970s there was, perhaps paradoxically, a proliferation of styles of dress linked to deviant sexualities. Gay Liberation (GLF) as a political movement began in Greenwich Village; brought to England it was the first political movement to elevate dress to the centre of its political practice. The gay liberationists of 1970 had yet to abandon their belief in sexual identity; they still believed that they 'were' homosexuals. The first and archetypal act for a member of GLF was therefore to 'come out' – publicly to declare himself gay. One of the most dramatic ways of doing this was to subvert the traditional 'drag' of the entertainment industry, and to wear – publicly – make-up and a frock. (The word 'frock' had languished in an old-fashioned limbo since the 1940s. It was retrieved by the hippies when they started to wear their secondhand forties finds.)

The GLF ideology was that forms of cross dressing broke down stereotyped gender roles; to wear a skirt and high heels was to give up 'male privilege'. But Gay Liberation went much further, even, than that. There was to be a general breaking down of all conventional divisions, and a revolutionary lifestyle in which individualism would be smashed:

Long nights were spent talking, crying, confessing, barriers came down with painful crashes. Egos took an incredible battering ... Because it was not always possible for us in the collective to be in one room all the time, we decided that if two or more of us got together and talked, then anything said should be repeated to whoever was missing. This helped us to fight couples and factions.

In practical terms some beautiful things started to happen. It was fabulous to see Richard walking around in Lorna's cardigan; Jenny in Richard's underpants; and Julia in my shoes. Soon it was possible not to feel that a particular article belonged to anyone.[35]

Because society had already made their sexuality into a problem, it was perhaps easier for young homosexuals to act out this attack on gender than it would have been for others. The problem with full scale drag still remained: although it caricatured traditional drag, it still often caricatured women as well, and could be offensively sexist.

Amongst gay men there was a movement towards the reassertion of masculinity. The homosexuals of the mid seventies wanted to make the statement that fags were not weeds, that manliness has no necessary connection with sexual orientation. Out of this came the 'clone' look. In a way, the clone was a caricature of masculinity. The clone wore jeans, lumber shirts and jackets, distressed leather and heavy boots, and although cleanshaven sported a moustache.[36] This almost uniform style had a number of advantages. The clone was instantly recognizable to other gay men, yet did not invite violence from queerbashers. The look would not offend at work for most colleagues would miss its significance; yet it gave the wearer the satisfaction of being able to feel that he was, in one sense, being openly gay even if most straights didn't realize it. The clone uniform emphasized the masculinity of gayness; it also had the advantage of ageing well. A bald clone looked much better than a bald ganymede, while the heavy belts and flying jackets could conceal a fair amount of paunch.

Leather freaks and s/m (sadomasochist) men and lesbians wore yet more daring styles. Some lesbians returned to the exaggerated 'butch' and 'femme' styles seen in the clubs and bars of the 1950s and 1960s but out of tune with the androgynous and feminist seventies. And, as is well known, American homosexuals even developed an elaborate sexual code based on the placing of handkerchiefs and bunches of keys. So while gender has been destabilized and – within avant-garde circles at least – it has become customary to downplay the permanency of sexual orientation, at the same time a more and more exquisitely specific scale of sexual desires is signalled with absolute precision.

Yet it would be a mistake to see this as more subversive than it really is. Suzy Menkes (*The Times*, 1 May 1984) wrote about the 1984 fashions for 'androgynous undies' and masculinity in women's dress, suggesting that these were 'the ultimate fashion statement about the sexual revolution'. Suzy Menkes goes on to reveal, however, that this form of 'cross dressing', which is opening up the way to 'gender-bending' unisex departments in exclusive fashion stores, is simply a new fad and that – significantly – the market it is aimed at is the market of affluent heterosexual *couples* for whom androgynous dress symbolizes not an attack on gender but merely a reaffirmation of middle-class togetherness.

Why should oppositional dress have been so recurrent a feature of life in the industrial world? In a fluid society, that is nevertheless still grossly unequal, individuals and groups find new ways to distinguish themselves; moreover individualism is encouraged, and dissent, up to a point, tolerated. In this 'democracy of wealth' in which everyone is free to make herself or himself unequal and in which society oscillates between the poles of public show and private self, a space opens up between the iron order of the body politic and the wayward lawlessness of the ego.

Of course, in such a society each new idea becomes grist to the mill of profit. Style deviance and style innovations are no exceptions to this rule, and s/he who dresses to shock must expect to be rapturously greeted as the latest thing. In late capitalism

> aesthetic production ... has become integrated into commodity production generally: the frantic urgency of producing fresh waves of ever more novel-seeming goods (from clothing to airplanes), at ever greater rates of turnover, now assigns an increasingly essential structural function and position to aesthetic innovation and experimentation.

What are the consequences of this?

> To argue that culture is today no longer endowed with the relative autonomy it once enjoyed ... is not necessarily to imply its disappearance or extinction. On the contrary: we must go on to affirm that the

dissolution of an autonomous sphere of culture is rather to be imagined as an explosion: a prodigious expansion of culture throughout the social realm, to the point at which everything in our social life . . . can be said to have become cultural.[37]

In this world, in which we are flooded with culture, oppositional styles continue, even more frenetically than before, their attempt to subvert dominant ideologies, using the very mass consumption means that constitute or contribute to the ideologies. Radicals such as Stuart and Elizabeth Ewen have condemned this, seeing in 'rebellion fashions' only a recuperation of protest:

> Where it might be argued that this desire for change would be more meaningfully pursued in the realm of concerted social action, fashion offered a continually changing outlet that located personal fulfilment, a sense of self, alongside the canals of social conformity.[38]

– the democracy of the image is only an image. Yet what this criticism misses is precisely the 'explosion' of the cultural that has taken place, and this particular condemnation of fashion can logically lead only to the Frankfurt School position – on which the critique implicitly rests – of wholesale condemnation of popular culture. The Ewens do not appreciate that in a world in which 'concerted social action' of a traditional kind may itself be gobbled up by post-modernist culture (so that even the Bolshevik revolution becomes a big box-office film, *Reds*, starring Warren Beatty and Diane Keaton) the cultural arte-facts to hand, however 'degraded' *must* be appropriated for any critique, even if there is always the danger, as George Melly – himself sympathetic to pop culture – suggests, that this will turn 'revolt into style'.

Walter Benjamin called this aestheticization of politics fascist in tendency.[39] When politics becomes aestheticized, when, that is, political activity is evaluated in terms of its 'beauty' rather than of its effects, then this produces a fascist elevation of style above humanity and of effect over suffering. Benjamin referred to the futurists, who hymned the 'beauty' of the pattern made by shells exploding and blowing up cavalry lines, killing and maiming men and horses. Another example would be Leni Riefenstahl's film of the Nuremberg Rally, which transformed the fanatical ranks of the Nazis into a compelling pattern of light and shade. This is a denial of the *meaning* of events, and a justification of cruelty and death in the name of style.

Post-modern culture generally, as defined by Jameson, must be open to this charge; while fashion in particular forever teeters on the edge of it. Yet because fashion, like capitalism itself, is so contradictory, it at least has the potential to challenge those ideologies in which it is itself enmeshed – as can all popular cultural forms, so long, that is, as we have some coherent political position (which post-modernist discourse lacks) from which to criticize.

Certainly the Bolshevik artists of the 1920s saw dress design as worthy of their attention. The constructivist Varvara Stepanova, a trained dress designer, spoke of fashion much as Patou or Chanel might have done when she said,

> Today's dress must be seen in action – beyond this there is no dress, just as the machine cannot be conceived outside the work it is supposed to be doing . . . the seams themselves – which are essential to the cut – give the dress form. Expose the ways in which the dress is sewn, its fasteners, etc., just as such things are clearly visible in a machine.[40]

Other constructivist artists who turned to dress design at this period were V. Tatlin and K. Malevich. Unfortunately, owing to the economic difficulties resulting from the Civil War, all these artists' designs, intended for mass production, never could be mass produced, but they represented prototypes of a new style of explicitly revolutionary dress, combining, as one writer put it in 1923, the versatility of peasant clothing and its lively colours with streamlined cut and fit suited to industrial work and city life. Soviet dress designers at this period were also interested in sportswear and its possible adaptation to daily life. But they equally aimed to combine industrial and traditional styles with the geometric modernism of 1920s *haute couture*.

The ideological importance of dress was not neglected, as a discussion in *Komsomol'skaya Pravda*, the newspaper of the Young Communist League, in June 1928 demonstrates. The writer is critical of the 'uniform' worn by the Komosomol, 'the monotonous khaki' in particular, since 'it threatens to become a barrier, dividing the . . . higher echelons of the Komosomol, who are better off, from the rest of the masses'. The answer, according to this writer, is the creation of genuine Soviet fashions, to compete with the foreign *haute couture* models displayed in shops in Moscow, and aped by 'dandies' amongst the young.[41]

More typical of 'revolutionary' approaches to fashion has been the attitude of the many utopian and socialist reformers who, thinking fashion unworthy of a progressive society, have sought to abolish it.

Revolutionary fashions of the Constructivists in the Soviet Union. Liubov Popova's design for magazine cover, 1924.

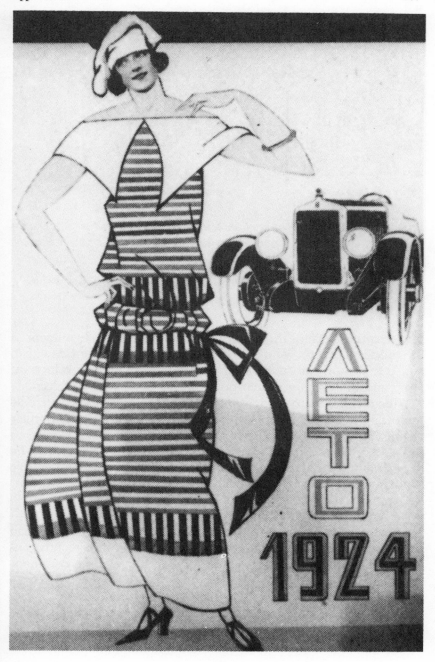

Chapter 10

Utopian Dress and Dress Reform

I'm just amazed by the power of makeup and costume ... I see image as a wrapping. Why not? It's something to play with, people take it far too seriously.

Annie Lennox, lead singer of The Eurythmics, *Sunday Times*, April 1984

The scientific spirit of the nineteenth century powerfully influenced the socialism that grew up out of the bowels of capitalism. Marxism aimed to demonstrate the *laws* of the capitalist mode of production; Marx and Engels named their political theory *scientific* socialism.

Nineteenth-century socialists gave dress a perhaps unexpectedly important place in their condemnation of capitalism and their visions of possible alternatives. Marxism as well as utilitarianism influenced Thorstein Veblen's work. It was from Marxism that he drew his understanding of the exploitation of women, their role both as property and as consumers. His work was a polemic against the oppression of women; it is unfortunate that his views on fashion got mixed up with feminism.

Dress reform – an undertaking uniquely expressive of Victorian earnestness of purpose (although it outlasted the nineteenth century) – was initially associated with some of the religious communities in the United States. In the earlier part of the nineteenth century there was a widespread interest in dress reform there, influenced, for example, by the plain dress of the Quakers; and dress reform was associated with other progressive views. Owenite and other communitarian settlements such as those at Brook Farm,

Oneida, and New Harmony, experimented with simplified dress, and women in such communities abandoned corsets, shortened their skirts and sometimes wore a form of trousers.[1] Women in the British Owenite communities appear also to have dressed in unconventional ways. The women of the Manea Fen community, for example, were described in a report by a local newspaper in 1840 as wearing trousers 'and the hair worn in ringlets' (although it is not clear whether 'ringlets' means short hair).[2] There were also socialist communities in France in the 1830s who: 'devised a uniform for both sexes which buttoned all the way down the back, so as to prevent one getting in or out of it on one's own, and this to further a sense of their interdependence.'[3]

Dress reform therefore easily came to be linked with feminism. The best known attempt at the reform of female dress was undertaken by a group of American feminists in 1851. The costume they adopted consisted of Turkish style trousers worn beneath a long, wide tunic, which was tied with a sash and had a bodice feminine in cut and style. It was christened the bloomer costume, after Amelia Bloomer, an American feminist, and her friend and fellow feminist Elizabeth Cady Stanton was responsible for its adoption for a time by a number of her fellow suffragists.[4] They were however forced to abandon it, since it caused so much ridicule of the feminist cause for which they were fighting. It set up a link between feminism and mannishness. In Britain *Punch* exploited this relentlessly to propagate a view of feminists as somehow unnatural, yet the clothes that were lampooned in *Punch* were often fashionable as much as they were feminist.[5]

In Britain there was another and different voice of opposition to the fashions of the period. This came from the artists of the pre-Raphaelite movement, which began in the 1840s. Their general aim was to depict nature truthfully. They were also influenced by the painting of the early Renaissance (hence their name), and developed a style of women's clothing based on their romantic vision of medieval simplicity of style. George Watts wrote about the aesthetic principles of dress. The mother of Millais researched and made costumes for his paintings; Elizabeth Siddal and Jane Morris, lovers and models of pre-Raphaelites, not only posed in but habitually wore a special style of dress. This abandoned both the crinoline and the fashionable dropped shoulder seam and tight lacing, which together prevented the fashionably dressed woman from raising her arms to their full height or extent. The pre-Raphaelite style incorporated sleeves with a very high armhole, and the sleeves themselves were often full at the top. Pre-Raphaelite women went uncorseted; Mrs Haweis, a doyenne of taste and style in the 1870s, emphasized this aspect of the style:

> The primary rule in beautiful dress is that it shall not contradict the natural form of the human frame ... One of the most important features is a graceful figure – hence one of the most conspicuous and valuable innovations of the Pre-Raphaelite school is the waist. The first aim is to have an 'antique waist' – which a vulgar mind would pronounce horribly thick – thick like the Venus de Medicis, thick like that of the far nobler Venus de Milo.[6]

It is significant that the examples chosen by Mrs Haweis come not from nature, but from classical art. Greek art deeply influenced the Victorians. E. W. Godwin, an architect of the later phase of the Victorian Greek revival, combined Hellenic style with the Japonaiserie fashionable in the last years of the nineteenth century. His mistress, Ellen Terry the actress, 'dressed either in Grecian robes or a kimono',[7] and a Liberty catalogue in the early 1900s demonstrated to its readers how to arrange a Greek style of dress.

These catalogues also depicted other varieties of period and almost fancy dress – evening gowns in medieval or eighteenth-century style, for example. In one sense this was the legacy of the Victorian love of dressing up. Modern life has increased self consciousness and this makes it difficult for men or women ever to feel fully at ease in their social roles. Possibly 'dressing up' offered a playful way to exorcize some of this unease. (It is related too to the way in which 'period costume' and a sense of correct periodization became important both on the stage and in painting.)

Yet at the same time the Victorians believed that the best art was that which most faithfully reflected the natural and the 'true'. Embedded in the whole history of the reform of dress, this confusion about the relationship between nature and art persists to this day. We have ceased to believe that art should copy the visible appearances of nature; yet there is still a strong wish to establish a

Amelia Bloomer 1851.
Reproduced courtesy of the Mary Evans Picture Library.

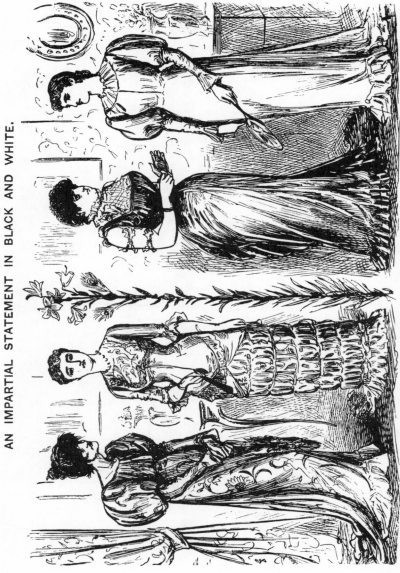

AN IMPARTIAL STATEMENT IN BLACK AND WHITE.

ÆSTHETIC LADY AND WOMAN OF FASHION. | WOMAN OF FASHION AND ÆSTHETIC LADY.

'natural' form of dress. The search for the 'natural' in dress must, however, be a wild goose chase, for such a project tries to deny, or at least does not recognize that dress is no mere accommodation to the body as a biological entity, nor to geography or climate; nor does it merely link the two. It is a complex cultural form, as is the human conception of the body itself.

Stella Mary Newton describes dress reform as 'one of the very few instances of an attempt to demolish [a] basic principle of civilization'. Yet not all dress reformers were resolutely against fashion itself. Ada Ballin, for example, writing in 1885, argued that dress reform had to take fashion into account, since 'women ... dread and have reason to dread ridicule'.[8] Her chief aim was less to abolish fashion than to render dress healthy, and she advocated exercise, and wool next to the skin because she believed cotton to be a poor absorber of moisture. She drew attention to the dangers of dyed clothes at a time when dyes did contain poisons, but she was of the view that 'a stout girl without stays looks very much like a shapeless and quivering mass of fat', and did not therefore oppose corsets. She also acknowledged the limits on dress reform set both by conservatism and by a desire for constant novelty.

Some members of the medical profession had campaigned since the early nineteenth century for healthier dress for both men and women. It was widely recognized that Victorian dress was unhygienic and restricting, and in 1884 an International Health Exhibition was held in South Kensington, London. Nicknamed 'the Healtheries', its popularity demonstrated the widespread interest in health and dress reform. The food and dress sections were especially popular; a divided skirt drew large crowds, and the exhibition of sweated labour (in the making of gloves and dresses) caused shocked comment. In the mid 1880s the Rational Dress Society was formed, its purpose the pursuit of a form of dress that would combine health, comfort and beauty.[9]

It was during this period that Dr Gustav Jaegar, Professor of Zoology and physiology at the University of Stuttgart, successfully promoted the idea that human beings should wear wool next to the skin (and sleep between woollen sheets) because animal fibres alone

Two views of Aesthetic Dress 1881.
Reproduced by kind permission of the proprietors of Punch.

could prevent the retention of the 'noxious exhalations' of the body. A contemporary report in *The Times* (4 October 1884, reprinted in *The Times*, 7 February 1984) refers to Jaegar's theory as being 'demonstrated by scientific experiments and proved by practical experience'. Jaegar's views, like those of so many dress reformers, were based on the erroneous belief that, 'being animals, we should wear animal clothing', that we would be healthier if we abandoned culture. He designed a special suit of sanitary clothing, entirely made of wool, and carefully designed so as to prevent all draughts reaching the skin. These combinations, or body suits, became wildly popular amongst the British intelligentsia. Oscar Wilde and George Bernard Shaw (said to look like a radish in his) were ardent disciples, and for a generation or more the precept 'wear wool next to the skin' became virtually a moral imperative.

Jaegar believed that commercial dyes, like vegetable fibres, had a literally poisonous effect on the human body. The pre-Raphaelites, by contrast, objected to chemical dyes for *aesthetic* reasons. Aniline dyes had been developed in Germany in the 1850s and 1860s from coal tar; they made possible a new range of loud, acid colours such as electric blue, magenta (named after a battle), lime green, mustard, sulphur yellow, Crimean blue and so on. The pre-Raphaelites, in revolt against what they considered to be this ugliness, emphasized natural, vegetable dyes, and used and promoted both rich, jewel colours and 'off', faded tones. Mrs Haweis quoted John Ruskin, the art historian, who had said, 'no colour harmony is of a high order unless it involve indescribable tints'; and she herself believed that colours were more beautiful when faded by age and not too pure in tone. Liberty was to translate this aesthetic into the characteristic 'greenery yallery' range lampooned by Gilbert and Sullivan in their operetta *Patience*, and described – with tongue in cheek – in women's magazines:

> Liberty's is the chosen resort of the artistic shopper. Note this lady robed in 'Liberty silk' of sad-coloured green, with rather more than a suspicion of yellow in ribbons, sash and hat (suggestive of a badly made salad) who talks learnedly to her young friend – clothed in russet

Liberty style in 1905 and in 1910.
Reproduced by kind permission of the Trustees of the Victoria and Albert Museum.

brown, with salmon pink reliefs showing in quaint slashings in un-expected places – of the 'value of tone' of negatives and positives, of delicious half tones.[10]

By the 1890s many features of aesthetic dress had been gradually incorporated into the fashionable dress of the day. Bustles as well as crinolines had at last ceded to the long, slender skirt, the high shoulder was fashionable, and soon to be exaggerated into the leg-of-mutton sleeve, and exercise, dancing and sport, together with changing views of women's role, were beginning to have their effect on high fashion. Katherine Anthony, writing in 1915, believed that Paul Poiret had been influenced by the reform dress of Scandi-navian and German feminists, although he himself nowhere admits this. But as early as 1900 it seems that the Belgian designer, Henry van der Velde, had shown 'reform clothes' at Kerfeld, centre of the German textile industry, and his designs, which scorned corsets, made use of high waists and built on 'architectural principles', sound very similar to Poiret's designs.[11]

Even the American Gibson girl, whom many feminists believed at the time to be a prototype for the 'new woman' of the 1890s and 1900s, may claim her descent from the pre-Raphaelites. Her creator, Charles Dana Gibson, visited George du Maurier while he was on a visit to Europe – and du Maurier, who became a leading illustrator for *Punch*, and was one of the best and best known lithographers of his day, 'had been one of the original members of the Pre-Raphaelite brotherhood'.[1]

In Britain in the 1890s, socialism was often linked to dress reform. The socialist artists Walter Crane and William Morris saw dress as an expression of social relations. E. Nesbit, writer of children's stories and wife of Hubert Bland, a prominent Fabian, had short hair and wore 'socialist gowns'. This sort of artistic or 'bohemian' apparel seems often to have been associated with a general rejection of the conventions and of bourgeois lifestyles. One socialist speaker at this period is described as 'free and unconventional in dress and manner, a disreputable hat crowning his shaggy locks, a picturesque cloak for wet weather'.[13] Edward Carpenter, the libertarian socialist,

---

The Agate by Joseph Southall 1910. This portrait by the artist of himself and his wife shows a mixture of fashionable and 'aesthetic' features, in particular the artist's breeches.

Reproduced by kind permission of Jane and David Livingstone.

homosexual and pro-feminist habitually wore knickerbockers and sandals. The sight of his bare feet in these articles of footwear caused consternation in the village in which he took up residence in search of a more authentic way of life. In 1894 a fellow socialist, who had emigrated to the West Coast of America wrote asking him for sandals; he 'enthused in his letter about the liberatory effect of emancipating feet from shoes ... "One begins to own one's body at last".'[14]

By this time, Stella Mary Newton suggests, there had been a subtle shift in the meanings of this kind of dress. Reform dress, she believes, was now no longer a moral and hygienic project, but had become a symbol of the wearer's tastes and politics. You wore a 'socialist gown' not only because it was, you hoped, both attractive and comfortable, but because it proclaimed what you *were*. It is this shift from clothing as part of a social project to clothing as part of an identity that really launches it into its most 'modern' manifestations.

Dress reform in relation to women's clothes became a dead issue after 1914, and in the 1920s the paring down of women's dress made it appear more rational and healthier than men's. Men continued to be imprisoned in high, stiff collars, heavy materials and constricting suits, underwear and boots, not to mention the trousers hated by dress reformers, who believed that they obscured the natural line of the leg as well as preventing sufficient ventilation. Before 1914 the dress reformers had favoured the alternative of breeches; now they advocated shorts for men.

J. C. Flugel, whose book on clothes appeared in 1930, was a dress reformer as well as a psychoanalyst. He wished dress to express democratic ideals and was a leading figure in the Men's Dress Reform Party. According to Flugel, the lengthening of women's skirts (initially by Jean Patou) at the end of the twenties did provoke a renewed interest in the reform of female clothing; he mentions a Sensible Dress Society, which 'was inspired directly by the desire to retain the short skirt'.

Flugel recognized that aesthetic considerations are important in dress, and believed that dress could express the democratic values he supported:

> Costume must be freed, alike from the ruinous competition and commercialism of fashion and from the unadaptable conservatism of 'fixed' dress. Reasonable consideration of ends and means, together

with an appeal to the highest standards of contemporary aesthetic taste, must replace a frantic search for novelty at any cost, or a blind adherence to tradition.[15]

Unlike most psychoanalysts, Flugel even remained calm at the prospect of an end to sexual differentiation in dress. He preferred to emphasize the many differences between individuals rather than the one difference of sex.

Flugel's book ends with his vision of a collectivist utopia in which clothing production is so regulated by the state as to produce garments that are elegant, functional and egalitarian, an anticipation, as it happens, of the Second World War Utility scheme. Indeed, he went further even than this, for his final arguments express an outlook widely held among scientifically minded intellectuals between the wars, and the popularity at that time of a strange ideal: not the abolition merely of fashion, but of clothes themselves:

> The reality principle demands ... that we consistently allow ourselves an undistorted recognition of our bodies. Thus aesthetic taste, as it develops, tends to be reconciled more and more to the natural human form and seeks to set off and reveal its beauties rather than to hide its deficiencies, or to substitute other beauties of a kind that are foreign to anatomy. If this process continues, it means that emphasis must tend to fall ever increasingly upon the body itself and less upon its clothes ... Complete reconciliation with the body would mean that the aesthetic variations, emendations and aggrandizements of the body that are produced by clothes would no longer be felt as necessary or desirable; in fact there would be no need for clothes ... Modesty ... when its essentially ambivalent nature is recognized can interpose no reasonable obstacle to nudity; nor in the long run can economics.[16]

The theory Flugel introduces to support this view is 'the new science of eugenics' which

> emphasizing the importance of sexual selection for future human welfare adds its own argument to those of hygiene and aesthetics and demands that we should duly value the body, if not for our own sake, at least for the sake of future generations.[17]

'Scientific breeding' was a major preoccupation right across the political spectrum in the 1930s. It was motivated by the desire to improve the human race by supposedly scientific rather than by social means, and saw the human race as genetically rather than as environmentally determined. It was as popular among Communist scientists as among those on the political right, and it influenced the kinds of utopias that writers then imagined.[18] Its obsession with racial improvement and therefore its association with fascist beliefs in racial purity discredited it after the Second World War.

Dress had always played a central part in literary utopias, and the view that a rational, just and happy society would have no fashion was not, in fact, new with the Victorians. Thomas More invented the word (it means 'no place' or 'nowhere' – hence William Morris's *News From Nowhere*); and the inhabitants of More's *Utopia* (1551) wore clothes that were uncoloured and all cut to the same pattern. This was an expression of puritanism and a critique of the extravagant display of the Tudor court, of the excesses of the aristocracy and the inequalities of Tudor mercantile capitalism. More was also influenced by the example of the simplicity of North American Indians, some of whom Amerigo Vespucci had already discovered and described.[19]

Such puritanism as More's was rational in a society that depended for its luxuries on handicraft. In More's *Utopia* no one was to work more than six hours a day, and this did not allow for the production of anything other than the necessities of life.

Daniel Defoe in *Robinson Crusoe* implicitly recognized the human need for adornment and clothing. Jonathan Swift, however, in *Gulliver's Travels*, had already arrived at a version even more extreme than Flugel's of the dress reformer's urge to rid the human race of clothes. For the ideal race in *Gulliver* is a superhuman breed of sublimely rational horses.

The political message of literary utopias changed with the passing centuries, and by the period of the romantic movement the utopian critique was invariably of capitalism. Henceforward, imagined societies were to express either aspirations towards socialism, or else attacks upon it.

The Fabian form of utilitarian socialism was especially sympathetic towards eugenics, to the selection of the fittest, and to a hyper-rationalistic view of life. The ultimate model for humans in many of the fictional futures of the early twentieth century was the machine, for after all machines are more rational than humans. Some writers equated socialism with science; they believed that social advancement would be brought about not by political endeavour but by 'miracles of science'.

H. G. Wells took this view. So did Gerald Heard. Heard later went to California and became a Buddhist (Christopher Isherwood became his disciple), but in 1924 he published *Narcissus: An Anatomy of Clothes*. In it, although dress clearly fascinated him, he argued for the abolition not only of apparel but also of the body itself. He suggested that clothing is somehow a projected form of the evolution of the body, which has reached the end of its own capacity to develop, so that clothing now has to take any further evolution forward. As this evolution proceeds still further,

> Will not architecture become what clothing has been? The main fabric will be given by a skeletal structure sustaining a circulatory system that already begins to imitate the elaboration of the body's ... If like a snail possessed we learn to carry a rushing home everywhere with us, it will be our costume and habit.[20]

Surgical and hormonal alterations to the body will be an improvement upon the 'blunt instruments of razor and corset', and ultimately

> Our bodies may be on the way to disappear ... Indeed what is to prevent us fulfilling Mr Wells' stupendous prophecy and becoming like the Martians only tentacled brains?[21]

J. D. Bernal, a prominent scientist and Communist Party member wrote a similar utopia in the late thirties. In his future world, too, rationalism would have triumphed; the 'flesh' of biology and the 'devil' of the human psyche would have been conquered at last by reason, and humanity would have become 'completely ethereal-ized'.[22] These curious views are simply an extreme form of a mechanical view of life founded upon over-scientific, over-rationalistic ideologies.

A different and more reasonable kind of reform involved protests and campaigns against cruelty to animals. The pelts, feathers and skins of animals, birds and reptiles have contributed much to the woman of fashion's appearance, and their slaughter on a world-wide scale was a feature of western domination. In the period roughly between 1860 and 1921 the fashion for plumage in women's hats led to a hideous carnage, first of British birds such as gulls and kittiwakes (sometimes their wings were pulled off the living birds which were then left to die in slow agony in the sea), later of the exotic species in the British Empire and the third world.

By 1898 the export of egret feathers from Venezuela had reached 2839 kilos and perhaps as many as two and a half million birds had been killed. And although ostriches were sometimes farmed, they, along with the bird of paradise and the even rarer lyre bird, rifle bird, quetzal and scarlet tanager, were thoughtlessly plundered.

In 1889 the Society for the Protection of Birds was formed, but not until 1921 was legislation passed in Britain to curb the traffic in feathers. By that time, however, the fashion for feathers in ladies' hats had passed.[23]

In recent years there has been renewed campaigning against cruelty to animals, for the preservation of endangered species in the wild, against the use of the pelts of rare animals for fur coats, of ivory for adornment purposes, and against cosmetics cruelly tested on animals or even based on animal products. This has become part of the wider campaign for animal liberation, in which the farming equally of mink for luxury furs or of battery hens for food has been recognized as just as cruel as the extermination of animals in the wild.

Another form of protest against unjust luxury, privilege and exploitation has been the refusal of formal, 'correct' wear in high places or on official occasions. Keir Hardie, the Independent Labour Party MP, horrified his colleagues by wearing a working man's cloth cap to the House of Commons in 1906. In the late forties Aneurin Bevan, a left winger in the Labour Party government of the period, refused to wear a dinner jacket when he went to dine at Buckingham Palace. More recently schools, professions, prisons and the church have all engaged in the struggle over relaxation in dress. It is the radical doctor who dresses informally, the most 'progressive' prisons that abandon uniform.

A studied flouting of conventions in dress denotes a distance from the norms of the role one is playing, or a refusal to commit oneself to the belief system involved. The social work profession, because its role is in any case ambiguous, illustrates this especially clearly. Social workers have often in recent years dressed informally as a gesture of solidarity with their clients, or to put them at their ease. This sometimes has discredited them in the eyes of police,

The hunting of ostriches (which cannot fly) in the 1870s.
Reproduced by courtesy of the Mansell Collection.

magistrates and the public. In 1983 *Community Care* reported an ongoing battle in one Greater London borough: 'Bexley's scruffy social workers have been told to smarten up'. The borough's chief social services officer sent out a memorandum to all social workers condemning 'excessive informality in their raiment or their propensity to tonsorial abstinence'. (Whether 'tonsorial abstinence' means baldness or too infrequent haircuts is unclear.) The Director of Sheffield Social Services was quoted as perceiving strange clothes as a London phenomenon, although he admitted that his own clothes had received censure in the past: 'As a newly appointed senior social worker I was told my steelworker's donkey jacket was not really fitting to my station' (*Community Care*, 16 June 1983.)

The social worker's status is uncertain, and it is probably for this reason that the social worker's attire causes unease. Along with school pupils and feminists, social workers face an ambiguity about sexuality. In their case this is because they are expected to form relationships of some confidence and intimacy with clients, from which sex must all the same be obviously excluded. Yet, unlike doctors and nurses, they have not built up a rigid sartorial system to establish distance.

The ambiguity of the social worker and the uncertain status of the social work profession is often explained by describing it as a 'women's profession' and a 'semi-profession'. The status of women when in public is itself uncertain. For this reason women in public life have always been concerned about dress, and have often felt very ambivalent about it. There were always some feminists who prided themselves on a well-turned-out and fashionable appearance. Elizabeth Garrett Anderson, for example, pioneer woman doctor in the nineteenth century, was always beautifully dressed, as was Emmeline Pankhurst. Elizabeth Cady Stanton was interested in clothes and proud of her appearance, and it was sometimes argued that feminists would win more support if their views were not almost always enunciated by 'platform women' dressed in dingy black.

The utopian theme, when interpreted by women, seemed more human than the masculine versions. In 1915 Charlotte Perkins Gilman, a feminist writer, published *Herland*,[24] a fictional utopia inhabited by women and girl children only. This race of women lived in the Latin American jungle, yet was not, like the mythical Amazons, warlike. They wore different weights of body suits, sometimes covered by tunics, a form of dress consistent both with feminism and with the ideals of dress reform, since it was healthy, comfortable to work in, aesthetically pleasing, and unchanging.

E. Nesbit in *The Amulet* (1901) described a future London in which 'the people's clothes were of bright, soft colours and all beautifully and very simply made. No-one seemed to have any hats or bonnets; but there were a great many Japanese looking sun-shades.'[25] This of course was a version of aesthetic dress.

After the First World War, a new generation of women appeared to reject many of the ideals of feminism. The dark aftermath of war still shadowed their lives, and there was a shortage of both men and jobs. No wonder that women, desperate to live life to the full, paid more attention to femininity than to feminism. But their indifference made some older women bitter:

> Some of those who had fought for the vote were not however pleased; those who fought for the emancipation of their sex and won it, look at the girl of today with a disappointment in which there is more than a hint of bitterness. Her bright appearance does not mollify them. They, in the fight, had no time to look nice; a good many of them, indeed, regarded and still regard any effort to look nice as part and parcel of the old technique of servitude. They smell sex appeal in it.[26]

After the Second World War, the New Look caused even greater consternation, and the Labour government itself became embroiled in the controversy surrounding this extravagant new fashion. Sir Stafford Cripps, President of the Board of Trade, begged the British Guild of Creative Designers to boycott it; women MPs from the Labour Party spoke out against its attack on the freedom of women, its 'caged bird' attitude and its emphasis on 'over sexiness';[27] and it caused a correspondence in the left-wing weekly, the *New Statesman and Nation*. Their diarist, 'Critic', commented on the sheep-like mentality of women in following the 'uncomely' new fashion (20 September 1947, p. 225). Molly Cochrane, a writer, replied (27 September 1947, p. 252), suggesting that men were as conformist as women, and that anyway longer skirts were both more convenient and more 'comely': 'the ballet has taught most of us the aesthetic advantages of a longer skirt'. Jill Craigie, journalist, and wife of Michael Foot who, in 1982, as leader of the Labour Party, got into trouble for his 'scruffy' attire at a remembrance ceremony for the dead of two world wars at the Cenotaph, also wrote in (4 October 1947, p. 270). Like Molly Cochrane she understood the lure of the New Look skirt, but felt duty bound to oppose it for its extravagant use of material because of the economic crisis, when British textiles were needed for the export drive. She bewailed the fact that the trousseau of Princess (now Queen) Elizabeth, who was married in the autumn of 1947, was to be calf length ('a major victory for the vested interests of the fashion houses'), and quoted George Orwell, who had written that class barriers were being broken down:

> He attributes this in part to the prevailing women's fashions which make working girls often almost indistinguishable from the wealthy. If the new fashion prevails it is obvious that the well to do will find the labour and the means to renovate their wardrobes whereas the majority of working girls will not. This may again tend to widen the gulf between the classes.

She noted, however, an encouraging rumour that the J. Arthur Rank film company was to continue to dress its stars in knee-length skirts, although MGM had succumbed to the new fashion.

In the United States, in fact, there appears to have been organized resistance to the new, long skirt. *Time* (September 1947) alleged that women across the land were flocking to the banners of resistance. In the summer of 1947, opinion polls had shown that American women didn't like the skirts; women in Dallas, Texas, actually demonstrated against the New Look; 1300 women formed a 'little below the knee club', and the legislature of Georgia announced its intention of introducing a bill to ban long skirts (just as some states had tried to make the showing of ankles illegal in the early twenties).[28]

The New Look appeared newer than it was because of the dislocation of war. Many Americans in the fashion industry may have been displeased to see French *haute couture* reassert its dominance so soon after the ending of hostilities, since it had been widely hoped that the United States would permanently oust Paris. In Britain, women seem to have welcomed the New Look as a relief from austerity, and one journalist has even explained it as a rebellion by women against men: a feminine protest against male imposed rationing and shortages.[29]

There were some signs of protest too when the midi skirt began to replace the mini skirt in the late 1960s. By that time, however, fashion was more pluralistic, and the lengthening of skirts had nothing like the same significance. In the 1950s, the New Look was the last stand of aristocratic dressing, and 'understated chic' had to be drummed into the readers of mass-circulation women's magazines precisely because the 'lady' was finally passing from view. In 1984 a Conservative MP could still complain about the sloppy dress of the Labour Party in the House of Commons and say of Harriet Harman (a member of the shadow cabinet): 'She came in the other day in a sweater and jeans. Any resemblance between her and a lady was entirely coincidental' (*Guardian*, 12 March 1984). But everyone knew he was just trying it on.

Harriet Harman, like many of the younger women in the Labour Party, has felt the influence of contemporary feminism. Not that the voice of feminism has been unequivocal about dress; yet it has been widely assumed that on the one hand feminists do dress in a particular way and on the other that they have a view about how all women should dress. A mistaken and ultimately reactionary philosophy has dominated this debate. To examine it is to raise wider issues about the whole aesthetic of dress, and the place of fashion in contemporary life.

Chapter II

Feminism and Fashion

Proust knew how much the fleeting expression of fashion ... can reflect something beyond its limited time, something that whispers of the nostalgia of human impermanence and mirrors man's ... destiny.

Cecil Beaton: *The Glass of Fashion*

One dimension to the history of fashion is the history of the individuals who created this world in which reality and fantasy mingle and become confused, a world in which we go adorned in our dreams. It is a world of microcosmic detail and of the grand gesture, of long term obsessions and love at first sight, of hysterical excitement and abject despair.

For everyone clothes are compulsory. This produces two kinds of individual at each extreme of the spectrum: those who hate it all, who, were it not for social pressure, would not bother with the aesthetics of their appearance and who experience fashion as a form of bondage; and those who live it as compulsion, the fashion freaks for whom dress is a source of passionate interest, who are its addicts; 'fashion victims', junkies of the art of self adornment.

Many addicts made a career from their obsession. In the London of the 1870s, Mary Eliza Haweis was the wife of a fashionable but impecunious clergyman. She supplemented the ever-failing family purse by writing articles and books on style, dress and interior decoration, some of which were best sellers. She loved fashion, and understood the horror of a faulty ensemble: 'After I had made myself killing,' she wrote in her diary before her marriage, 'all my roses and silver were in vain, I had forgotten my white shoes and had to creak about and dance in my walking Oxfords! Awful.' She regarded persons of taste and sensitivity as a persecuted minority:

> Those whose taste has been cultivated by having beautiful things always about them are incredibly sensitive to awkward forms and inappropriate colours in inharmonious combinations. To such persons [these] ... cause not only the mere feeling of disapprobation but even a kind of physical pain.[1]

Today, the Italian fashion journalist, Anna Piaggi, has taken the addiction to even further extremes. As reported in the *Observer* (1 May 1983):

> She is a fashion phenomenon. The most dedicated follower of fashion pales into insignificance beside a woman who has spent months travelling by train because the exaggerated crinolines she was affecting at the time would not fit through the door of an aeroplane.

Many men as well as women have made not simply a career but a life work out of being fashion addicts. The supreme example was perhaps Beau Brummell, for whom perfection in dress was a symbolic philosophy. There was Paul Poiret, a great impresario of fashion. There was a whole coterie of artists and designers in Paris in the 1930s and 1940s: Christian Bérard, Jean Cocteau, Christian Dior.

Many of these men and women paid dearly for their addiction, gave their lives, in a sense, to 'that most difficult of all causes – to make oneself a work of art'.[2] Poiret died in the poorhouse, as did Beau Brummell. Many of the beauties died young, mysteriously of rare illnesses, tragically of drink or drugs, or both. Some became the walking epitome of their epoch, and could not move on when times changed. There sometimes seems something almost mad about these women and men who dedicated their lives to the 'tragic game' of being chic.

Secrecy – addiction – obsession: these words gesture towards our feeling that a love of fashion is not quite respectable. Halfway between hobby and ritual it is indulged in the 'privacy of the home', yet flaunted in the public world, is stigmatized by its uncertain status as not quite art, yet certainly not really life.

Caught between the addicts and the puritans, however, many, perhaps most, individuals experience above all an intense ambivalence about fashion and a love of fine dressing. This ambivalence has reproduced itself within contemporary feminism in a specific way.

It is difficult to discuss fashion in relation to the feminism of today, because the ideologies about dress that have circulated within the women's movement seem never to have been made explicit. This may be one reason for the intense irritation and confusion that the subject provoked from the beginning of the women's liberation movement in 1970, and still provokes.

One cause for irritation has been that from the earliest days of contemporary feminism the mass media promoted a caricature of feminists – the bra-burning 'women's libbers' who hated men but dressed just like them; a caricature virtually unchanged from nineteenth-century *Punch*. It seems that bra-burning was an invention of the media. There were, however, many demonstrations, both in England and in America, against sexism in the media, against the way in which stereotyped ideals of beauty were forced on women, and against the way in which women were seen only as sexual objects, not as people.[3] This was an important theme in the early years of the contemporary women's movement but the mass media consistently and wilfully confused anti-sexism with being anti-sex.

Meanwhile, two different ways of understanding culture emerged within feminism. The first of these was a whole-hearted condemnation of every aspect of culture that reproduced sexist ideas and images of women and femininity, all of which came to seem in some sense 'violent' and 'pornographic'; the other, by contrast, was a populist liberalism which argued that it would be élitist to criticize any popular pastime which the majority of women enjoyed, whether it were reading pulp romances or dressing in smart clothes, an approach that was an offshoot of a general intellectual interest in popular culture, discussed earlier.

Underlying these two approaches were hidden discourses rooted in the history of culture. On the one hand there was the continuing effect of the nineteenth-century cult of the natural sciences, which I discussed in relation to utopias; yet simultaneously feminists were influenced by the beliefs of nineteenth-century liberalism and its twentieth-century reinterpretations, although these contradict the more authoritarian 'Fabian utilitarianism'. These two views are mutually inconsistent, although no debate within feminism has fully brought this out. They possibly reflect a deeper division, which, it has been suggested, underlies many current political debates – a division between

> on the one hand, those committed to 'cultures of identity' and the achievement of true self and expression. On the other hand, those who act on the basis that human interaction depends on dissimulation, who insist on the central value of the city, its unpredictability, the fluidity of its codes and the subversive play with them.[4]

This division between the 'authentic' and the 'modernist' can be applied to many of the fashions I have discussed, and especially to contemporary counter-cultural fashions. The hippie, for example, would be 'authentic', the punk, as I suggested, 'modernist'. The nineteenth-century dress reformers were 'authentic', but the dandies, like the courtesans of the French Second Empire, were 'modernists' – preoccupied with the creation of an image, not the discovery of the 'true' self. The division suggests two radically divergent ways of seeing the world – and fashion – and two radically different kinds of politics. Is fashionable dress part of the oppression of women, or is it a form of adult play? Is it part of the empty consumerism, or is it a site of struggle symbolized in dress codes? Does it muffle the self, or create it?

An unresolved tension between 'authenticity' and 'modernism' haunts contemporary feminism. The recurring theme of women's relationship to nature, of women's utopias, and of the vision of a wholly other world in which 'women's values' hold sway suggests a longing for a more 'authentic' world, closely bound to 'nature', in which we will find our true selves. Engagement in the political battle, the use of avant-garde art, the appropriation of jazz and rock by women's bands and of an anarchic tradition of humour by women comics, and the belief in the social construction of the gendered self represent the 'modernist' approach. (Sometimes the two converge, as at Greenham.)

This unresolved tension marks a number of feminist debates, for example the debate about heterosexual love, the controversies over pornography and romantic fiction, and the debate about dress and feminist attitudes to personal adornment. Some feminists, for example, have defined men – men at least in so-called 'patriarchal society' – as the oppressors of women, and the construction of female sexuality as the core of female subordination; since they have also acknowledged that most women, including most feminists, do wish to relate sexually and emotionally to men, they have set up an insoluble problem. Thesis and antithesis can never dissolve into a synthesis; the dialectic simply leaves a wound. Others, of course, have argued that it is fine for women to pursue their desires in whatever direction they lead; lesbian sado-masochism has been the practice most frequently justified, but the arguments apply equally to heterosexuality in any form.[5]

In the sphere of literature, while some feminists have argued that pornography constitutes actual violence towards women, others have asserted our right to look, and, indeed, to be turned on by it. In discussions about pulp fiction there is a similar dispute between the moralists who denounce it as promoting false values and as being a form of ideological subordination of women, and the hedonists who emphasize its fantasy and erotic potential.

Similarly with dress: the thesis is that fashion is oppressive, the antithesis that we find it pleasurable; again no synthesis is possible. In all these arguments the alternatives posed are between moralism and hedonism; either doing your own thing is okay, or else it convicts you of false consciousness. Either the products of popular culture are the supports of a monolithic male ideology, or they are there to be enjoyed and justified.

A slightly different version of these arguments acknowledges that desires for the 'unworthier' artefacts of the consumer society have been somehow implanted in us, and that we must try to resolve the resulting guilt by steering some moderate middle way. To care about dress and our appearance *is* oppressive, this argument goes, and our love of clothes *is* a form of false consciousness – yet, since we *do* love them we are locked in a contradiction. The best we can then do, according to this scenario, is to try to find some form of reasonably attractive dress that will avoid the worst pitfalls of extravagance, self-objectification and snobbery, while avoiding also becoming 'platform women in dingy black'.

Susan Brownmiller's *Femininity* exemplifies this false logic. She defines the erotically appealing as being in direct conflict with the

Some feminists *have* managed to design and make clothing that is stylish and reasonably priced, and which avoids the exploitation on which so much low-price clothing depends – as these illustrations from the Ragged Robin Catalogue show.
Reproduced by kind permission of the Ragged Robin Cooperative.

serious and the functional, and offers feminists only the choice
between the two:

> Why do I persist in not wearing skirts? Because I don't like this artificial
> gender distinction. Because I don't wish to start shaving my legs again.
> Because I don't want to return to the expense and aggravation of
> nylons. Because I will not reacquaint myself with the discomfort of
> feminine shoes . . . Because the nature of feminine dressing is superficial
> in essence.[6]

Yet she finds unshaven legs unappealing, and low-heeled shoes
unerotic (although they were certainly *fashionable* in 1984, the year
the book was published) and longs for the gracefulness and pretty
colours of her discarded gowns.

Neither a puritanical moralism, nor a hedonism that supports *any*
practice in the name of 'freedom' is an adequate politics of popular
culture. The body of theory, or ideology, that I have called 'utilitarianism' contributed to the construction of this impasse with the
unacknowledged, and unrecognized, influence of its machine philosophy, its glorification of the work ethic and its inability to grant
pleasure a proper place in human culture – the influence of Veblen.
Later nineteenth-century feminism was marked by this Fabian spirit
which posed use against beauty; the same utilitarianism marks it
today. The logic of this view is ultimately that the only justification
for clothing is function – utility.

The emphasis on function leads to an image of what is 'natural'
which is inseparably locked into this debate. The belief that nature
is superior to culture was enshrined within the Romantic reaction
to the industrial revolution. Janet Radcliffe Richards, one of the
few writers to have examined feminist attitudes to dress, suggests
that underlying feminist contempt for fashion and cosmetics is a
'muddle' about 'the natural person being the real thing'.[7] She
argues that feminists share what is actually a conservative view: that
to try to 'make the most of oneself' is to create a *false* impression,
somehow to deceive the world.

Human beings, however, are not natural. They do not live primarily by instinct. They live in socially constructed cultures. To
suggest, therefore, as Professor Jaegar did, that we would do better
to dress as much as possible like sheep, since we, like sheep, are
mammals, is to make a fundamental mistake about what human
existence is.

To set up the 'natural' as superior to the 'artificial' (as if the very concept of human culture were not artificial) is a view also influenced by some of the non-conformist, puritan versions of Christianity, which confused the natural with simplicity, and so the uncorrupt. These, like Fabianism, have influenced British and American non-Marxist socialism. Since contemporary feminism, in Britain at least, has been greatly influenced by the socialist tradition, it is hardly surprising that the feminist debate about dress has been marked by this counter-liberatory ideology. One side of the stifled debate about dress has been simply a re-run in very different circumstances of the whole nineteenth-century dress reform project: to *get out of* fashion.

It would be wrong to deny the rational aspects of this view: the dreadful exploitation of garment workers throughout the world is a reality, and feminists should support campaigns against it. In the United States, for example there is a label in clothes made by properly unionized labour stating that fact. Ultimately only progressive economic policies can end this exploitation, and in that sense the clothes we wear are part of a wider struggle that doesn't necessarily imply a rejection of finery as such. There is also the issue of the way in which certain styles of female dress are held to signal sexuality in a way that invites sexual harassment, makes women vulnerable (when they wear high heels, for example, so that they can't run away from a rapist, or to catch a bus) and also punishes them by making them uncomfortable.

Yet these arguments are often used not rationally, but as rationalizations. Exploitation in the electronics industry does not lead feminists to reject the use of videos and word-processors; the horrors of the agri-industry in no way restrict their enjoyment of gourmet food.[8] Those who can afford foreign holidays usually take them, notwithstanding the despoliation that international tourism inflicts on the third world. The quite special rage reserved for fashionable dressing tells us that dress speaks the irrational-unconscious in a special way.

This relates also to an attitude of persistent hostility to the fine arts that has been evident in certain veins of progressive thought. A 'progressive' condemnation of fashion can extend to a general denigration of 'bourgeois art'. Aesthetes are then equated with the degenerate upper classes, and their preoccupations become suspect. To care or know about traditional art, classical music or 'high culture' generally is often to be convicted of pretentiousness and a damaging involvement with the norms of bourgeois culture. The ultimate example of such an attitude is the radical feminist who dismisses Tintoretto and Rubens as 'all tits and bums' or as 'pornography'.[9]

The self-righteousness of such attitudes surfaces whenever, as happened several times in recent years, 'serious' British newspapers carried articles about feminism and fashion. One correspondent (a man) wrote to the *Guardian* in response to such a piece:[10]

> The strength of the feminist movement lies in the fact that they do not need to rely on such superficiality – they gain their sisterhood through being women in a patriarchal environment. They are fighting the oppression of society – a fight they will never win if they feel obliged to conform to the fashions that society imposes on them.

while a woman responded:

> I can't be the only woman who reaches for the first t-shirt and skirt/ trousers that come to hand in the morning, adding a jumper (knitted by Mum from age-old patterns) when it looks chilly ... I'm wearing the same summer frocks that I've worn for the past two years. Well, they're not worn out, are they? I have absolutely no idea what is going on in the distant, nonsensical world of fashion. And oddly enough I don't think I'm the one out of touch.

More recently the same issue surfaced in the pages of *Spare Rib*, a feminist magazine. One woman wrote to the letters page (*Spare Rib* no. 139, November 1983):

> Recently I have been the target of a lot of criticism from women ... because they do not like the way that I dress and wear my hair (i.e. Mohican, Bondage, etc.). They tell me that I am ignoring its racist and sexist overtones, that it is not 'feminist', and that I am allowing myself to be exploited by the fashion market ...
>
> Do you criticize your sisters because they don't wear dungarees and Kickers? Is a woman any less emancipated because she 'chooses' to wear make-up and stilettos?
>
> Is not the whole point of feminism to help a woman to realise her right to control her own life and make decisions for herself?
>
> If so, why are we as feminists oppressing women with a new set of rules ... Would anyone with any individuality call that liberation?

Other readers wrote in to agree with her.

This letter shows how, coexisting with a tradition of puritanism (a word not used as a term of abuse, but to indicate a specific historical tradition) is a wholly other ideology of individualism and free choice. While feminists with one voice condemn the consumerist poison of fashion, with another they praise the individualism made possible by dress. 'I thought that the feminist ideal was to dress according to personal preference and choice, and not according to a set of rules,' wrote a correspondent to the *Sunday Times* (29 August 1982) in response to an article (*Sunday Times*, 22 August 1982) in which Adrianne Blue had tried to *describe* feminist styles of dress. Although she made no attempt to tell anyone what to wear, the writers of several letters published appeared to object to the very attempt even to classify 'feminist' ways of dressing, perhaps partly because it seemed to confirm stereotypes, but also, I suspect, because it subtly undermined the 'free choice' ideology.

Liberated dress, according to this ideology, means 'doing your own thing'. The idea of free choice has contributed significantly to contemporary feminism. Perhaps feminists should have questioned it more than they have. Perhaps feminists haven't dared to, because the idea of free choice is so powerful in western societies. Yet 'free choice' is really a myth, and is inconsistent with the belief, to which all feminists pay at least lip service, that human beings are 'socially constructed'. The concept of social construction is based on the view that at birth a baby has the potential to develop in a variety of ways, limited to some extent by genetic heritage, but equally, or more importantly, dependent on the environmental influences that shape its experience and provide a comparatively favourable or unfavourable soil for growth. Many of the most important aspects of this development occur in early childhood. By the time we become adults, therefore, our capacity to choose freely is greatly restricted by the way in which our personality has developed. It is also equally restricted by external circumstances such as class, wealth, gender, age, and where we live.

Despite their apparent acceptance of this 'social construction' model, many feminists continue to discuss moral choice as though

Following page: The Rebirth of Venus.
Reproduced by kind permission of Posy Simmonds

we were all free agents, as if they had never heard of the well-worn but sensible aphorism: 'men make their history, but they do so in circumstances that are not of their own choosing.' In the realm of aesthetics the very idea of 'free choice' is inappropriate; styles of dress are not dictated simply by economics or sexist ideology but are, as I have argued, intrinsically related to contemporary art styles.

In so far as feminists have dressed differently from other women (and most have not) their style of dress has still borne a close relationship to currently circulating styles. The initial 'look' of movement women was the counter-cultural look of the student movement at the end of the 1960s when mini-skirts and Egyptian wig hairstyles (by then slightly out of date) coexisted with hippie robes and curls. Feminists wore floor length dresses in dusty tints, and long, pre-Raphaelite hair. Soon, to cut off your hair curtains became a symbol of liberation, and make-up was seldom worn – but then naturalism was fashionable in the mainstream.

If liberated dress meant doing your own thing, no one ever commented on how strange it was that everyone wanted to do the *same* thing. In the early seventies alternative lifestyle gear varied only within a narrow and predictable range of ethnic blouses, cheesecloth skirts, Biba sleeves, Laura Ashley smocks, bell-bottomed denims and cords and woolly sweaters with that special matted jumble sale finish. (Fifteen years later a different set of aesthetic conventions dictated trousers that are either much baggier or much tighter, bold colours and black and grey instead of Biba greenery-yallery, and hair that is dyed in flashes instead of being hennaed.)

In pioneering thrift-shop styles and retro-chic, feminism was innovative rather than anti-fashion. The hacking jacket worn with a flower skirt (1977), the trilby hat (1979) and the old-fashioned handmade sweaters were fashions that feminism initiated and the mainstream copied.

Some feminists did disdain skirts and high heels, and the popular public stereotype of the feminist was of a stalwart woman in dunga-rees or boiler suit and Dr Martens boots. Some feminists did wear such clothes, perhaps partly in order to avoid sexual harassment. Some lesbians had always worn boyish or 'butch' styles, and lesbian feminists sometimes took over these styles as a way of proudly proclaiming their sexuality.

Even feminists who never wore a skirt or make-up went crazy

about Kickers, or wore beautifully hand-painted boots in rainbow colours; they adorned themselves with rings and long, bright earrings made of feathers, beads or metal – drawing attention with all these, and with their brightly flashed hair, away from the body and towards its periphery. Fashion, banished from clothing, reappeared surreptitiously in forms of adornment that were less obviously feminine or sexualized.

Dungarees and boiler suits can in any case – and have been – redefined as 'fashionable' and 'sexy'. Yet the very idea of them has sometimes seemed to send men into a frenzy of agitation. In the spring of 1979 a debate was staged in London between Arthur Scargill, later President of the National Union of Miners, and Anna Coote, a feminist journalist, following an article in the *Morning Star* which had attacked the *Yorkshire Miner*, the newspaper of the most militant section of the National Union of Miners, for its policy of having 'page three' pin-ups. Maurice Jones, then editor of the *Yorkshire Miner*, who was also on the platform, at one stage in the proceedings worked himself up into an incoherent frenzy at the outrage of women in dungarees (of whom there were none in an audience consisting in large part of feminists). Such irrational rage could only indicate some deep seated fear, presumably because 'dungarees' when associated with 'feminists' has become shorthand for rejection of men, for the most menacing (to men) aspect of lesbianism.[11]

The rage of men such as Maurice Jones suggests that it may well be important for women to challenge norms of feminine dress, and even if there is nothing especially political about wearing 'whatever you like', women (and men) should be able to choose not to dress fashionably in so far as this is possible – I have argued that it is not really possible. Nevertheless it is mistaken to set up something called 'alternative fashion' as a morally superior ideal, as another series of correspondents in the *Guardian* (25 October 1983) tried to do:

> I'm sick of being patronized by ... subtle propaganda ... It's no news to me and millions of other women who wear bright, cheap clothes, that overalls per se are not revolutionary. What matters is dressing to please ourselves and to say what we want. Men may like 'impossible heels' – we want to walk and run, not deform our spines ... Let's hear about who runs the fashion industry and why it's there at all.

So wrote one London woman. Another, from Yorkshire, bewailed
the absence of alternative fashion in the north of England:

> High street chic is the ultimate fashion goal for young women. The
> linched waist, dolman sleeve and three-quarter length leather boot is
> more eagerly sought than any amount of [alternative fashion].
>
> Why is it ... that despite dwindling incomes and few jobs people
> want conformist fashion instead of cheaper, imaginative and experi-
> mental apparel? Can alternative fashion only exist if it is under-written
> by well established sub-cultures? Or do people prefer to display the
> badges of achievement and status in mainstream society, no matter how
> precarious their own position is?

Some pertinent questions are asked; but the writers seem not to
doubt that their own mode of dressing is both freely chosen and
rationally superior. They thus manage to collapse together the two
opposed traditions of liberal free choice and utilitarianism. This
doesn't resolve the contradiction, the ambivalence; it merely
expunges it with the false claim that there exists some form of
'alternative dress' that *is* both these things.

To the extent that a feminist style does exist, it has to be understood as a sub-theme of the general fashion discourse. Boiler suits
and dungarees are after all fashion garments, not just a feminist
uniform. They are commercially marketed items of casual chic; and
the contortions necessary in the lavatory, and the discomfort in cold
weather of having to undress completely in order to relieve oneself,
should prove conclusively that this form of dress is worn not to
promote rational apparel, but to announce the wearer's feminism in
public. In urban society, clothes are the poster for one's act. In the
pre-industrial world clothes were the badge of rank, profession or
trade. As classes fragment we revert to a state in which our clothes
once more informally define us. Feminism, in evolving a style
among these styles, joins the discourse rather than breaking with
it, capitulates rather than transcends – which it could in any case
never do.

Feminist style relates to a wider social structure. It is the style of
dress adopted by intellectuals and white-collar workers of a certain
status, what might be called polytechnic dressing (if 'polytechnic'
wasn't used as a term of abuse along with 'feminist'). Anita
Brookner again mistakes this form of dressing for an expression of
freedom:

A five-minute survey of my immediate community reveals a preponder-
ance of blue jeans, dungarees, pullovers, tennis shoes, boots, shawls,
odd waistcoats, long skirts, plaid blouses ... To be sure academic
gatherings are not noted for their elegance, but ... there are several
messages to be read here ...

The first is that all degrees of seniority are obliterated in the desire to
look as young, as carefree, as natural as possible. The second is that
these unreconstructed dressers, although brought together for purposes
of work ... are dressed for play ... The rules have disappeared ... there
does not seem to be the slightest awareness of the purpose of dressing:
there is no disguise, no self-consciousness − and certainly no shame.
(*London Review of Books*, 15 April–5 May 1982)

Yet, in the environment described, this form of dress is virtually
compulsory, and does conform to a set of unspoken rules, of which
one is the pseudo-democracy of 1960s liberal views on education:
that it is possible to abolish the hierarchic distinctions between
teachers and taught. In reality, the differences in status and power
have changed little since the student rebellions; it is simply that now
the informal dress of teachers gestures rather placatingly towards
some alternative ideal. Angela Carter is nearer the mark when she
suggests that 'Jeans have lost their outlaw chic since the class of '68
took them into the senior common room by a natural progression.
They are now ... a sign of grumpy middle age' (*New Society*, 13
January 1983).

The casual dress described by Anita Brookner, far from being the
inspiration of free spirits, is the latter-day version of the Fabian
style, of the vegetarians and socialists in sandals and hairy knickerbockers whom George Orwell used to refer to as 'gruff lesbians',
'sandals wearers', 'orange juice drinkers', 'pansies' and other 'cranks'
unfortunately attracted to socialism. Orwell's caricatures are offensive; moreover these 'cranks' *had* been innovative. For example, it
was liberating when Edward Carpenter wore open sandals. Then he
broke a taboo; now casual dress may surely be optional. The idea
that casual dress must be both freely chosen and somehow 'better' is
mixed up with another ideology from the 1960s: that formality is
always repressive. We confuse opposition to the repressive rituals of
our society with opposition to all ritual.

In relation to dress, some feminists, mostly American, have tried
to retrieve fashion as one amongst other traditional female skills.

They would argue that women's creativity in the art of dress has been underrated, as have most feminine skills. Lois Banner uses a slightly different argument in suggesting that 'the pursuit of beauty and of its attendant features, fashion and dress, has more than any other factor bound together women of different classes, regions and ethnic groups, and constituted a key element in women's separate experience of life'.[12] She offers no evidence for this, and it would be as easy to argue that dress, beauty and fashion have promoted competitiveness and envy among women.

I have suggested that more typical of feminist discourse on dress has been its tendency to set up a kind of syllogism that cannot be resolved. It attempts to address and to resolve the ambivalence that is such a widespread response to fashion; yet the terms of the debate inevitably perpetuate that very ambivalence.

I have argued that to understand all 'uncomfortable' dress as merely one aspect of the oppression of women, is fatally to over-simplify; that dress is never primarily functional, and that it is certainly not natural. I have argued, against those who see fashion as one form of capitalist 'consumerism', that these critics fail to understand that women and men may use the 'unworthiest' items of capitalist culture to criticize and transcend that culture. The dis-affected use bizarre dress to thumb the nose at consumerism and to create jeering cartoons of society's most cherished conventions. But the fashionably dressed and the more traditionally glamorous are not therefore to be dismissed as necessarily the slaves of consumer-ism. Socially determined we may be, yet we consistently search for the crevices in culture that open to us moments of freedom. Precise-ly because fashion is at one level a game (although it is not *just* a game), it can be played for pleasure.

This perspective on fashion is diametrically opposed to that of those radicals who make a root and branch attack on 'consumerism'. Many radicals do advocate a return to 'use values'. We should struggle for a world, they argue, in which we would respect craft-made objects and lovingly *use* them. The beauty of pottery, fabrics and furniture – and of course clothes – resides in their simplicity and functionalism. Such critics contrast this sturdy 'use' with modern culture in which we 'consume', that is, 'use up'. Consumer-ism then comes to have destructive and voracious implications. Theodor Adorno and other cultural critics of the 'Frankfurt School' developed a deeply pessimistic view of consumer culture, seeing its very diversity, hedonism and inventiveness as a hidden form of uniformity – as I discussed earlier. But the political implication of this was 'repressive tolerance' and the idea that *every* aspect of consumer culture duped and doped the masses: consumer culture was a form of 'false consciousness'. These critics used psycho-analysis – a theory of the *unconscious*, to try to explain the way in which this false consciousness takes over the individual. Consumer-ism becomes a compulsive form of behaviour, over which we have little conscious control. According to this puritanical view, we are squeezed between the imperatives of the market and the urges of an unconscious whose desires are warped and invalidated by the cul-ture in which we live. Fashionable dressing and our pleasure in it then becomes one example of a mass outbreak of inauthenticity.

I believe that, on the contrary, fashion is one among many forms of aesthetic creativity which make possible the exploration of alter-natives. For after all, fashion is more than a game; it is an art form and a symbolic social system:

> Once literacy and a rich vocabulary of visual, aural and dramatic expressions exist, then society has a permanently available ... resource in which all the tabooed, fantastic, possible and impossible dreams of humanity can be explored in blueprint.[13]

This is a far more democratic view than the élitism of the radicals – whether these are the Frankfurt School, Christopher Lasch, Stuart and Elizabeth Ewen or some feminists – who see consumer culture as nothing more than 'false consciousness'. Apart from anything else, it is clear that while the modern educational system, based ultimately on élitist principles, has failed many of its pupils, these same young men and women have managed to develop what is often an extremely knowing and sophisticated visual taste and a capacity to use images and the adorned person to make complex – if often cynical and nihilist – commentaries on contemporary life.

The pointlessness of fashion, what Veblen hated, is precisely what makes it valuable. It is in this marginalized area of the contin-gent, the decorative, the futile, that not simply a new aesthetic but a new cultural order may seed itself. Out of the cracks in the pave-ments of cities grow the weeds that begin to rot the fabric.

In the sense, therefore, that we can use and play with fashion, we should reject feminist ambivalence as an inappropriate if under-standable response. Yet there is another sense in which fashion elicits an ambivalent response, and that has to do with an ambivalence that runs deeper and is more tightly embedded in fashion itself.

Fashion acts as a vehicle for fantasy. The utopias both of right and left, which were themselves fantasies, implied an end to fantasy in the perfect world of the future. There will, however, never be a human world without fantasy, which expresses the unconscious unfulfillable. All art draws on unconscious fantasy; the performance that is fashion is one road from the inner to the outer world. Hence its compulsiveness, hence our ambivalence, hence the immense psychological (and material) *work* that goes into the production of the social self, of which clothes are an indispensable part.

In this sense, ambivalence *is* an appropriate response to dress; and in this sense 'modernism' is a more adequate response than the 'cult of the authentic', since the latter allows for no ambivalence:

> Take the example of nudity as it is presented in ... the mass media's discovery of the body and sex. This nudity claims to be rational, progressive: it claims to rediscover the truth of the body, its natural reason, beyond clothing, taboos and fashion. In fact, it is too rationalistic, and bypasses the body ... and the true path of desire, which is always ambivalent, love and death simultaneously.[14]

This ambivalence is that of contradictory and irreconcilable desires, inscribed in the human psyche by that very 'social construction' that decrees such a long period of cultural development for the human ego. Fashion – a performance art – acts as vehicle for this ambivalence; the daring of fashion speaks dread as well as desire; the shell of chic, the aura of glamour, always hide a wound.

Fashion reflects also the ambivalence of the fissured culture of modernity, is only like all modern art in expressing a flawed culture. The dilemma of fashion is the dilemma of all modern art: what is its purpose and how is it to be used in the world of 'mechanical reproduction'? Where fashion differs from some forms of art is that whereas in some fields high art and popular culture have veered further and further apart, in dress the opposite has happened. High fashion has become to some extent demotic. All chic is now gutter chic.

Like all art, it has a troubled relationship with morality, is almost always in danger of being denounced as immoral. Yet also, like all art, it is likely to become most 'immoral' when it comes closest to the truth. Utilitarian dress, like conventional 'good' clothes and academic art, expresses conservatism. The progressive project is not to search for some aesthetically pleasing form of utilitarian dress, for that would be to abandon the medium; rather we should use dress to express and explore our more daring aspirations, while respecting those who use it to disguise personal inadequacies, real or imagined, or to make themselves feel confident or important.

Art is always seeking new ways to illuminate our dilemmas; dress, however tainted a medium – from its association with the body and with daily life and behaviour – nevertheless does this too. Fashion is ambivalent – for when we dress we wear inscribed upon our bodies the often obscure relationship of art, personal psychology and the social order. And that is why we remain endlessly troubled by fashion – drawn to it, yet repelled by a fear of what we might find hidden within its purposes, masked by the enigma of its Mona Lisa smile.

References

Chapter One

1. Dickens, Charles (1976), 'Meditations in Monmouth Street', in *Selected Short Fiction*, Harmondsworth: Penguin, pp. 106–7. (Originally published in 1836.)
2. Polhemus, Ted (ed.) (1978), 'Introduction', *Social Aspects of the Body*, Harmondsworth: Penguin, p. 28.
3. Douglas, Mary (1966), *Purity and Danger*, Harmondsworth: Penguin.
4. Carlyle, Thomas (1931), *Sartor Resartus*, London: Curwen Press. (Originally published in 1831.)
5. Sévigné, Madame de (1982), *Selected Letters*, Harmondsworth: Penguin, p. 74.
6. Bell, Quentin (1947), *On Human Finery*, London: The Hogarth Press, p. 14.
7. Hollander, Anne (1975), *Seeing Through Clothes*, New York: Avon Books.
8. Jameson, Fredric (1981) *The Political Unconscious: Narrative as Socially Symbolic Act*, London: Methuen, p. 79.
9. Moretti, Franco (1983), 'Homo Palpitans: Balzac's Novels and Urban Personality', *Signs Taken for Wonders*, London: Verso, p. 113.
10. Martin, Bernice (1981), *A Sociology of Contemporary Cultural Change*, Oxford: Basil Blackwell, p. 28.
11. Jameson, Fredric (1984), 'Postmodernism, or the Cultural Logic of Late Capitalism', *New Left Review*, no. 146, July/August.
12. Elias, Norbert (1978), *The Civilizing Process: The History of Manners*, Vol. I, translated by Edmund Jephcott, Oxford: Basil Blackwell, p. 50.

Chapter Two

1. Newton, Stella Mary (1976), 'Couture and Society', *Times Literary Supplement*, 12 November.
2. Hiler, Hilaire (1929), *From Nudity to Raiment*, London: Foyles.
3. Von Boehn, Max (1932), *Modes and Manners, Vol. I: From the Decline of the Ancient World to the Renaissance*, London: Harrap, p. 168.
4. Gibbon, Edward (1952), *The Portable Gibbon: The Decline and Fall of the Roman Empire*, Harmondsworth: Penguin, pp. 204–5.
5. Runciman, Steven (1975), *Byzantine Style and Civilization*, Harmondsworth: Penguin, p. 121.
6. ibid., p. 123.
7. Laver, James (1969a), *A Concise History of Costume*, London: Thames and Hudson, p. 62.
8. ibid.
9. Mukerji, Chandra (1983), *From Graven Images: Patterns of Modern Materialism*, New York: Columbia University Press, ch. 5. My thanks to Hilda Scott for directing my attention to this book.
10. My thanks to Tony Halliday for this suggestion. I have relied on Laver, James, op. cit., for my account of Cretan costume.
11. Cunnington, Phillis and Lucas, Catherine (1967), *Occupational Costume in England from the Eleventh Century to 1914*, London: Adam and Charles Black.
12. ibid., p. 204.
13. Von Boehn, Max, op. cit.
14. Cunnington, Phillis and Lucas, Catherine, op. cit.
15. Baldwin, Frances Elizabeth (1926), *Sumptuary Legislation and Personal Regulation in England*, Baltimore: John Hopkins Press.
16. Burckhardt, Jacob (1955), *The Civilisation of the Renaissance in Italy*, London; Phaidon Press, pp. 223–4. (Originally published in 1860.)
17. Quoted in Berman, Marshall (1983), *All That is Solid Melts into Air: The Experience of Modernity*, London: Verso.
18. ibid.
19. Laver, James (1969b), *Modesty in Dress: An Inquiry into the Fundamentals of Fashion*, London: Heinemann, p. 44.
20. Flugel, J. C. (1930), *The Psychology of Clothes*, London: Hogarth Press.
21. See Bray, Alan (1983), *Homosexuality in Renaissance England*,

London: Gay Men's Press; and Weeks, Jeffrey (1977), *Coming Out*, London: Quartet.

22. Delbourg-Delphis, Marylène (1981), *Le Chic et le Look: Histoire de la Mode Féminine et des Moeurs de 1850 à nos Jours*, Paris: Hachette.

23. Quoted in Moers, Ellen (1960), *The Dandy: Brummell to Beerbohm*, London: Secker and Warburg.

24. Saunders, Edith (1954), *The Age of Worth*, London: Longmans, p. 75.

25. Banner, Lois (1983), *American Beauty*, New York: Alfred A. Knopf.

26. Benjamin, Walter (1973a), *Charles Baudelaire: A Lyric Poet in the Era of High Capitalism*, London: New Left Books, p. 47.

27. Cunnington, Phillis and Lucas, Catherine, op. cit.

28. Byron, George Gordon, Lord (1982), *Selected Prose*, letter to Francis Hodgson, 25 September 1811, Harmondsworth: Penguin, p. 95.

29. Charles-Roux, Edmonde (1975), *Chanel*, London: Jonathan Cape, translated by Nancy Amphoux.

30. Beaton, Cecil (1954), *The Glass of Fashion*, London: Weidenfeld and Nicolson.

31. Etherington-Smith, Meredith (1983), *Patou*, London: Hutchinson.

32. Waugh, Evelyn (1928), *Decline and Fall*, Harmondsworth: Penguin, p. 75.

33. Lee, Sarah Tomalin (1975), *American Fashion*, London: André Deutsch, p. 218.

34. Chisholm, Anne (1981), *Nancy Cunard*, Harmondsworth: Penguin.

35. In Britain, clothing was rationed ('on coupons') during the Second World War, and for several years afterwards. Each individual was issued with a book of coupons, which had to last for one year; most items of clothing were valued in coupons; hats, however, were exempt.

Chapter Three

1. Newton, Stella Mary (1975), 'Fashions in Fashion History', *Times Literary Supplement*, 21 March, argues that fashion history lags behind other branches of art history, and is 'unlikely to catch up'.

2. Moore, Doris Langley (1949), *The Woman in Fashion*, London: Batsford. 'As it happens all the psychological enquiries into fashion are predominantly concerned with feminine fashion, and the band of theorists has without exception been male.' (p. 1.)

3. Cunnington, Cecil Willett (1950), *Women* (Pleasures of Life Series), London: Burke.

4. Cunnington, Cecil Willett (1941), *Why Women Wear Clothes*, London: Faber and Faber, pp. 260–61.

5. Bell, Quentin (1947), *On Human Finery*, London: The Hogarth Press, p. 128.

6. Moore, Doris Langley, op. cit.

7. Veblen, Thorstein (1957), *The Theory of the Leisure Class*, London: Allen and Unwin, pp. 179–82. (Originally published in 1899.)

8. Adorno, Theodor (1967), 'Veblen's Attack on Culture', *Prisms*, Cambridge, Ma.: The MIT Press; translated by Samuel and Sherry Weber, p. 77.

9. See Chapters Ten and Eleven.

10. Lasch, Christopher (1979), *The Culture of Narcissism*, New York: Warner Books.

11. Ewen, Stuart and Ewen, Elizabeth (1982), *Channels of Desire: Mass Images and the Shaping of the American Consciousness*, New York: McGraw Hill.

12. Baudrillard, Jean (1981), *For a Critique of the Political Economy of the Sign*, St Louis, Mo.: Telos Press, p. 79; translated by Charles Levin.

13. ibid., p. 51n.

14. Mukerji, Chandra (1983), *From Graven Images: Patterns of Modern Materialism*, New York: Columbia University Press, pp. 2, 188.

15. Carlyle, Thomas (1931), *Sartor Resartus*, London: Curwen Press, p. 48. (Originally published in 1831.)

16. Darwin, Charles (1959), *The Voyage of the Beagle*, London: J. M. Dent and Sons, pp. 202–3, 210. (Originally published in 1845.)

17. Quoted in Laver, James (1969b), op. cit., p. 9.

18. Bell, Quentin, op. cit., p. 13.

19. Lurie, Alison (1981), *The Language of Clothes*, London: Heinemann.

20. Barthes, Roland (1967), *Système de la Mode*, Paris: Éditions du Seuil.

21. Culler, Jonathan (1975), *Structuralist Poetics*, London: Routledge and Kegan Paul.

22. Barthes, Roland, op. cit., p. 256.

23. König, René (1973), *The Restless Image*, London: George Allen and Unwin.

24. The quotation comes from *The Communist Manifesto* (1848), quoted in Berman, Marshall (1983), *All That is Solid Melts into Air: The Experience of Modernity*, London: Verso.

25. Mallarmé, Stéphane (1933), *La Dernière Mode*, with an introduction by S. A. Rhodes. New York: Publications of the Institute of French Studies, Inc.

26. Greenberg, Clement (1982), 'Modernist Painting', in Frascina, Frances and Harrison, Charles (eds.), *Modern Art and Modernism: A Critical Anthology*, London: Harper and Row.

27. Anderson, Perry (1984), 'Modernity and Revolution', *New Left Review*, no. 144, March/April.

28. Horkheimer, Max and Adorno, Theodor (1979), *The Dialectic of Enlightenment*, translated by John Cumming, London: Verso, p. 154. (Originally published in 1944.)

Chapter Four

1. Thompson, E. P. (1968), *The Making of the English Working Class*, Harmondsworth: Penguin; Foster, John (1974), *Class Struggle and the Industrial Revolution*, London: Methuen.

2. Fraser, Grace Lovat (1948), *Textiles by Britain*, London: Allen and Unwin, gives this derivation. Taylor, Lou (1983), *Mourning Dress: A Costume and Social History*, London: Allen and Unwin, states that the name 'jeans' is supposed to derive from Jaen in Spain.

3. Mukerji, Chandra (1983), *From Graven Images: Patterns of Modern Materialism*, New York: Columbia University Press, ch. 5; Fraser, Grace Lovat, op. cit.

4. George, M. Dorothy (1966), *London Life in the Eighteenth Century*, Harmondsworth: Penguin. (Originally published in 1925.)

5. Taylor, Lou, op. cit., however, suggests that when, as frequently happened, whole courts were plunged into mourning, the general silk trade was severely affected and workers thrown out of employment.

6. Briscoe, Lynden (1971), *The Textile and Clothing Industries of the U.K.*, Manchester: Manchester University Press.

7. Stewart, Margaret and Hunter, Leslie (1964), *The Needle is Threaded: The History of an Industry*, London: Heinemann.

8. Engels, Friedrich (1973), *The Condition of the Working Class in England*, Moscow: Progress Publishers, pp. 245–6. (Originally published in 1844.)

9. Ewen, Stuart and Ewen, Elizabeth (1982), *Channels of Desire: Mass Images and the Shaping of the American Consciousness*, New York: McGraw Hill.

10. Taylor, Barbara (1983a), '"The Men are as Bad as their Masters ...": Socialism, Feminism and Sexual Antagonism in the London Tailoring Trade of the 1830s', in Newton, Judith, Ryan, Mary P., and

Walkowitz, Judith R. (1983), *Sex and Class in Women's History*, London: Routledge and Kegan Paul, p. 206.

11. Alexander, Sally (1976), 'Women's Work in Nineteenth Century London: A Study of the Years 1820–1850', in Mitchell, Juliet and Oakley, Ann (1976), *The Rights and Wrongs of Women*, Harmondsworth: Penguin.

12. Black, Clementina (1983), *Married Women's Work: Being the Report of an Enquiry Undertaken by the Women's Industrial Council*, London: Virago, with an introduction by Ellen F. Mappen. (Originally published in 1915.)

13. Stewart, Margaret and Hunter, Leslie, op. cit., p. 128.

14. Chase, Edna Woolman (1954), *Always in Vogue*, London: Gollancz.

15. Black, Clementina, op. cit.

16. Bennett, Arnold (Jacob Tonson) (1917), *Books and Persons*, quoted in Gross, John (1969), *The Rise and Fall of the Man of Letters: Aspects of English Literary Life Since 1800*, London: Weidenfeld and Nicolson.

17. Ewen, Stuart and Ewen, Elizabeth, op. cit., pp. 210–11.

18. Dobbs, J. L. (1928), *The Clothing Workers of Great Britain*, London: Routledge and Kegan Paul.

19. Disher, M. L. (1947), *American Factory Production of Women's Clothing*, London: Deveraux Publications, p. 5. See also Dooley, William H. (1934), *Economics of Clothing and Textiles*, Boston: DC Heath.

20. Ewing, Elizabeth (1974), *History of Twentieth Century Fashion*, London: Batsford.

21. ibid., p. 202.

22. Briscoe, Lynden, op. cit., p. 176.

23. National Union of Tailors and Garment Workers (NUTGW). I am most grateful to Neil Kearney, Information and Research Officer of NUTGW, for giving me his time and so much helpful information.

24. Campbell, Beatrix (1979), 'Lining Their Pockets', *Time Out*, 13–19 July.

25. Coyle, Angela (1982), 'Sex and Skill in the Organization of the Clothing Industry', in West, Jackie (ed.), *Work, Women and the Labour Market*, London: Routledge and Kegan Paul, p. 11.

26. Hamilton, M. (1951), *Women at Work*, London: Routledge and Kegan Paul, p. 130.

27. Briscoe, Lynden, op. cit. Modernization and the installation of increasingly complex automatic machinery led to the employment of

skilled engineers (male), particularly in the hosiery and knitted goods sector. Investment in capital intensive plant meant that shift work was increasingly introduced (to recoup and reap the profits) and male immigrant labour replaced women workers.

28. See Chapkis, Wendy and Enloe, Cynthia (1983), *Of Common Cloth: Women in the Global Textile Industry*, Amsterdam: Transnational Institute. These authors, however, discuss import controls only as an isolated form of protectionism, not as part of an overall 'Alternative Economic Strategy' that would include new trading initiatives with developing and socialist countries.

29. NUTGW.

30. Elson, Diane and Pearson, Ruth (1981), '"Nimble Fingers Make Cheap Workers": An Analysis of Women's Employment in Third World Export Manufacturing', *Feminist Review*, no. 7, Spring.

31. NUTGW.

32. Chapkis, Wendy and Enloe, Cynthia, op. cit.

33. Poiret, Paul (1931), *My First Fifty Years*, London: Gollancz.

34. Ewen, Stuart and Ewen, Elizabeth, op. cit.

35. Dior, Christian (1957), *Dior by Dior*, London: Weidenfeld and Nicolson.

36. ibid., p. 17.

37. Bertin, Célia (1956), *Paris à la Mode: A Voyage of Discovery*, London: Gollancz.

38. See Suzy Menkes in *The Times*, 5 July 1983, and Nathalie Mont-Servan in *Le Monde*, 26 May 1984.

Chapter Five

1. Laver, James (1969b), *Modesty in Dress: An Inquiry into the Fundamentals of Fashion*, London: Heinemann.

2. Flugel, J. C. (1930), *The Psychology of Clothes*, London: Hogarth Press.

3. In psychoanalytic terms, a reaction formation is a defence mechanism. Forbidden wishes and fantasies are denied; the reaction formation is the development of strong feelings against what was previously desired. For example, homophobia is, according to psychoanalytic thought, a reaction formation against homosexual wishes that have become unconscious.

4. Bergler, Edmund (1953), *Fashion and the Unconscious*, New York: Robert Brunner.

5. ibid., p. 289.
6. Baudrillard, Jean (1981), *For a Critique of the Political Economy of the Sign*, St Louis, Mo.: Telos Press, p. 91.
7. Freud, Sigmund (1953), 'Three Essays on The Theory of Sexuality', *The Standard Edition of the Complete Psychological Works*, Vol. VII (1953), London: The Hogarth Press and the Institute of Psychoanalysis. Translated by James Strachey. (Originally published in 1905.)
8. Morris, Ivan (1964), *The World of the Shining Prince*, Harmondsworth: Penguin, p. 216.
9. Flaubert, Gustave (1972), *Madame Bovary*, Paris: Livre de Poche, p. 20. (Originally published in 1857.)
10. ibid., p. 186.
11. Tanner, Tony (1979), *Adultery and the Novel*, Baltimore: Johns Hopkins University Press.
12. Laver, James, op. cit., p. 115.
13. Kunzle, David (1982), *Fashion and Fetishism*, Totowa, New Jersey: Rowman and Littlefield.
14. Roberts, Hélène (1977), 'The Exquisite Slave: The Role of Clothes in the Making of the Victorian Woman', *Signs*, Vol. 2, no. 3, Spring, p. 557.
15. Tinling, Teddy (1983), *Sixty Years in Tennis*, London: Sidgwick and Jackson, p. 24.
16. Faust, Beatrice (1981), *Women, Sex and Pornography*, Harmondsworth: Penguin, p. 49. Thanks to Ruby Rich for drawing my attention to this passage.
17. See Chapter Eleven.
18. Réage, Pauline (1954), *The Story of O*, London: The Olympia Press, pp. 16, 60, 61–2, 62.
19. Cunnington, C. Willett and Cunnington, Phillis (1951), *The History of Underclothes*, London: Michael Joseph, p. 11.
20. Duff Gordon, Lucy, Lady (1932), *Discretions and Indiscretions*, London: Jarrolds, p. 45.
21. Wharton, Edith (1952), *The House of Mirth*, London: Oxford University Press, pp. 298–302. (Originally published in 1905.)
22. Laver, James, op. cit., pp. 110–11.
23. Ewing, Elizabeth (1978), *Dress and Undress: A History of Women's Underwear*, London: Batsford, p. 173.
24. Carter, Angela (1982), 'The Bridled Sweeties', *Nothing Sacred*, London: Virago.

25. See Kolbowski, Silvia (1984), '(Di)vested Interests: The Calvin Klein Ads', *ZG*, no. 10, Spring.
26. Cunnington, Cecil Willett and Cunnington, Phillis, op. cit., p. 12.
27. Angeloglou, Maggie (1970), *A History of Makeup*, London: Studio Vista.
28. Dickens, Charles (1970), *Dombey and Son*, Harmondsworth: Penguin, p. 472. (Originally published in 1848.)
29. Banner, Lois (1983), *American Beauty*, New York: Alfred A. Knopf, p. 42.
30. Rubinstein, Helena (1930), *The Art of Feminine Beauty*, London: Gollancz.
31. Anderson, Jervis (1982), *Harlem: The Great Black Way 1900–1950*, London: Orbis.
32. Lewis, Alfred and Woodworth, Constance (1973), *Miss Elizabeth Arden*, W. H. Allen.
33. Rubinstein, Helena, op. cit., pp. 25–6.
34. ibid., p. 34.
35. Osborne, John (1982), *A Better Class of Person: An Autobiography 1929–1956*, Harmondsworth: Penguin, pp. 35–6.
36. White, Doris (1980), *D For Doris, V For Victory*, Milton Keynes: Oakleaf Books, p. 63.
37. Banner, Lois, op. cit.
38. Turner, Bryan (1982), 'The Discourse of Diet', *Theory, Culture and Society*, Vol. 1, no. 1, Spring.
39. Byron, George Gordon, Lord (1982), *Selected Prose*, letter to his mother, 25 June 1811, Harmondsworth: Penguin, p. 82.
40. Hollander, Anne (1975), *Seeing Through Clothes*, New York: Avon Books.

Chapter Six

1. Baldwin, Frances Elizabeth (1926), *Sumptuary Legislation and Personal Regulation in England*, Baltimore: John Hopkins Press.
2. Squire, Geoffrey (1974), *Dress, Art and Society: 1560–1970*, London: Studio Vista.
3. Elias, Norbert (1978), *The Civilizing Process: The History of Manners*, Oxford: Basil Blackwell.
4. Zeldin, Theodore (1977), *France 1848–1945: Taste and Corruption*, Oxford: University Press, p. 94.
5. Freud, Sigmund (1973), 'Femininity', *New Introductory Lectures on*

Psychoanalysis, Harmondsworth: Penguin, p. 165. (Originally published in 1933.)

6. Ackroyd, Peter (1979), *Dressing Up: Transvestism and Drag: The History of an Obsession*, London: Thames and Hudson, p. 37.

7. Cobbe, Frances Power (1869), 'The Final Cause of Women', in Butler, Josephine (ed.) (1869), *Woman's Work and Woman's Culture*, London: Macmillan, pp. 10–11.

8. Nystrom, Paul (1928), *Economics of Fashion*, New York: Ronald Press, pp. 479–80.

9. Turim, Maureen (1983), 'Fashion Shapes: Film, The Fashion Industry and the Image of Women', *Socialist Review*, no. 71 (Vol. 13, no. 5), pp. 86–7.

10. Beauvoir, Simone de (1953), *The Second Sex*, London: Jonathan Cape, p. 505.

11. ibid., p. 509.

12. ibid., p. 512.

13. ibid.

14. Beaton, Cecil (1982), *Self Portrait with Friends: The Selected Diaries of Cecil Beaton 1926–1974*, ed. Richard Buckle, Harmondsworth: Penguin, p. 14.

15. Benjamin, Walter (1973a), *Charles Baudelaire: A Lyric Poet in the Era of High Capitalism*, London: New Left Books, pp. 90, 95.

16. Haweis, Mary Eliza (1878), *The Art of Beauty*, London: Chatto and Windus, p. 274.

17. Roberts, Michèle (1983), *The Visitation*, London: The Women's Press.

18. Fitzgerald, Scott (1934), *Tender is the Night*, Harmondsworth: Penguin, p. 14.

19. Beaton, Cecil (1954), *The Glass of Fashion*, London: Weidenfeld and Nicolson.

20. Michelson, Peter (1970), 'An Apology for Porn', in Hughes, Douglas (ed.) *Perspectives on Pornography*, New York: Macmillan.

21. Sartre, Jean-Paul (1969), *Being and Nothingness*, London: Methuen, p. 609. See also, Douglas, Mary (1966), *Purity and Danger*, Harmondsworth: Penguin.

Chapter Seven

1. Balzac, Honoré de, (1971), *Lost Illusions,* Harmondsworth: Penguin, p. 165.

2. Engels, Friedrich (1973), *The Condition of the Working Class in England*, Moscow: Progress Publishers, p. 64. (Originally published in 1844.)

3. Simmel, Georg (1958), *Soziologie*, p. 486; quoted in Benjamin, Walter (1973a), *Charles Baudelaire: A Lyric Poet in the Era of High Capitalism*, London: New Left Books.

4. Benjamin, Walter, op. cit., p. 38.

5. Proust, Marcel (1981), *Remembrance of Things Past: Vol. II: The Guermantes Way*, translated by C. K. Scott Moncrieff and Terence Kilmartin, London: Chatto and Windus, p. 147. (Originally published in 1920.)

6. Sennett, Richard (1974), *The Fall of Public Man*, Cambridge: Cambridge University Press, p. 166. (I have drawn extensively on Sennett in this passage.)

7. Boswell, James (1966), *Boswell's London Journal 1762–1763*, Harmondsworth: Penguin, p. 201.

8. Simmel, Georg (1971), *On Individuality and Social Forms: Selected Writings*, ed. Donald N. Levine, Chicago: Chicago University Press, p. 311.

9. Proust, Marcel, op. cit., *Vol. I: Swann's Way*, p. 460.

10. Lee, Sarah Tomalin (1975), *American Fashion*, London: André Deutsch.

11. Stead, Christina (1945), *A Little Tea, A Little Chat*, London: Virago, pp. 59–60, 284–5.

12. Fiedorek, Mary B. (1983), *Executive Style: Looking It, Living It*, Piscataway, New Jersey: New Century Publishers; Molloy, John T. (1977), *The Women's Dress for Success Book*, Chicago: Follet Publishing Co.

13. My thanks to Lennie Goodings for drawing my attention to this article.

14. Berman, Marshall (1983), *All That is Solid Melts into Air: The Experience of Modernity*, London: Verso.

15. Jameson, Fredric (1984), 'Postmodernism, or the Cultural Logic of Late Capitalism', *New Left Review*, no. 146, July/August, p. 89.

16. Lasch, Christopher (1979), *The Culture of Narcissism*, New York: Warner Books, p. 167.

17. Quoted in Adburgham, Alison (1981), *Shops and Shopping: 1800–1914*, London: Allen and Unwin, p. 103.

18. Bloch, Ivan (1958), *Sexual Life in England*, London: Corgi Books, p. 109.

19. Adburgham, Alison, op. cit.
20. Hower, Ralph M. (1946), *History of Macy's of New York: 1858–1919*, Cambridge, Ma.: Harvard University Press.
21. Adburgham, Alison, op. cit.
22. Ferry, John (1960), *A History of the Department Store*, New York: Macmillan.
23. Miller, Michael (1981), *The* Bon Marché*: Bourgeois Culture and the Department Store: 1869–1920*, London: Allen and Unwin.
24. Adburgham, Alison, op. cit.
25. Ferry, John, op. cit.
26. Miller, Michael, op. cit.
27. Rees, Goronwy (1969), *St Michael: A History of Marks and Spencer*, London: Weidenfeld and Nicolson.
28. Sally Brampton of the *Observer*, reporting (6 November 1983) on a recent survey of shopping preferences undertaken by Source Information Marketing, wrote that its findings suggested that customers now perceive the department store as 'anonymous', and are demanding the 'old-fashioned' services of intimate surroundings and personal attention formerly associated precisely with the department store, and from which the 1960s boutiques broke away.
29. See the *Guardian*, 6 September 1984.

Chapter Eight

1. Braudel, Fernand (1981), *Civilization and Capitalism: Fifteenth to Eighteenth Centuries: Vol. I: The Structures of Everyday Life: The Limits of the Possible*, London: Collins, p. 313.
2. Pinchbeck, Ivy (1981), *Women Workers and the Industrial Revolution: 1750–1850*, with a new introduction by Kerry Hamilton, London: Virago, p. 312. (Originally published in 1930.)
3. Barlee, Ellen (1863), *A Visit to Lancashire in December 1862*, London: Seeley and Co., pp. 25–7.
4. Stanley, Liz (ed.) (1984), *The Diaries of Hannah Cullwick, Victorian Maidservant*, London: Virago, p. 231.
5. Ewen, Stuart and Ewen, Elizabeth (1982), *Channels of Desire: Mass Images and the Shaping of the American Consciousness*, New York: McGraw Hill.
6. Hollander, Anne (1975), *Seeing Through Clothes,* New York: Avon Books.
7. Adburgham, Alison (1981), *Shops and Shopping: 1800–1914*, London: Allen and Unwin.

8. See Chapter Ten.
9. Marx, Karl (1970), *Capital*, Vol. I, London: Lawrence and Wishart, p. 399. (Originally published in translation in 1886.) The quotation is taken from Dr H. J. Hunter's Report on rural housing, P.P. 1864 (3416) XXVIII, *6th Report of the Medical Officer of the Privy Council*, Apps. 13–14, p. 456.
10. Rhondda, Margaret Haigh, Viscountess (1933), *This Was My World*, London: Macmillan, p. 278.
11. Fitzgibbon, Theodora (1983), *With Love: An Autobiography 1938–1946*, London: Pan Books.
12. Mitford, Nancy (1974), *The Pursuit of Love*, in *The Best Novels of Nancy Mitford*, London: Hamish Hamilton, p. 134. (Originally published in 1945.)
13. Kunzle, David (1982), *Fashion and Fetishism*, Totowa, New Jersey: Rowman and Littlefield, pp. 84–5.
14. Beaton, Cecil, op. cit.
15. Anderson, Jervis (1982), *Harlem: The Great Black Way 1900–1950*, London: Orbis, p. 72.
16. Benthall, Jeremy (1976), *The Body Electric: Patterns of Western Industrial Culture*, London: Thames and Hudson.
17. Bailey, Margaret J. (1981), *Those Glorious Glamour Years*, Secaucus, New Jersey: Citadel Press, quotes figures of as little as $16.50 for a forty-hour week for a seamstress, and the starting salary of Edith Head, who later became a major MGM designer, was $30.00 as a sketcher, again for a six-day week. See also Hertzog, Charlotte and Gaines, Jane (1983), 'Hollywood, Costumes and the Fashion Industry', *Triangle Cinema Programme*, Birmingham, April–June.
18. Hollander, Anne, op. cit., pp. 342–3.
19. Eckert, Charles (1978), 'The Carole Lombard in Macy's Window', *Quarterly Review of Film Studies*, Winter; Gustafson, Robert (1982), 'The Power of the Screen: The Influence of Edith Head's Film Designs on the Retail Fashion Market', *The Velvet Light Trap: Review of Cinema*, no. 19.
20. Jameson, Fredric (1984), 'Postmodernism, or the Cultural Logic of Late Capitalism', *New Left Review*, no. 146, July/August, p. 65.
21. Warhol, Andy and Hackett, Pat (1980), *POPism: The Warhol '60s*, New York: Harcourt Brace Jovanovich, p. 43.
22. Ironside, Janey (1973), *Janey: An Autobiography*, London: Michael Joseph, p. 126.
23. Quant, Mary (1966), *Quant by Quant*, London: Cassell, p. 2.

24. Melly, George (1972), *Revolt Into Style: The Pop Arts in Britain*, Harmondsworth: Penguin, p. 147.
25. Quant, Mary, op. cit., p. 75.
26. Melly, George, op. cit., p. 148.
27. Warhol, Andy and Hackett, Pat, op. cit., p. 163.

Chapter Nine

1. Melly, George (1972), *Revolt Into Style: The Pop Arts in Britain*, Harmondsworth: Penguin.
2. Laver, James (1968), *Dandies*, London: Weidenfeld and Nicolson; Moers, Ellen (1960), *The Dandy: Brummell to Beerbohm*, London: Secker and Warburg.
3. Laver, James, op. cit. (1968), p. 21.
4. Moers, Ellen, op. cit.
5. Goffman, Erving (1969), *The Presentation of Self in Everyday Life*, London: Allen Lane, p. 29.
6. Smith, James (*c.* 1820), note appended to seventeenth edition of *Rejected Addresses*. I am indebted to Tony Halliday for this reference.
7. Baudelaire, Charles (1859), 'Le Dandy', *Ecrits sur l'Art*, Tome 2, Paris: Le Livre de Poche, p. 175.
8. ibid.
9. Cowley, Malcolm (1951), *Exile's Return*, New York: Viking, p. 55. See also Parry, Albert (1960), *Garrets and Pretenders: A History of Bohemianism in America*, New York: Dover Publications. (Originally published in 1933.)
10. Field, Andrew (1983), *The Formidable Miss Barnes: The Life of Djuna Barnes*, London: Secker and Warburg, p. 59.
11. ibid., p. 83.
12. Cowley, Malcolm, op. cit., p. 62. See also Ware, Carolin (1935), *Greenwich Village 1920–1930: A Comment on American Civilisation in the Postwar Years*, Boston: Houghton Miflin.
13. Spalding, Frances (1983), *Vanessa Bell*, London: Weidenfeld and Nicolson, pp. 244–5.
14. Ironside, Janey (1973), *Janey: An Autobiography*, London: Michael Joseph, p. 39.
15. Fitzgibbon, Theodora (1983), *With Love: An Autobiography 1938–1946*, London: Pan Books, p. 124.
16. Beauvoir, Simone de (1963), *Force of Circumstance*, Harmondsworth: Penguin, p. 47.

17. ibid., pp. 151–2.
18. Taylor, Lou (1983), *Mourning Dress: A Costume and Social History*, London: Allen and Unwin.
19. Proust, Marcel (1981), *Remembrance of Things Past: Vol. III: Time Regained*, p. 744.
20. Frith, Simon (1983), *Sound Effects: Youth, Leisure and the Politics of Rock and Roll*, London: Constable.
21. Priestley, J. B. (1934), *English Journey*, Harmondsworth: Penguin, p. 375.
22. Frith, Simon, op. cit.
23. MacInnes, Colin (1959), *Absolute Beginners*, London: Allison and Busby, p. 17.
24. ibid., p. 62.
25. Fyvel, T. R. (1961), *The Insecure Offenders*, London: Chatto and Windus.
26. Melly, George, op. cit., p. 150.
27. Frith, Simon, op. cit., p. 220.
28. Hebdige, Dick (1979), *Subculture: The Meaning of Style*, London: Methuen, p. 107.
29. ibid.
30. Sampson, Kevin and Rimmer, David (1983), 'The Ins and Outs of High Street Fashion', *The Face*, July, pp. 20–22.
31. Cosgrove, Stuart (1984), 'The Zoot Suit and Style Warfare', *History Workshop Journal*, Issue 18, Autumn.
32. Malcolm X (1965), *The Autobiography of Malcolm X*, Harmondsworth: Penguin, pp. 164, 137–8.
33. Keenan, Brigid (1977), *The Women We Wanted to Look Like*, New York: St Martins Press, p. 178.
34. Goldman, A. (1974), *Ladies and Gentlemen, Lenny Bruce*, London: Panther, quoted in Hebdige, Dick, op. cit.
35. Walter, Aubrey (ed.) (1981), 'Fuck the Family', *Come Together: The Years of Gay Liberation 1970–1973*, London: Gay Men's Press, pp. 156–7.
36. See Altman, Dennis (1982), *The Homosexualization of America*, Boston: Beacon Press.
37. Jameson, Fredric (1984), 'Postmodernism or the Cultural Logic of Late Capitalism', *New Left Review*, no. 146, July/August, pp. 56, 87.
38. Ewen, Stuart and Ewen, Elizabeth (1982), *Channels of Desire: Mass Images and the Shaping of the American Consciousness*, New York: McGraw Hill, p. 237.

39. Benjamin, Walter (1973b), 'The Work of Art in the Age of Mechanical Reproduction', *Illuminations*, London: Fontana, pp. 243–4.

40. Anscombe, Isabelle (1984), *A Woman's Touch: Women in Design from 1860 to The Present Day*, London: Virago, p. 95.

41. Museum of Modern Art, Oxford (1984), *Art Into Production: Soviet Textiles, Fashion and Ceramics 1917–1935*, Oxford: Museum of Modern Art.

Chapter Ten

1. Banner, Lois (1983), *American Beauty*, New York: Alfred A. Knopf.

2. Taylor, Barbara (1983b), *Eve and the New Jerusalem*, London: Virago, p. 255.

3. Kunzle, David (1982), *Fashion and Fetishism*, Totowa, New Jersey: Rowman and Littlefield, p. 122.

4. Banner, Lois, op. cit.

5. Adburgham, Alison (1961), *A* Punch *History of Manners and Modes*, London: Hutchinson.

6. Haweis, Mary Eliza (1878), 'Pre-Raphaelite Dress', quoted in Newton, Stella Mary (1974), *Health, Art and Reason: Dress Reformers of the Nineteenth Century*, London: John Murray, p. 53.

7. Jenkyns, Richard (1980), *The Victorians and Ancient Greece*, Oxford: Basil Blackwell, p. 301.

8. Ballin, Ada (1885), *The Science of Dress in Theory and Practice*, London: Sampson Low.

9. Newton, Stella Mary (1976), 'Couture and Society', *Times Literary Supplement*, 12 November.

10. ibid.

11. Katherine Anthony is quoted in Banner, Lois, op. cit. For the reference to Henry van der Velde, see Anscombe, Isabelle (1984), *A Woman's Touch: Women in Design from 1860 to the Present Day*, London: Virago, p. 95.

12. Banner, Lois, op. cit.

13. Rowbotham, Sheila and Weeks, Jeffrey (1977), *Socialism and the New Life: The Personal and Sexual Politics of Edward Carpenter and Havelock Ellis*, London: Pluto, p. 68.

14. ibid., p. 116.

15. Flugel, J. C. (1930), *The Psychology of Clothes*, London: Hogarth Press, p. 218.

16. ibid., pp. 234–5.

17. ibid., p. 233.
18. For an extended discussion of eugenicism and the left, see Werskey, Gary (1978), *The Visible College: A Collective Biography of British Scientists and Socialists of the 1930s*, London: Allen Lane.
19. Morton, A. L. (1952), *The English Utopia*, London: Lawrence and Wishart.
20. Heard, Gerald (1924), *Narcissus: An Anatomy of Clothes*, London: Kegan Paul, p. 142.
21. ibid., p. 155.
22. Bernal, J. D. (1929), *The World the Flesh and the Devil: An Enquiry Into The Three Enemies of the Rational Soul*, London: Kegan Paul, p. 57. Quoted in Wood, Neal (1959), *Communism and British Intellectuals*, London: Victor Gollancz, p. 139.
23. Haynes, Alan (1983), 'Murderous Millinery: The Struggle for the Plumage Act, 1921', *History Today*, July, pp. 26–31.
24. Gilman, Charlotte Perkins (1979), *Herland*, London: The Women's Press. (Originally published in 1915.)
25. Nesbit, E. (1959), *The Story of the Amulet*, Harmondsworth: Penguin, p. 224. (Originally published in 1901.) See also, Moore, Doris Langley (1967), *E. Nesbit: A Biography*, London: Ernest Benn.
26. Hamilton, Mary Agnes (1936), 'Changes in Social Life', in Strachey, Ray (ed.) (1936), *Our Freedom and Its Results*, London: Hogarth Press, p. 237.
27. Quoted in Phillips, Pearson (1963), 'The New Look', in Sissons, Michael and French, Philip (1963), *The Age of Austerity 1945–1951*, Harmondsworth: Penguin.
28. Lang, Kurt and Lang, Gladys (1961), 'Fashion: Identification and Differentiation in the Mass Society', in Roach, Mary Ellen and Eicher, Jane Bubolz (1965), *Dress Adornment and the Social Order*, New York: John Wiley.
29. Phillips, Pearson, op. cit.

Chapter Eleven

1. Haweis, Mary Eliza (1818), 'Pre-Raphaelite Dress', quoted in Newton, Stella Mary (1974), *Health, Art and Reason: Dress Reformers of the Nineteenth Century*, London: John Murray, p. 9. The diary quotation comes from Howe, Bea (1967), *Arbiter of Elegance*, London: The Harvill Press, p. 69.
2. Beaton, Cecil, op. cit.

3. I thought I remembered reading of a demonstration that was staged on Wall Street, New York City, at which bras were symbolically burned. An account of a demonstration against the Miss America Contest, which took place in Atlantic City in August 1968, is accompanied by a note from the editor of the anthology in which it appears saying 'Bras were never burned'; however, one feature of the demonstration was 'a huge Freedom Trash Can (into which we will throw bras, girdles, curlers, false eyelashes, wigs, and representative issues of *Cosmopolitan, Ladies' Home Journal, Family Circle*, etc. Bring any such woman-garbage you have around the house)'. See Morgan, Robin (ed.) (1970), *Sisterhood is Powerful: An Anthology of Writings from the Women's Liberation Movement*, New York: Random House, p. 521. See also O'Sullivan, Sue (1982), 'Passionate Beginnings: Ideological Politics 1969–82', *Feminist Review*, no. 11, for an account of the English demonstration against the Miss World Contest at the Albert Hall, London, in November 1970.

4. Chalmers, Martin (1983), 'Politics of Crisis', in *City Limits*, 19–25 August.

5. See Snitow, Ann, Stansell, Christine and Thompson, Sharon (1984), *Desire: The Politics of Sexuality*, London: Virago, for a discussion of some of these issues.

6. Brownmiller, Susan (1984), *Femininity*, New York: Linden Press, Simon and Schuster. I am indebted for the information about Susan Brownmiller's book to Chapkis, Wendy (1984), 'The Gender Divide: A Discussion of *Femininity* by Susan Brownmiller', Unpublished paper.

7. Radcliffe Richards, Janet (1980), *The Sceptical Feminist*, London: Routledge and Kegan Paul.

8. I have avoided the discussion of vegetarianism here. There is, of course, a whole series of preoccupations surrounding food, some of which are, supposedly at any rate, concerned with health, some with the exploitation of animals, some with conditions in the developing countries. The point still seems to me to stand – that western radical culture is far less ascetic about food – or drink – than it is about dress.

9. I have myself heard women refer to all nude paintings in the National Gallery, London, as pornography. Bel Mooney tells a similar anecdote in the *Sunday Times* (March 1984). Obviously this is a generalization on the basis of anecdote and open to criticism on that score; but such views do flavour parts of the radical scene.

10. The original article was Wilson, Elizabeth (1982), 'If You're so Sure You're a Feminist, Why do you read the Fashion Page?', *Guardian*, 26 July. The letters appeared on 2 August 1982.

11. For a description of this event, see Wilson, Elizabeth (1982), *What is to be Done about Violence towards Women?*, Harmondsworth: Penguin.

12. Banner, Lois (1983), *American Beauty*, New York: Alfred Knopf.

13. Martin, Bernice (1981), *A Sociology of Contemporary Cultural Change*, Oxford: Basil Blackwell, p. 51.

14. Baudrillard, Jean (1981), *For a Critique of the Political Economy of the Sign*, St Louis, Mo.: Telos Press, p. 97.

Bibliography

Ackroyd, Peter (1979), *Dressing Up: Transvestism and Drag: The History of an Obsession*, London: Thames and Hudson.

Adburgham, Alison (1961), *A* Punch *History of Manners and Modes*, London: Hutchinson.

—— (1981), *Shops and Shopping 1800–1914*, London: Allen and Unwin.

Adorno, Theodor (1967), *Prisms*, Cambridge Ma: The MIT Press.

Alexander, Sally (1976), 'Women's Work in Nineteenth Century London: A Study of the Years 1820–1850', in Mitchell, Juliet and Oakley, Ann (eds.), *The Rights and Wrongs of Women*, Harmondsworth: Penguin.

Altman, Denis (1982), *The Homosexualization of America*, Boston: Beacon Press.

Anderson, Jervis (1982), *Harlem: The Great Black Way 1900-1950*, London: Orbis.

Anderson, Perry (1984), 'Modernity and Revolution', *New Left Review*, no. 144.

Anscombe, Isabelle (1984), *A Woman's Touch: Women in Design from 1860 to the Present Day*, London: Virago.

Angeloglou, Maggie (1970), *A History of Makeup*, London: Studio Vista.

Bailey, Margaret (1981), *Those Glorious Glamour Years*, Secaucus, NJ: Citadel Press.

Baldwin, Frances Elizabeth (1926), *Sumptuary Legislation and Personal Regulation in England*, Baltimore: Johns Hopkins Press.

Ballin, Ada (1885), *The Science of Dress in Theory and Practice*, London: Sampson and Low.

Balzac, Honoré de (1971), *Lost Illusions*, Harmondsworth: Penguin.

Banner, Lois (1983), *American Beauty*, New York: Alfred Knopf.

Barlee, Ellen (1863), *A Visit to Lancashire in December 1862*, London: Seeley and Co.

Barthes, Roland (1967), *Système de la Mode*, Paris: Éditions du Seuil.

Baudelaire, Charles (1859), 'Le Dandy', *Écrits Sur L'Art*, Tome 2, Paris: Livre de Poche.

Baudrillard, Jean (1981), *For A Critique of the Political Economy of the Sign*, St Louis, Mo.: Telos Press.

Beaton, Cecil (1954), *The Glass of Fashion*, London: Weidenfeld and Nicolson.

(1982), *Self Portrait with Friends: The Selected Diaries of Cecil Beaton 1926–1974*, Harmondsworth: Penguin.

Beauvoir, Simone de (1953), *The Second Sex*, London: Jonathan Cape.

(1963), *The Prime of Life*, Harmondsworth: Penguin.

(1965), *Force of Circumstance*, Harmondsworth: Penguin.

Bell, Quentin (1947), *On Human Finery*, London: The Hogarth Press.

Benjamin, Walter (1973a), *Charles Baudelaire: A Lyric Poet in the Era of High Capitalism*, London: New Left Books.

(1973b), 'The Work of Art in the Age of Mechanical Reproduction', in *Illuminations*, London: Fontana/Collins.

Bennett, Arnold (Jacob Tonson) (1917), *Books and Persons*, quoted in Gross, John (1969), *The Rise and Fall of the Man of Letters: Aspects of English Literary Life Since 1800*, London: Weidenfeld and Nicolson.

Benthall, Jeremy (1976), *The Body Electric: Patterns of Western Industrial Culture*, London: Thames and Hudson.

Bergler, Edmund (1953), *Fashion and the Unconscious*, New York: Robert Brunner.

Berman, Marshall (1983), *All That is Solid Melts into Air: The Experience of Modernity*, London: Verso.

Bernal, J. D. (1929), *The World the Flesh and the Devil: An Enquiry into the Three Enemies of the Rational Soul*, London: Kegan Paul.

Bertin, Célia (1956), *Paris à la Mode: A Voyage of Discovery*, London: Gollancz.

Black, Clementina (1983), *Married Women's Work: Being the Report of an Enquiry Undertaken by the Women's Industrial Council*, London: Virago. (Originally published in 1915.)

Bloch, Ivan (1958), *Sexual Life in England*, London: Corgi Books.

Boswell, James (1966), *Boswell's London Journal 1762–1763*, Harmondsworth: Penguin.

Braudel, Fernand (1981), *Civilization and Capitalism from the Fifteenth to the Eighteenth Century Vol. I: The Structures of Everyday Life: The Limits of the Possible*, London: Collins.

Bray, Alan (1983), *Homosexuality in Renaissance England*, London: Gay Men's Press.

Briscoe, Lynden (1971), *The Textile and Clothing Industries of the United Kingdom*, Manchester: Manchester University Press.

Brownmiller, Susan (1984), *Femininity*, New York: Linden Press, Simon and Schuster.

Burckhardt, Jacob (1955), *The Civilization of the Renaissance in Italy*, London: Phaidon Press. (Originally published in 1860.)

Butler, Josephine (ed.) (1869), *Woman's Work and Woman's Culture*, London: Macmillan.

Byron, George Gordon, Lord (1982), *Selected Prose*, Harmondsworth: Penguin.

Campbell, Beatrix (1979), 'Lining Their Pockets', *Time Out*, 13–19 July.

Carlyle, Thomas (1831), *Sartor Resartus*, London: Curwen Press.

Carter, Angela (1982), *Nothing Sacred*, London: Virago.

Chalmers, Martin (1983), 'Politics of Crisis', *City Limits*, 19–25 August.

Chapkis, Wendy and Enloe, Cynthia (1983), *Of Common Cloth: Women in the Global Textile Industry*, Amsterdam: Transnational Institute.

Charles-Roux, Edmonde (1975), *Chanel*, London: Jonathan Cape.

Chase, Edna Woolman (1954), *Always in Vogue*, London: Gollancz.

Chisholm, Anne (1981), *Nancy Cunard*, Harmondsworth: Penguin.

Cobbe, Frances Power (1869), 'The Final Cause of Women', in Butler, Josephine (ed.), *Woman's Work and Woman's Culture*, London: Macmillan.

Cowley, Malcolm (1951), *Exile's Return*, New York: Viking.

Coyle, Angela (1982), 'Sex and Skill in the Organization of the Clothing Industry', in West, Jackie (ed.), *Work, Women and the Labour Market*, London: Routledge and Kegan Paul.

Culler, Jonathan (1975), *Structuralist Poetics*, London: Routledge and Kegan Paul.

Cunnington, Cecil Willett (1941), *Why Women Wear Clothes*, London: Faber and Faber.

(1950), *Women*, 'Pleasures of Life Series', London: Burke.

and Cunnington, Phillis (1951), *The History of Underclothes*, London: Michael Joseph.

Cunnington, Phillis and Lucas, Catherine (1967), *Occupational Costume in England from the Eleventh Century to 1914*, London: Adam and Charles Black.

Darwin, Charles (1845), *The Voyage of the Beagle*, London: J. M. Dent and Sons.

Delbourg-Delphis, Marylène (1981), *Le Chic et le Look: Histoire de la Mode Féminine et des Moeurs de 1850 à nos Jours*, Paris: Hachette.

Dickens, Charles (1970), *Dombey and Son*, Harmondsworth: Penguin. (Originally published in 1848.)

(1976), 'Meditations In Monmouth Street', *Selected Short Fiction*, Harmondsworth: Penguin. (Originally published in 1836.)

Dior, Christian (1957), *Dior by Dior*, London: Weidenfeld and Nicolson.

Disher, M. L. (1947), *American Factory Production of Women's Clothing*, London: Deveraux Publications.

Dobbs, J. L. (1928), *The Clothing Workers of Great Britain*, London: Routledge and Kegan Paul.

Dooley, William H. (1934), *Economics of Clothing and Textiles*, Boston: D.C. Heath.

Douglas, Mary (1966), *Purity and Danger: An Analysis of Concepts of Pollution and Taboo*, Harmondsworth: Penguin.

Duff Gordon, Lucy, Lady (1932), *Discretions and Indiscretions*, London: Jarrolds.

Eckert, Charles (1978), 'The Carole Lombard in Macy's Window', *Quarterly Review of Film Studies*, Winter.

Elias, Norbert (1978), *The Civilizing Process: The History of Manners*, translated by Edmund Jephcott, Oxford: Basil Blackwell. (Originally published in 1939 as *Uber den Prozess der Zivilisation*.)

Elson, Diane and Pearson, Ruth (1981), '"Nimble Fingers Make Cheap Workers": An Analysis of Women's Employment in Third World Export Manufacturing', *Feminist Review*, no. 7, Spring.

Engels, Friedrich (1844), *The Condition of the Working Class in England*, Moscow: Progress Publishers.

Etherington Smith, Meredith (1983), *Patou*, London: Hutchinson.

Ewen, Stuart and Ewen, Elizabeth (1982), *Channels of Desire: Mass Images of the Shaping of the American Consciousness*, New York: McGraw Hill.

Ewing, Elizabeth (1978), *Dress and Undress: A History of Women's Underwear*, London: Batsford.

(1974), *History of Twenteith Century Fashion*, London: Batsford.

Faust, Beatrice (1981), *Women, Sex and Pornography*, Harmondsworth: Penguin.

Ferry, John (1960), *A History of the Department Store*, New York: Macmillan.

Field, Andrew (1983), *The Formidable Miss Barnes: The Life of Djuna Barnes*, London: Secker and Warburg.

Fiedorek, Mary B. (1983), *Executive Style: Looking It, Living It*, Piscataway, New Jersey: New Century Publishers.

Fitzgerald, Scott (1934), *Tender is the Night*, Harmondsworth: Penguin.

Flaubert, Gustave (1857), *Madame Bovary*, Paris: Livre de Poche.

Foster, John (1974), *Class Struggle and the Industrial Revolution*, London: Methuen.

Foucault, Michel (1979), *The History of Sexuality: Vol. I An Introduction*, Harmondsworth: Penguin.

Frascina, Francis and Harrison, Charles (eds.) (1982), *Modern Art and Modernism: A Critical Anthology*, London: Harper Row.

Fraser, Grace Lovat (1948), *Textiles by Britain*, London: George Allen and Unwin.

Freud, Sigmund (1953), 'Three Essays on the Theory of Sexuality', in *Standard Edition of the Complete Psychological Works Vol. VII*, London: Hogarth Press and the Institute of Psychoanalysis. (Originally published in 1905.)

—— (1973), 'Femininity', *New Introductory Lectures on Psychoanalysis*, Harmondsworth: Penguin. (Originally published in 1933.)

Frith, Simon (1983), *Sound Effects: Youth Leisure and the Politics of Rock and Roll*, London: Constable.

Fyvel, T. R. (1961), *The Insecure Offenders*, London: Chatto and Windus.

George, M. Dorothy (1925), *London Life in the Eighteenth Century*, Harmondsworth: Penguin.

Gibbon, Edward (1952), *The Portable Gibbon: The Decline and Fall of The Roman Empire*, Harmondsworth: Penguin.

Gilman, Charlotte Perkins (1979), *Herland*, London: The Women's Press. (Originally published in 1915.)

Goffman, Erving (1969), *The Presentation of Self in Everyday Life*, London: Allen Lane.

Goldman, A. (1974), *Ladies and Gentlemen, Lenny Bruce*, London: Panther.

Greenberg, Clement (1982), 'Modernist Painting', in Frascina, Francis and Harrison, Charles (eds.), *Modern Art and Modernism: A Critical Anthology*, London: Harper and Row.

Gross, John (1969), *The Rise and Fall of the Man of Letters: Aspects of English Literary Life Since 1800*, London: Weidenfeld and Nicolson.

Gustafson, Robert (1982), 'The Power of the Screen: The Influence of Edith Head's Film Designs on the Retail Fashion Market', *The Velvet Light Trap: Review of Cinema*, no. 19.

Hamilton, Mary Agnes (1936), 'Changes in Social Life', in Strachey, Ray (ed.), *Our Freedom and its Results*, London: Hogarth Press.

Hamilton, M. (1941), *Women at Work*, London: Routledge and Kegan Paul.

Haweis, Mary Eliza (1878), *The Art of Beauty*, London: Chatto and Windus.

Haynes, Alan (1983), 'Murderous Millinery: The Struggle for the Plumage Act 1921', *History Today*, July.

Heard, Gerald (1924), *Narcissus: An Anatomy of Clothes*, London: Kegan Paul.

Hebdige, Dick (1979), *Subculture: The Meaning of Style*, London: Methuen.

Hertzog, Charlotte and Gaines, Jane (1983), 'Hollywood, Costumes and the Fashion Industry', *Triangle Cinema Programme*, Birmingham, May.

Hiler, Hilaire (1929), *From Nudity to Raiment*, London: Foyles.

Hollander, Anne (1975), *Seeing Through Clothes*, New York: Avon Books.

Horkheimer, Max and Adorno, Theodor (1979), *The Dialectic of Enlightenment*, London: Verso. (Originally published in 1944.)

Howe, Bea (1967), *Arbiter of Elegance*, London: The Harvill Press.

Hower, Ralph M. (1946), *History of Macy's of New York: 1858–1919*, Cambridge, Ma.: Harvard University Press.

Hughes, Douglas (ed.) (1970), *Perspectives on Pornography*, New York: Macmillan.

Ironside, Janey (1973), *Janey: An Autobiography*, London: Michael Joseph.

Jameson, Fredric (1981), *The Political Unconscious: Narrative as Socially Symbolic Act*, London: Methuen.

Jameson, Fredric (1984), 'Postmodernism, or the Cultural Logic of Late Capitalism', *New Left Review*, no. 146, July–August.

Jenkyns, Richard (1980), *The Victorians and Ancient Greece*, Oxford: Basil Blackwell.

Keenan, Brigid (1977), *The Women We Wanted to Look Like*, New York: St Martins Press.

Kolbowski, Silvia (1984), '(Di)vested Interests: The Calvin Klein Ads', *ZG*, no. 10, Spring.

König, René (1973), *The Restless Image*, London: George Allen and Unwin.

Kunzle, David (1982), *Fashion and Fetishism*, Totowa, New Jersey: Rowman and Littlefield.

Lang, Kurt and Lang, Gladys (1961), 'Fashion: Identification and Differentiation in the Mass Society', in Roach, Mary Ellen and Eicher, Jane Bubolz (1965), *Dress Adornment and the Social Order*, New York: John Wiley.

Lasch, Christopher (1979), *The Culture of Narcissism*, New York: Warner Books.

Laver, James (1968), *Dandies*, London: Weidenfeld and Nicolson.

(1969a), *A Concise History of Costume*, London: Thames and Hudson.

(1969b), *Modesty in Dress: An Inquiry into the Fundamentals of Fashion*, London: Heinemann.

Lee, Sarah Tomalin (1975), *American Fashion*, London: André Deutsch.

Lewis, Alfred and Woodworth, Constance (1973), *Miss Elizabeth Arden*, London: W. H. Allen.

Lurie, Alison (1981), *The Language of Clothes*, London: Heinemann.

MacInnes, Colin (1959), *Absolute Beginners*, London: Allison and Busby.

Malcolm X (1965), *The Autobiography of Malcolm X*, Harmondsworth: Penguin.

Mallarmé, Stéphane (1933), *La Dernière Mode*, with an introduction by S. A. Rhodes, New York: Publications of the Institute of French Studies Inc.

Martin, Bernice (1981), *A Sociology of Contemporary Cultural Change*, Oxford: Basil Blackwell.

Marx, Karl (1970), *Capital*, Vol. I, London: Lawrence and Wishart. (Originally published in translation in 1886.)

Melly, George (1972), *Revolt into Style: The Pop Arts in Britain*, Harmondsworth: Penguin.

Michelson, Peter (1970), 'An Apology for Porn', in Hughes, Douglas (ed.), *Perspectives on Pornography*, New York: Macmillan.

Miller, Michael (1981), *The* Bon Marché: *Bourgeois Culture and the Department Store 1869–1920*, London: Allen and Unwin.

Mitchell, Juliet and Oakley, Anne (eds.) (1976), *The Rights and Wrongs of Women*, Harmondsworth: Penguin.

Mitford, Nancy (1974), *The Best Novels of Nancy Mitford*, London: Hamish Hamilton.

Moers, Ellen (1960), *The Dandy: Brummell to Beerbohm*, London: Secker and Warburg.

Molloy, John T. (1977), *The Women's Dress For Success Book*, Chicago: Follet Publishing Co.

Moore, Doris Langley (1949), *The Woman in Fashion*, London: Batsford. (1967), *E. Nesbit: A Biography*, London: Ernest Benn.

Moretti, Franco (1983), *Signs Taken for Wonders*, London: Verso.

Morgan, Robin (ed.) (1970), *Sisterhood is Powerful: An Anthology of Writings from the Women's Liberation Movement*, New York: Random House.

Morris, Ivan (1964), *The World of the Shining Prince*, Harmondsworth: Penguin.

Morton, A. L. (1952), *The English Utopia*, London: Lawrence and Wishart.

Mukerji, Chandra (1983), *From Graven Images: Patterns of Modern Materialism*, New York: Columbia University Press.

Nesbit, E. (1901), *The Story of the Amulet*, Harmondsworth: Penguin.

Newton, Judith, Rayan Mary P. and Walkowitz, Judith (1983), *Sex and Class in Women's History*, London: Routledge and Kegan Paul.

Newton, Stella Mary (1974), *Health Art and Reason: Dress Reformers of the Nineteenth Century*, London: John Murray.

— (1975), 'Fashion in Fashion History', *Times Literary Supplement*, 21 March.

— (1976), 'Couture and Society', *Times Literary Supplement*, 12 November.

Nystrom, Paul (1928), *Economics of Fashion*, New York: Ronald Press.

Osborne, John (1982), *A Better Class of Person: An Autobiography 1929–1956*, Harmondsworth: Penguin.

O'Sullivan, Sue (1982), 'Passionate Beginnings: Ideological Politics 1969–82', *Feminist Review*, no. 11.

Parry, Alfred (1960), *Garrets and Pretenders: A History of Bohemianism in America*, New York: Dover Publications. (Originally published in 1933.)

Phillips, Pearson (1963), 'The New Look', in Sissions Michael and French, Philip (eds.), *The Age of Austerity 1945–51*, Harmondsworth: Penguin.

Pinchbeck, Ivy (1981), *Women Workers and the Industrial Revolution 1750–1850*, London: Virago. (Originally published in 1930.)

Poiret, Paul (1931), *My First Fifty Years*, London: Victor Gollancz.

Polhemus, Ted (ed.) (1978), *Social Aspects of the Human Body*, Harmondsworth: Penguin.

Proust, Marcel (1981), *Remembrance of Things Past Vols. I, II, and III*, London: Chatto and Windus. (Originally published 1908–1925.)

Quant, Mary (1966), *Quant by Quant*, London: Cassell.

Radcliffe Richards, Janet (1980), *The Sceptical Feminist*, London: Routledge and Kegan Paul.

Réage, Pauline (1954), *The Story of O*, London: The Olympia Press.

Rees, Goronwy (1969), *St Michael: A History of Marks and Spencer*, London: Weidenfeld and Nicolson.

Rhondda, Margaret Haig, Viscountess (1933), *This Was My World*, London: Macmillan.

Roach, Mary Ellen and Eicher, Jane Bubolz (1965), *Dress Adornment and the Social Order*, New York: John Wiley.

Roberts, Hélène (1977), 'The Exquisite Slave: The Role of Clothes in the Making of the Victorian Woman', *Signs*, Vol. 2, no. 3, Spring.

Roberts, Michèle (1983), *The Visitation*, London: The Women's Press.

Rowbotham, Sheila and Weeks, Jeffrey (1977), *Socialism and the New Life; The Personal and Sexual Politics of Edward Carpenter and Havelock Ellis*, London: Pluto Press.

Rubinstein, Helena (1930), *The Art of Feminine Beauty*, London: Victor Gollancz.

Runciman, Steven (1975), *Byzantine Style and Civilisation*, Harmondsworth: Penguin.

Sampson, Kevin and Rimmer, David (1983), 'The Ins and Outs of High Street Fashion', *The Face*, July.

Sartre, Jean-Paul (1968), *Being and Nothingness*, London: Methuen.

Saunders, Edith (1954), *The Age of Worth*, London: Longmans.

Sennett, Richard (1974), *The Fall of Public Man*, Cmabridge: Cambridge University Press.

Sévigné, Madame de (1982), *Selected Letters,* translated by Leonard Tancock, Harmondsworth: Penguin.

Simmel, Georg (1971), 'On Individuality and Social Forms', in *Selected Writings,* Chicago: Chicago University Press.

Sissons, Michael and French, Philip (eds.) (1963), *The Age of Austerity 1945–1951,* Harmondsworth: Penguin.

Snitow, Ann, Stansell, Christine and Thompson, Sharon (1984), *Desire: The Politics of Sexuality,* London: Virago.

Sontag, Susan (1979), *On Photography,* Harmondsworth: Penguin.

Spalding, Frances (1983), *Vanessa Bell,* London: Weidenfeld and Nicolson.

Squire, Geoffrey (1974), *Dress, Art and Society 1560–1970*, London: Studio Vista.

Stanley, Liz (ed.) (1984), *The Diaries of Hannah Cullwick*, London: Virago.

Stead, Christina (1945), *A Little Tea A Little Chat,* London: Virago.

Stewart, Margaret and Hunter, Leslie (1964), *The Needle is Threaded: The History of an Industry*, London: Heinemann.

Strachey, Ray (ed.) (1936), *Our Freedom and its Results,* London: Hogarth Press.

Tanner, Tony (1979), *Adultery and the Novel,* Baltimore: Johns Hopkins University Press.

Taylor, Barbara (1983a), '"The Men are as Bad as their Masters" ...: Socialism, Feminism and Sexual Antagonism in the London Tailoring Trade of the 1830s', in Newton, Judith, Ryan, Mary and Walkowitz, Judith (eds.), *Sex and Class in Women's History*, London: Routledge and Kegan Paul.

(1983b), *Eve and the New Jerusalem,* London: Virago Press.

Taylor, Lou (1983), *Mourning Dress: A Costume and Social History,* London: Allen and Unwin.

Thompson, E. P. (1968), *The Making of the English Working Class,* Harmondsworth: Penguin.

Tinling, Teddy (1983), *Sixty Years in Tennis,* London: Sidgwick and Jackson.

Turim, Maureen (1983), 'Fashion Shapes: Film, the Fashion Industry and the Image of Women', *Socialist Review,* no. 71 (Vol. 13, no. 5).

Turner, Bryan (1982), 'The Discourse of Diet', *Theory, Culture and Society,* Vol. 1 no. 1, Spring.

Veblen, Thorstein (1957), *The Theory of the Leisure Class,* London: Allen and Unwin. (Originally published in 1899.)

Von Boehn, Max (1932), *Modes and Manners Vol. I: From the Decline of the Ancient World to the Renaissance,* London: Harrap.

Walter, Aubrey (1981), *Come Together: The Years of Gay Liberation 1970–1973,* London: Gay Men's Press.

Warhol, Andy and Hackett, Pat (1980), *POPism: The Warhol '60s,* New York: Harcourt Brace Jovanovich.

Waugh, Evelyn (1928), *Decline and Fall,* Harmondsworth: Penguin.

Weeks, Jeffrey (1977), *Coming Out,* London: Quartet.

Werskey, Gary (1978), *The Visible College: A Collective Biography of British Scientists of the 1930s,* London: Allen Lane.

West, Jackie (ed.) (1982), *Work, Women and the Labour Market,* London: Routledge and Kegan Paul.

Wharton, Edith (1952), *The House of Mirth,* London: Oxford University Press. (Originally published in 1905.)

White, Doris (1980), *D For Doris, V For Victory,* Milton Keynes: Oakleaf Books.

Wilson, Elizabeth (1982), 'If You're so Sure You're a Feminist, Why do you read the Fashion Page?', *Guardian,* 26 July.

(1983), *What is to be Done about Violence Towards Women?,* Harmondsworth: Penguin.

Wood, Neal (1959), *Communism and British Intellectuals,* London: Victor Gollancz.

Zeldin, Theodor (1977), *France 1848–1945: Taste and Corruption,* Oxford: Oxford University Press.

Index